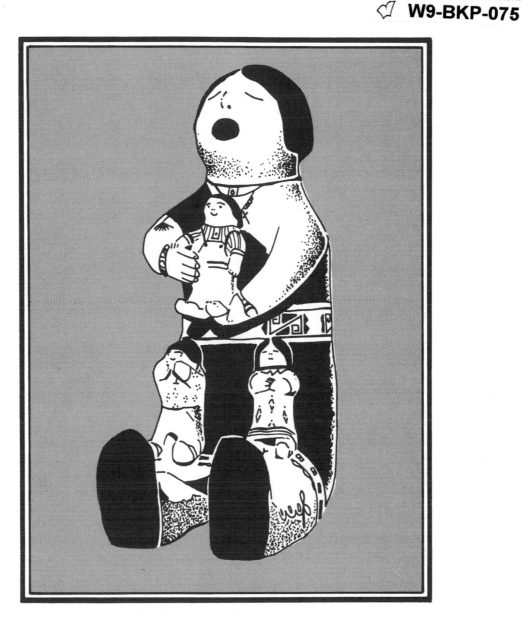

HEARD IN THE KITCHEN
THE HEARD MUSEUM GUILD COOKBOOK
PHOENIX • ARIZONA

Storyteller Figures

Native Americans have made clay figures for many centuries to depict various activities in their life cycle. Today's storyteller figures are part of that tradition. In 1964, Helen Cordero, of Cochiti Pueblo in New Mexico, became the innovator of the modern storyteller figure. Previously, known for her mother and child figures, often called "singing mothers," Mrs. Cordero was encouraged to make a doll with many children. She created a male figure with five children on his lap and shoulders in memory of her grandfather, who was famous for the legends and stories he shared with his grandchildren. Older people enjoyed the storytelling as much as the children. Most of the stories recalled traditions that were handed down, usually in the form of a "lesson" for the children. Storytellers continue to perpetuate the legends and traditions of Native Americans. Contemporary storyteller figures are being created by artists from the villages of Acoma, Zuni, and Hopi, and the Rio Grande Pueblos.

This cookbook is a collection of favorite recipes, which are not necessarily original recipes.

Published by: The Heard Museum Guild

Copyright 1994 The Heard Museum
22 East Monte Vista Road
Phoenix, Arizona 85004-1480

Edited and Printed by: Favorite Recipes® Press
P.O. Box 305142
Nashville, Tennessee 37230
1-800-358-0560

Manufactured in the United States of America
First Printing: 1994, 10,000 copies

Heard in the kitchen : the Heard Museum Guild cookbook.
     p.   cm.
   Includes index.
   ISBN 0-934351-43-0
    1. Cookery, American.   2. Cookery, Indian.   I. Heard Museum Guild.
TX715.H3967   1993
641.5973—dc20   93-46620
                                              CIP

Contents

Acknowledgments

Cover: Ceramic "Storyteller" figure by Helen Cordero of Cochiti Pueblo, New Mexico; The Heard Museum Collection

Photograph by John C. Cacheris

Art Consultant: Diane P. Kopp

The Heard Museum Guild expresses its appreciation to the Cookbook Committee members who contributed endless time and energy to the completion of the cookbook:

Chairman . . . . Irene Kline 1989-1992
Co-Chairman . . . . Betty F. Neal 1989-1992

Chairman . . . . Mary Rainey 1992-1993

Co-Chairmen . . . . Helen Cacheris 1993-1994
                            Betty F. Neal 1993-1994

Ginger Allingham
Kit Applegate
Dorothy Bennett
Rose Brigid Berry
Marie Borgmann
Martha Cozzi
Anne Girand
Mary Guilford
Polly Hartzler
Diane Kopp

Barbara Maiwurm
Faye Mitchell
Arlene Nygren
Vivian Price
Lois Rogers
Louise Slotta
Nan Steiner
Anne Suguitan
Isabelle Taylor
Virginia Yates

The Cookbook Committee and the Guild thank the members of
The Heard Museum staff for their support and assistance, particularly:
Ann Marshall, Assistant to the Director
Gina Laczko, Educational Services Manager
Mary Brennan, Communications Coordinator
Lisa MacCollum, Exhibits Coordinator/Graphics
Janice Decker, Membership/Marketing Coordinator
and Mario Klimiades, Librarian/Archivist

The Heard Museum

The Heard Museum was founded in 1929 by Dwight B. and Maie Bartlett Heard, who were avid collectors of native artifacts and art, especially of the Southwest. The Heards built the Museum in order to share their exemplary collection. Today, The Heard Museum is internationally recognized for its collections of artifacts documenting the history of southwestern Native Americans. Equally impressive are the Museum's collections of historical and contemporary paintings and sculpture by native artists. Each year, thousands of visitors come to the Museum to experience its innovative exhibits, its entertaining events, and its thought-provoking education programs and workshops.

The Heard Museum Guild History

From a casual suggestion in 1956 and a 30-member group of founders, the Heard Museum Guild has grown to a dynamic membership of more than 700.

While the goals of the founding group were the same as ours today, the Guild has seen tremendous strides in all endeavors.

The Las Guias training program has progressed from several one-hour lectures to a highly structured program lasting from September to May. Its graduates are prepared to serve as guides in any gallery in the Museum. Upon completion of a shorter study program, Gallery Interpreters specialize in just one gallery. Guild members also assist the Museum Librarian and the Curator of Collections; work at Visitor Services; participate in the Speakers' Bureau; staff a special event; or work in the Museum Shop. The appeal of the Guild is enhanced by study programs, field trips and social events for its members.

The Indian Fair and Market, held annually since 1958, has grown in size and scope to attract visitors worldwide. The Exhibitors Juried Competition, held in conjunction with the Fair, is a welcome addition.

The Museum Shop, from a small start in 1958, has become highly respected by collectors of Native American art and crafts for the quality and authenticity of its merchandise. In recent years, other fund-raising activities such as the Lecture Series have been added. The Guild allots a part of its earnings each year to the H. Thomas Cain Endowment Fund.

Each spring the Native American Student Arts and Crafts Show encourages students in Grades 3 through 12 to create their finest works by awarding prizes for excellence and providing an opportunity for the sale of entries. Ten award winning students in Grades 7 through 12 are invited to participate in a summer workshop at the Museum, led by a noted Native American artist.

As The Heard Museum has grown from a very small one-curator museum to one of national and international importance and prestige, so has the Guild developed its abilities and resources to contribute greatly to that growth.

Historical Overview of The Heard Museum

In 1895, Dwight B. and Maie Bartlett Heard left Chicago to settle in Phoenix, Arizona. Soon after their arrival, the couple began collecting Native American artifacts. Their acquisitions centered on arts and crafts that exhibited the diversity, as well as the quality, of the artisans and artists.

Numerous trips around the country and the world enabled the Heards to add many fine pieces to their eclectic collection. By the time the collection was moved to the Museum in 1929, it numbered more than 3,000 items, 800 of which were baskets. Many of these items were used for gathering, preparing and storing food.

The idea of a museum was suggested by the couple's daughter-in-law, Winifred Heard, when the Heards' collection outgrew their home, Casa Blanca. With the help of a Phoenix architect, Herbert H. Green, the building was designed in the Spanish Colonial Revival Style. The many books on Spanish and Mediterranean architecture which inspired the design can be found in the Museum library.

The original building consisted of only 73 by 95 feet in total area, including the courtyard and cloisters surrounding it. The original courtyard still welcomes visitors to the Museum. In addition, there were six exhibition rooms, a library, auditorium, apartment and kitchen, and a small workshop for curatorial work. The initial blueprints called for "undesignated exhibit rooms" on the second floor which were quickly filled with the extensive collection.

In 1958, with limited area for exhibitions and no real storage or curatorial space, David Murdock, a Phoenix financier, donated money for a one-story, 2,200-square-foot exhibition wing on the southwest corner of the existing building. On the west side of the building, an enclosed Palm Courtyard was added. It was not until 1961 that air conditioning was installed, allowing the Museum to remain open year round.

In 1964, Barry Goldwater donated his collection of 400 kachina dolls to the Museum. This invaluable collection overwhelmed the storage, curatorial and exhibition facilities of the Museum. From 1966 to 1968, a successful fund raising for a "Home for the Goldwater Collection," was undertaken. The funds provided for a three-story, L-shaped addition along the east side of the building. The addition encompassed two large galleries, a projection room, elevator, library, auditorium and much needed curatorial and storage space in a full basement. The two-story Gallery of Indian Art was added on the southwest corner. This Gallery continues to exhibit fine art by Native Americans. The gallery's facade along Monte Vista Road mirrors the Spanish Colonial Revival Style architecture of the original building. The additions more than doubled the existing Heard Museum building to 37,000 square feet.

A $3.5 million expansion program in 1983-1984 again doubled the available space of the Museum. Another three-story addition of 9,000 square feet per floor was built in the northwest corner of the old Palm Courtyard. A walled garden, the Dr. Dean Nichols Memorial Sculpture Court, on the west side of the building was designed to present outdoor sculpture by Native American artists. Another wing was added east of the Goldwater wing, housing the much expanded Heard Museum Guild Shop, a mini-courtyard, a 350-seat auditorium and a large commercial kitchen.

Including a kitchen was unusual in museums built in Arizona during the early 1900s but Maie Heard foresaw a need for kitchen facilities in the original Heard Museum. She and her husband had become very active in Phoenix business and cultural activities, and often were called upon to entertain business and political friends. The original plans of the Museum included a full-sized kitchen, measuring 13 by 14 feet. In the kitchen were wooden cabinets and counters, a sink, a gas stove and a six-foot refrigerator with an "ice-box drain." The kitchen was located under the stairs to the second floor, next to the original auditorium, now the Sandra Day O'Connor Gallery. The kitchen provided catering space for the black-tie dinners and refreshments for the many concerts and lectures offered to the community by the Heards at the Museum.

Introduction

In spite of all the experiments undertaken by modern botanists, Native American peoples remain the developers of the world's largest array of nutritious foods and the primary contributors to the world's varied cuisines. In fact, Native Americans have given the world three-fifths of all the food crops now under cultivation.

Columbus left Spain with bread, wine, meat and fish. Along the way, he caught crab, tuna and dolphin. But from the minute he made contact with the Arawak peoples of the Caribbean, the culinary history of the world changed. Columbus' diary is full of information about new foods that he enthusiastically sampled and then took back to the court of Spain. Thus, the rest of the world was introduced to tomatoes, potatoes, chiles, chocolate, vanilla, sweet potatoes, avocados, pineapple, grapefruit, peanuts, manioc, maize and dozens of other foods. In turn, the Spanish brought some new foods and animals to this hemisphere.

What is sometimes overlooked is the technology of food production that the Europeans learned from the Native peoples. From the indigenous farmers, for example, the Europeans adopted the idea of planting seeds, rather than sowing them. Native Americans planted corn by placing the kernels firmly in the ground. They selected each seed to be planted, rather than merely grabbing a handful of seed from a bag and casting them on the ground. This process of individualized seed selection was one reason that Native Americans have been such successful farmers. In addition, they realized that planting corn, beans and squash in the same field not only reduced the destruction of the plants by insects and other pests, but also helped to retain the soil's fertility.

The "discovery" of the Americas resulted in a culinary revolution and greater, balanced nutrition for the world's population. The staple diet of corn, beans, and squash, often revered as the "three sisters" by Native peoples, contributes significantly to a balanced diet. Only a fraction of the foods domesticated in the Americas has been adopted worldwide. Still available in traditional cuisines are "new" foods that can feed an increasingly hungry world. From the highland Andean mountains and lowland drainages of the Amazon, from the remote villages of Chiapas and the scattered ramadas of the Sonoran Desert, Native peoples are still using foods discovered by their ancestors.

This publication includes more than 400 recipes which utilize many of the Old and New World foods in today's varied cuisines, as well as, traditional Native American recipes. Section dividers provide a brief history of the New World foods discovered by Columbus. Also interspersed throughout the book are vignettes on nutritious Native foods still being used by Native Americans in the Southwest.

Navajo Squash Blossom

Appetizers

Avocados

Until recently the avocado was virtually ignored by cooks outside Latin America. The semi-tropical plant has a thin skin and does not travel well.

It was not a profitable crop until rapid transportation made it possible to move the fruit from South America, Florida, Puerto Rico and California to urban markets very quickly and without damage to the fruit. It is possible that the English name for the fruit, "alligator pear," was also a stumbling block to its acceptance. When the name was changed to avocado (which is derived from the Aztec name *ahuacatl*), public acceptance rose dramatically.

The avocado has been eaten in the United States since at least 1776. The Aztecs enjoyed guacamole, made with avocado, tomato, chiles and agave worms. Guacamole, minus the worms, is probably the most popular way to eat avocados today.

Avocados are now grown in Israel, Kenya and the Americas for both domestic consumption and export. Europeans, however, still regard the avocado as a novelty food and have not assigned it the culinary role it has in the Americas.

Squash

Squash (from the Algonkin *askootasquash*) is, along with corn or maize and beans, one of the primary foods of the Native peoples of Central and North America. The native name means "something you eat raw." The colonists, however, preferred squash cooked, and in 1664 a shortened form of the word, squash, entered the English language. While widely accepted in the Americas, squash does not play an important culinary role in other cuisines. In fact, in Great Britain, "squash" is a term for a citrus drink. The Italians enjoyed a long, thin green squash which they named zucchini. Zucchini is the diminutive form of *zucca,* meaning gourd.

Baked Brie

1   8 to 12-ounce whole Brie or
       Camembert
1   teaspoon butter
2   tablespoons slivered almonds
2   tablespoons brown sugar

Yield: 8 to 12 servings

Place cheese on ovenproof serving dish; cover with moist paper towel. Bake in preheated 350-degree oven for 10 minutes; remove paper towel. Top with butter and almonds; sprinkle with brown sugar. Broil 6 inches from heat source until bubbly, watching closely to prevent burning; brown sugar caramelizes very quickly. Serve immediately with French bread rounds or crackers.

This is also a nice dessert served with fresh fruit and crackers.

Hot Jezebel Appetizer

2   cups apricot-pineapple preserves or
       1 cup each apricot and pineapple
       preserves
1¼   cups prepared horseradish, drained
1   tablespoon dry mustard
1   teaspoon pepper
1   8-ounce package cream cheese,
       softened

Yield: 3½ cups

Combine preserves, horseradish, dry mustard and pepper in bowl; mix well. Place cream cheese on serving plate. Spoon preserve mixture over top. Serve with crackers or Melba toast rounds.

This may also be used as a glaze on ham or broiled chicken.

Caviar Mold Appetizer

1   8-ounce round container of
      chive-flavor cream cheese
1   small onion, finely chopped
2   hard-cooked eggs, chopped
2   tablespoons mayonnaise
1/2 cup sour cream
1   2-ounce jar caviar, drained

Yield: 2¹/₂ cups

Unmold cream cheese carefully to retain
shape; sprinkle with onion. Combine eggs
and mayonnaise in small bowl; mix well.
Spread over cream cheese; frost top with
sour cream. Chill, wrapped in plastic wrap,
until firm. Unwrap and place on serving plate.
Top with caviar.

Chili-Pecan Rolls

8   ounces process American cheese,
      shredded, softened
3   3-ounce packages cream cheese,
      softened
1/2 teaspoon salt
1/2 teaspoon instant minced onion
1/4 teaspoon instant minced garlic
      Ground red pepper to taste
2   teaspoons fresh lemon juice
3/4 cup finely chopped pecans
3   tablespoons chili powder

Yield: 36 servings

Combine cheeses in food processor or mixer
bowl; process or beat until well mixed. Add
salt, instant onion, instant garlic, red pepper,
lemon juice and pecans; mix well. Shape
into rolls 4 inches long and 1¹/₂ inches in
diameter. Chill for 30 minutes. Coat rolls with
chili powder; wrap individually in foil. Chill
until firm. Slice rolls ¹/₈ inch thick and serve
on round crackers.

Herring Dip

1	16-ounce jar plain or wine-pack herring pieces
1	6-ounce jar marinated artichoke hearts
1	4-ounce can chopped black olives, drained
1	medium red bell pepper, chopped
1	medium red onion, chopped
1	12-ounce bottle of chili sauce

Yield: 5 cups

Drain and chop herring and artichoke hearts. Combine with black olives, bell pepper, onion and chili sauce in bowl; mix well. Chill until serving time.

May store in refrigerator for weeks.

Shrimp Dip

1	pint small curd cottage cheese
1	4½-ounce can tiny whole shrimp
¼	cup mayonnaise
1	tablespoon fresh lemon juice
3	green onions with tops, chopped
3	tablespoons instant minced onion
1	tablespoon Worcestershire sauce
½	teaspoon curry powder
½	teaspoon seasoned salt

Yield: 3 cups

Process cottage cheese in blender for 2 minutes. Add shrimp, mayonnaise, lemon juice, green onions, onion, Worcestershire sauce, curry powder and seasoned salt. Process for 20 to 30 seconds or until smooth. Serve with chips or crackers.

This is also good as a sandwich spread.

Louisiana Shrimp Dip

1/4	cup fresh lemon juice
1	8-ounce package cream cheese, softened
1	pound shrimp, cooked, peeled, coarsely chopped
1 1/4	cups finely chopped green onions
1	cup mayonnaise
2	tablespoons hot red pepper sauce
1/8	teaspoon cayenne pepper
1	tablespoon Worcestershire sauce
	Salt to taste

Yield: 5 cups

Combine lemon juice and cream cheese in bowl; mix until smooth. Stir in shrimp and green onions. Add mayonnaise, pepper sauce, cayenne pepper, Worcestershire sauce and salt; mix well. Chill until serving time. Serve with crackers, bagel chips or Melba toast rounds.

This is best chilled overnight.

Seafood Appetizer Mold

2	envelopes unflavored gelatin
1/2	cup cold water
1	3-ounce package cream cheese, softened
1 1/4	cups mayonnaise
1	tablespoon fresh lemon juice
2	teaspoons minced parsley
1	cup finely chopped celery
1	teaspoon minced onion
	Garlic salt to taste
2	cups cooked tiny shrimp
1	cup flaked crab meat

Yield: 4 cups

Soften gelatin in cold water in double boiler. Heat over hot water until gelatin dissolves, stirring constantly. Beat cream cheese in mixer bowl until light. Add gelatin gradually; mix well. Add mayonnaise and lemon juice; mix well. Fold in parsley, celery, onion, garlic salt, shrimp and crab meat. Pour into oiled 1-quart mold. Chill until set. Unmold onto serving plate; serve with bagel chips or Melba toast rounds.

It is not necessary to oil a plastic mold.

Crab Appetizer

1	8-ounce package cream cheese, softened
1	tablespoon milk
8	ounces crab meat
1	12-ounce bottle of cocktail sauce

Yield: 8 servings

Combine cream cheese and milk in bowl; mix until smooth. Spread in serving dish. Sprinkle evenly with crab meat; spoon cocktail sauce over top. Chill until serving time. Serve with Melba toast rounds.

Smoked Oyster Dip

1	8-ounce package cream cheese, softened
1	4-ounce can chopped black olives, drained
1	3³/₄-ounce can smoked oysters, drained, chopped
¹/₂	cup sour cream
¹/₂	cup mayonnaise
5	dashes of hot pepper sauce
1	tablespoon fresh lemon juice

Yield: 2 cups

Combine cream cheese, olives, oysters, sour cream, mayonnaise, pepper sauce and lemon juice in bowl; mix well. Chill until serving time. Serve with crackers.

Salmon Ball

1	15-ounce can salmon
1	8-ounce package cream cheese, softened
³/₄	teaspoon dillweed
¹/₂	teaspoon liquid smoke
	Garlic salt and pepper to taste
1	tablespoon fresh lemon juice
¹/₂	cup chopped pecans
¹/₄	cup chopped parsley

Yield: 2 cups

Drain salmon, discarding skin and bones. Combine with cream cheese, dillweed, liquid smoke, garlic salt, pepper and lemon juice in bowl; stir until well mixed. Shape into ball or log; coat with mixture of pecans and parsley. Serve with Melba toast rounds or crackers.

Party Pâté

1	pound Braunschweiger or goose liver
2	tablespoons mayonnaise
1	small onion, finely chopped
	Freshly ground pepper to taste
2	cups sour cream
1	2-ounce jar caviar

Yield: 2 cups

Remove casing from Braunschweiger or goose liver; blend with mayonnaise in bowl. Add onion and pepper; mix well. Shape into ball. Chill, wrapped with plastic wrap, until serving time. Place ball on serving plate. Press depression in top of ball with back of spoon. Frost ball with sour cream, leaving depression unfrosted. Fill depression with caviar. Garnish with lemon leaves or parsley. Serve with butter crackers or cocktail rye.

Liver Paste

1	pound chicken livers
1	teaspoon salt
	Cayenne pepper to taste
3/4	cup butter, softened
1/8	teaspoon nutmeg
1/8	teaspoon dry mustard
1/8	teaspoon ground cloves
2	tablespoons grated onion

Yield: 2 cups

Rinse chicken livers in cold water. Combine with fresh water to cover in saucepan. Cook, covered, for 15 minutes. Drain, reserving a small amount of cooking liquid. Cool livers. Combine livers, salt, cayenne pepper, butter, nutmeg, dry mustard, cloves and onion in blender container; process until smooth, adding enough reserved cooking liquid to make of desired consistency. Spoon into 2-cup mold. Chill until firm. Unmold onto serving plate. Serve with chips, French bread or crackers.

May make in advance and freeze.

Party Pâté with Mushrooms

8	ounces fresh mushrooms, chopped
1/2	teaspoon salt
1/2	teaspoon pepper
1/4	cup butter
8	ounces liver sausage, at room temperature
1	8-ounce package cream cheese, softened

Yield: 4 cups

Sauté mushrooms with salt and pepper in butter in skillet. Combine with liver sausage and cream cheese in blender or food processor container; process until smooth. Pack into crock or mold. Chill, covered, for 4 hours or longer. Place or unmold on serving plate. Serve with crackers or dark bread.

Chopped Vegetable Salsa

3	medium tomatoes, chopped
1	medium green bell pepper, chopped
1	medium onion, chopped
1	4¹/₂-ounce can chopped black olives, drained
1	4-ounce can chopped green chiles
1	4-ounce can chopped mushrooms, drained
1/3	cup wine vinegar
1	tablespoon vegetable oil
	Salt and pepper to taste

Yield: 4¹/₂ cups

Combine tomatoes, green pepper, onion, black olives, undrained green chiles and mushrooms in bowl. Mix vinegar, oil, salt and pepper in small bowl. Add to vegetable mixture. Let stand for 1 to 2 hours. Serve with tortilla chips.

May also serve as sauce for chicken.

Sunflower ∼

The sunflower is a common roadside weed. Sunflower seeds are one of the Southwest's earliest food plants. The seeds, high in oil, were roasted and ground into meal for use in soups, stews, bread and gravy. A popular method for using sunflower seeds today is to roast them in a slow oven, salt them, and use them as you would peanuts. They are an excellent source of protein.

Mushroom Caviar

8	ounces fresh mushrooms, finely chopped
1	medium onion, finely chopped
2	tablespoons butter
	Nutmeg to taste
1/2	teaspoon salt
	Pepper to taste
1	teaspoon fresh lemon juice
1/2	cup sour cream

Yield: 1 1/2 cups

Sauté mushrooms and onion in butter in skillet until moisture has nearly evaporated. Sprinkle with nutmeg, salt and pepper. Stir in lemon juice; remove from heat. Stir in sour cream. Spoon into serving dish. Chill until serving time. Let stand until room temperature to serve.

Artichoke Dip

1	6-ounce can plain or marinated artichoke hearts, drained, chopped
1	cup grated Parmesan cheese
1	cup mayonnaise
1	7-ounce can chopped green chiles

Yield: 3 cups

Combine artichoke hearts, Parmesan cheese, mayonnaise and green chiles in bowl; mix well. Spoon into 8-inch baking dish. Bake at 350 degrees for 20 to 25 minutes or until bubbly. Serve with corn chips.

Mock Crab Spread

2	cups shredded Swiss cheese
2	tablespoons chopped stuffed green olives
2	tablespoons finely chopped green bell pepper
1/2	cup chopped seeded tomato
1/2	cup mayonnaise
	Salt and pepper to taste

Yield: 3 cups

Combine cheese, olives, green pepper, tomato, mayonnaise, salt and pepper in bowl; mix well. Chill until serving time. Serve with flat bread (Lahvosh).

Glazed Horseradish Meatballs

1	pound lean ground beef
1/2	cup water
1	egg
1/2	cup dry bread crumbs
2	tablespoons horseradish
1	cup finely chopped water chestnuts
1/2	teaspoon salt
	Marmalade Sauce

Yield: 3 dozen

Combine ground beef, 1/2 cup water, egg, bread crumbs, horseradish, water chestnuts and salt in bowl; mix well. Shape into 1-inch meatballs. Place in baking dish. Bake at 350 degrees for 30 minutes; drain and place in saucepan. Add Marmalade Sauce. Simmer for 10 minutes. Serve from chafing dish.

Marmalade Sauce

1/3	cup orange marmalade
1	clove of garlic, minced
1	cup soy sauce
2	tablespoons fresh lemon juice
1/3	cup water

Yield: 1 1/2 cups

Combine marmalade, garlic, soy sauce, lemon juice and 1/3 cup water in bowl; mix well.

Polynesian Meatballs

1	pound lean ground beef
1/2	cup fine dry bread crumbs
1	small onion, minced
1	teaspoon cornstarch
1	teaspoon salt
	Allspice to taste
1	egg, beaten
3/4	cup half and half
1	12-ounce bottle of chili sauce
1/2	cup grape jelly

Yield: 3 dozen

Combine ground beef, bread crumbs, onion, cornstarch, salt, allspice, egg and half and half in bowl; mix well. Shape into 1-inch meatballs. Arrange in 9x13-inch baking dish. Combine chili sauce and jelly in saucepan. Bring to a boil; reduce heat. Simmer for 5 minutes, stirring to mix well. Pour over meatballs. Bake at 300 degrees for 1 hour.

Marmalade-Glazed Chicken Wings

3	pounds chicken wings
1/2	cup Tequila
1/2	cup chopped cilantro
1/4	cup lime or lemon marmalade
1/4	cup olive oil
2	tablespoons fresh lime juice
1	tablespoon coarsely ground pepper
2	medium cloves of garlic, minced
2	teaspoons hot pepper sauce
1	teaspoon salt
1/2	teaspoon grated lime zest
1/4	cup lime or lemon marmalade
2	tablespoons fresh lime juice
1	teaspoon grated lime zest
2	limes, cut into wedges
	Sprigs of fresh cilantro

Yield: 8 to 10 servings

Cut each chicken wing into 3 parts, discarding tip portions. Rinse chicken and pat dry; place in shallow dish. Combine Tequila, chopped cilantro, 1/4 cup marmalade, olive oil, 2 tablespoons lime juice, pepper, garlic, pepper sauce, salt and 1/2 teaspoon lime zest in bowl; mix well. Pour over chicken. Marinate, covered, overnight, turning occasionally. Drain chicken, reserving marinade; arrange chicken in large shallow baking pan. Bake in preheated 350-degree oven for 30 minutes, turning after 15 minutes. Strain reserved marinade into saucepan. Cook for 5 minutes or until reduced by 1/2, stirring occasionally. Add 1/4 cup marmalade, 2 tablespoons lime juice and 1 teaspoon lime zest. Boil for 1 minute. Brush over chicken. Broil in preheated oven until crisp and brown, turning and basting with marinade sauce several times. Place on serving platter; add lime wedges and cilantro sprigs.

This can be prepared ahead of time and reheated in 300-degree oven.

Crab Bites

1/2	cup butter or margarine
1/4	teaspoon garlic salt
1 1/2	tablespoons mayonnaise
1	6-ounce can crab meat or shrimp
1	5-ounce jar Old English cheese spread
6	English muffins, split

Yield: 72 servings

Let ingredients stand until room temperature. Combine butter, garlic salt, mayonnaise, crab meat and cheese spread in bowl; mix well. Spread on muffin halves; cut each half into 6 wedges. Place on baking sheet. Freeze until firm; store in plastic bag in freezer. Place on baking sheet. Bake in preheated 400-degree oven for 10 minutes.

Tuna Antipasto

1	cup sliced fresh mushrooms
2	tablespoons mixed pickling spices
2	13-ounce cans albacore tuna, drained, flaked
2	cups small onions, boiled
2	cups small stuffed green olives
1	12-ounce bottle of catsup
1/2	cup vegetable oil
3	cloves of garlic, minced

Yield: 10 to 12 servings

Sauté mushrooms in skillet until tender; drain. Tie pickling spices in cheesecloth bag. Combine with tuna, onions, olives, sautéed mushrooms, catsup, oil and garlic in 3-quart saucepan; mix well. Simmer for 2 hours; remove spice bag. Cool to room temperature. Spoon into serving bowl. Chill for 48 hours or longer. Serve with crackers or cocktail rye bread.

Smoked Salmon Canapés

1   **8-ounce package light cream cheese,
        softened**
4   **green onions, minced**
1/2   **cup finely chopped chives**
1/2   **cup finely chopped parsley**
2   **teaspoons dried thyme, crumbled**
1   **clove of garlic, minced**
1   **tablespoon dillweed**
1   **loaf sliced party rye bread, toasted**
8   **ounces smoked salmon, thinly sliced**
1   **4-ounce jar capers, drained**

Yield: 36 servings

Combine cream cheese, green onions, chives, parsley, thyme, garlic and dillweed in bowl; mix well. Reserve some of the cream cheese mixture. Spread remaining cream cheese mixture on toasted bread. Top with small slice of salmon, a dollop of reserved cream cheese mixture and several capers. Arrange on serving plate. Chill, covered, until serving time.

Bleu Cheese Stuffed Mushrooms

1   **pound fresh mushrooms**
3   **green onions with tops, chopped**
1/4   **cup butter**
1/2   **cup fresh bread crumbs**
3   **tablespoons crumbled bleu cheese**
1   **tablespoon minced parsley**
1   **tablespoon fresh lemon juice**
1/2   **teaspoon salt**
      Paprika to taste

Yield: 20 to 24 servings

Remove and chop mushroom stems, reserving mushroom caps. Sauté chopped stems and green onions in butter in skillet. Add bread crumbs, cheese, parsley, lemon juice and salt; mix well. Spoon into reserved mushroom caps. Arrange in shallow baking pan; sprinkle with paprika. Bake at 450 degrees for 8 minutes or until light brown. Serve hot.

Festive Florentine Crescents

1   10-ounce package frozen chopped
        spinach, thawed, well drained
8   ounces Velveeta cheese, cubed
1/4   cup dry bread crumbs
3   slices bacon, crisp-fried, crumbled
2   8-ounce cans crescent rolls
1   egg, beaten

Yield: 32 servings

Combine spinach, cheese, bread crumbs and bacon in 1½-quart saucepan. Cook over low heat until cheese melts, stirring occasionally. Separate roll dough into 16 triangles; cut each triangle into halves lengthwise to form 32 triangles. Spread with spinach mixture; roll up from wide end to enclose filling. Place on greased baking sheet. Brush with egg. Bake at 375 degrees for 11 to 13 minutes or until golden brown.

Fried Zucchini

1   pound zucchini
        Salt to taste
2/3   cup (about) flour
1   cup (about) water
        Vegetable oil for frying

Yield: 6 servings

Slice zucchini ⅛ inch thick; sprinkle with salt. Let stand for 30 minutes. Drain and pat dry. Blend flour gradually into water in bowl, whisking constantly and adjusting amounts of flour and water as needed for desired consistency. Fill skillet halfway with oil. Heat until very hot. Dip zucchini slices into batter; drop a few at a time into heated oil. Fry until golden brown; drain on paper towels. Adjust salt if desired. Serve immediately.

Chile Rounds

2	eggs
1/2	cup milk
4	ounces Cheddar or Monterey Jack cheese, shredded
1	4-ounce can chopped green chiles
1	10-count can flaky biscuits

Yield: 30 servings

Combine eggs, milk, cheese and green chiles in bowl; mix well. Separate each biscuit into 3 layers; press into miniature muffin cups. Fill with chili mixture. Bake at 375 degrees for 20 minutes.

Cheese-Wrapped Grapes

1	8-ounce package cream cheese, softened
8	ounces sharp Cheddar cheese, shredded, softened
1/4	cup butter, softened
1	tablespoon prepared mustard
1/2	teaspoon Worcestershire sauce
50	large seedless grapes
	Paprika to taste
1	cup finely chopped walnuts or pecans

Yield: 50 servings

Combine cheeses, butter, mustard and Worcestershire sauce in bowl; beat until well mixed. Shape a small amount of cheese mixture around each grape with damp hands, enclosing grape completely. Coat with paprika and walnuts. Place on serving plate. Chill until serving time.

Frosted Dill Pickles

8	large dill pickles, chilled
2	8-ounce packages cream cheese, softened
1	5-ounce jar dried beef, finely chopped

Yield: 80 slices

Drain pickles well and pat dry. Spread evenly with cream cheese; coat with beef. Wrap individually in foil; chill overnight. Slice pickles 3/8 inch thick; arrange slices on platter to serve.

Stuffed Celery

1	8-ounce package cream cheese, softened
1/4	cup chopped green olives
1/4	cup chopped pecans
	Milk
1	large bunch celery

Yield: 16 to 20 servings

Combine cream cheese with olives and pecans in bowl; mix well. Add milk if needed for desired consistency; mix well. Chill, covered, overnight. Spoon into celery; cut into desired lengths. Arrange on serving plate.

Cheddar and Walnut Toast

3	cups shredded sharp Cheddar cheese
1/4	cup unsalted butter, softened
1/4	cup medium dry sherry
1/2	teaspoon salt
4–5	drops of hot pepper sauce
1 1/2	cups finely chopped walnuts
4	6-inch pita bread rounds

Yield: 64 servings

Combine cheese, butter, wine, salt and pepper sauce in mixer bowl; beat until smooth. Stir in walnuts. Split pita rounds horizontally into 2 pieces. Spread each round with cheese mixture, covering completely. Cut each round into 8 wedges; place on baking sheet. Broil 2 inches from heat source until light brown and bubbly.

Parched Corn ～

   Hopi women prepare parched corn in the traditional manner at the Heard Museum Guild Indian Fair and Market each year. Split wood is used to make a hot fire. Clean sand is placed in a kettle and heated thoroughly. The sand maintains an even heat which prevents the corn from burning. The kettle is set at an angle so that when the corn pops it hits the upper side of the kettle and falls back in. Corn is added to the hot sand and stirred constantly until the corn stops popping. The parched corn is removed with a metal sifter, scooping corn and sand together. The sand is sifted directly back into the kettle, leaving the corn. The parched corn is then placed in a shallow sifter basket and shaken well. To season it with salt, a corn cob is dipped into salt water and rubbed over the kernels, coating all surfaces. Parched corn keeps well and is similar to "corn nuts" available at food stores.

Feta Cheese Pastries

1   16-ounce package frozen phyllo
     dough, thawed
1¼   cups melted butter or margarine
     Feta Filling

Yield: 6 dozen

Place 2 sheets of phyllo dough on work surface; brush with butter. Cut lengthwise into 2-inch wide strips. Place 1 teaspoon Feta Filling at end of each strip. Fold corner over to form triangle; continue to fold in triangles to end of strip. Place on ungreased baking sheet. Bake at 350 degrees for 20 minutes or until golden brown. Serve hot.

These may be baked in advance, cooled and chilled or frozen; reheat at 350 degrees for 10 minutes.

Feta Filling

2   8-ounce packages cream cheese,
     softened
8   ounces feta cheese, crumbled
1   egg
3   tablespoons melted butter or
     margarine

Yield: 3 cups

Combine cream cheese, feta cheese, egg and butter in small mixer bowl. Beat at medium speed until smooth.

Navajo Running Water

Beverages

Chocolate

Cacao beans, the basis for chocolate, were used by the Aztecs as currency. Only the highest levels of society were permitted to grind up the beans and make a beverage flavored with chocolate. The Spanish introduced chocolate to Europe in 1528, and cacao became Spain's most important export from Mexico in the 16th and 17th centuries.

The passion for chocolate spread to Italy in 1606 and to France in 1660. Tea and chocolate were both introduced into England in 1657. Coffee had debuted just seven years earlier. And Mrs. White's Chocolate House, which opened in London in 1698, became Great Britain's first private club. Chocolate houses sprang up where society gathered afternoons to gossip and drink the new delicacy.

Chocolate is not naturally sweet, and it is used as a seasoning in many Mexican dishes, such as *mole poblano*. The Swiss added milk and sugar to chocolate to create the delicious candy known today. Baker's chocolate plant, founded in 1765, is the oldest food company in the United States. And Milton Hershey began selling his chocolate bars in 1894.

Arizona Punch

1	12-ounce can frozen orange juice concentrate
2	cups cold water
1	cup pineapple juice
1/4	cup maraschino cherry juice
2	quarts ginger ale

Yield: 15 servings

Combine orange juice concentrate, cold water, pineapple juice and maraschino cherry juice in large pitcher or punch bowl; mix well. Add ginger ale gently. Add ice ring or ice cubes.

Banana Slush

2	cups sugar
3	cups water
1 1/2	cups fresh orange juice
4–5	very ripe bananas, mashed
1/4	cup fresh lemon juice
1	46-ounce can pineapple juice
1	12-ounce can lemon-lime soda
1 1/2	quarts ginger ale

Yield: 20 (6-ounce) servings

Bring sugar and water to a boil in saucepan; reduce heat. Simmer for 20 minutes. Combine with orange juice, mashed bananas, lemon juice and pineapple juice in freezer container; mix well. Freeze. Place in punch bowl 1 hour before serving time. Add lemon-lime soda. Let stand for 1 hour. Mash until slushy. Add ginger ale; mix gently.

Chia ~

Chia was an important food used by Native Americans. A thick mucilaginous drink was made by steeping the seeds in water. It was a nutritious drink that provided protein, carbohydrates, fat and calcium. The seeds were also parched or ground, mixed with wheat and sugar and pounded together to make pinole, a tasty meal.

Chia is also know as desert sage or simply sage because it was believed that these plants had the power to make a person "wise" or "sage."

Blushing Fruit Punch

1	10-ounce package frozen strawberries, partially thawed
1	13-ounce can crushed pineapple
1	6-ounce can frozen lemonade concentrate, thawed
2	16-ounce bottles of ginger ale

Yield: 2 quarts

Combine strawberries, undrained pineapple and lemonade concentrate in blender container; process for 1 minute. Chill until serving time. Combine with ginger ale in pitcher; mix well. Serve over ice cubes.

Open House Punch

1	fifth of Southern Comfort, chilled
6	ounces fresh lemon juice, chilled
1	6-ounce can frozen lemonade concentrate, thawed
1	6-ounce can frozen orange juice concentrate, thawed
1	6-ounce can frozen grapefruit juice concentrate, thawed
3	quarts lemon-lime soda, chilled
1	lemon, sliced
1	orange, sliced

Yield: 36 servings

Combine Southern Comfort, lemon juice, lemonade concentrate, orange juice concentrate and grapefruit juice concentrate in punch bowl. Mix in lemon-lime soda gently. Add fruit slices. May add ice ring if desired.

"Tomatillos" ~

The berries of the wolfberry shrubs were eaten raw or cooked in water to make beverages, soups, and sauces by Native Americans in the Southwest. The berries were called "tomatillos" meaning little tomatoes because that is what they look like. They are juicy and somewhat bitter.

The Navajo boiled the berries to a thick consistency which was then dried by spreading it on rocks. The dried tomatillos were stored and eaten later. The Pima made a beverage by boiling and mashing the berries.

Cranberry Cooler

5   cups cranberry juice cocktail, chilled
1   cup grapefruit juice, chilled
3/4 cup vodka
2   limes, sliced

Yield: 6 (3/4-cup) servings

Combine cranberry juice, grapefruit juice and vodka in large pitcher. Pour over cracked ice into glasses. Place 1 lime slice on rim of each glass.

Fruit Mimosas

1   6-ounce can frozen strawberry
        daiquiri mix
1   6-ounce can frozen lemonade
        concentrate, thawed
1/2   6-ounce can frozen limeade
        concentrate, thawed
1   12-ounce can frozen orange juice
        concentrate, thawed
2   cups cold water
2   quarts Champagne or club soda,
        chilled

Yield: 16 (6-ounce) servings

Prepare daiquiri mix using directions on can. Combine with lemonade concentrate, limeade concentrate, orange juice concentrate and water in large pitcher; mix well. Pour over ice in glasses, filling half full. Fill with Champagne or club soda; mix gently. Garnish with orange slice or strawberry.

This is great for brunch or for any festive occasion. It can be served from a punch bowl.

Wine Punch

2	quarts rosé
1	6-ounce can frozen limeade concentrate, thawed
3/4	cup apricot nectar
1	1-quart bottle of lemon-lime soda, chilled
2	limes, thinly sliced

Yield: 3¹/₂ quarts

Combine wine, limeade concentrate and apricot nectar in pitcher; mix well. Chill in refrigerator. Pour over ice in punch bowl. Add soda; mix gently. Add lime slices.

May add Champagne.

Honey Fresh Orangeade

6	tablespoons fresh orange juice
1	tablespoon fresh lemon juice
2	tablespoons clover honey
1	cup club soda or mineral water

Yield: 1 serving

Combine orange juice, lemon juice and honey in glass; mix well. Add club soda; mix gently. Fill glass with ice. Let stand for 3 minutes before serving.

Orange Blossom Cooler

1	12-ounce can frozen lemonade concentrate, thawed
1	6-ounce can frozen orange juice concentrate, thawed
5	cups cold water
1	quart pineapple or orange sherbet
1	quart ginger ale, chilled

Yield: 25 to 30 servings

Combine juice concentrates and water in pitcher; mix well. Place sherbet in punch bowl; cut up with spoon. Add juice mixture; mix gently. Add ginger ale just before serving.

Golden Mint Punch

30–35	sprigs of mint
2	cups sugar
2	quarts boiling water
2$^1/_3$	cups fresh lemon juice, chilled
2	quarts fresh orange juice, chilled
2	cups pineapple tidbits, chilled
1	quart ginger ale, chilled
1	quart sparkling water, chilled
12	sprigs of mint
$^1/_4$	cup grated lemon zest

Yield: 50 servings

Combine 30 to 35 sprigs of mint with sugar and boiling water in 4-quart saucepan. Simmer, uncovered, for 10 minutes. Chill in refrigerator. Combine lemon juice, orange juice and pineapple in punch bowl. Strain mint syrup into punch bowl. Add ginger ale and sparkling water; mix gently. Add 12 mint sprigs and lemon zest.

May substitute Champagne for sparkling water if desired.

Saguaro ⁓

The saguaro is so important to the Tohono O'odham that they begin their calendar year with the harvest of the fruit during late June or early July. Although saguaro fruit is no longer as important a part of the regular food supply, some Tohono O'odham families still set up a harvest camp. This includes a ramada that provides a work area shaded from the sun.

To pick the fruit, long poles are made of saguaro ribs. Short cross pieces are then tied at an angle near one end. Fruit that is beginning to turn pink is dislodged from the plant. It is cut open and the red pulp and its many black seeds are scooped out of the shell. The fruit, high in carbohydrate, is made into juice, syrup, jam and wine. The flavor is a blend of watermelon and fresh figs. The black seeds, high in protein, are separated from the pulp, parched and ground into meal. The saguaro juice is allowed to ferment into a wine called "tiswin" which traditionally is made and used ceremonially during the prayers for rain.

Holiday Punch

1	cup sugar
1	cup water
2	cups fresh grapefruit juice, chilled
1/2	cup fresh lemon juice, chilled
1/2	cup fresh lime juice, chilled
1/2	cup fresh orange juice, chilled
2	cups club soda, chilled
1 1/2	quarts dry to moderately sweet white wine

Yield: 3 1/4 quarts

Bring sugar and water to a boil in 2-quart saucepan. Cook until sugar dissolves, stirring constantly. Cool to room temperature. Chill in refrigerator. Combine with grapefruit juice, lemon juice, lime juice and orange juice in 5 to 6-quart punch bowl. Add club soda and wine; mix gently. Add ice; garnish with orange, lemon and lime slices.

May substitute ginger ale for wine.

Iced Tea Punch

3	large tea bags
3	quarts boiling water
1/2	cup sugar
1	12-ounce can frozen lemonade concentrate, thawed
1	33-ounce bottle of ginger ale, chilled

Yield: 4 1/2 quarts

Steep tea bags in boiling water in pitcher for 8 minutes; remove tea bags. Stir in sugar and lemonade concentrate. Chill in refrigerator. Add ginger ale at serving time. Serve over ice.

Spicy Tomato Sipper

1	46-ounce can tomato juice
1/2	cup water
1/4	cup fresh lemon juice
1	tablespoon prepared horseradish
1/8	teaspoon lemon pepper

Yield: 6 (3/4-cup) servings

Combine tomato juice, water, lemon juice, horseradish and lemon pepper in pitcher; mix well. Chill for several hours to blend flavors.

This is a great base for Bloody Marys.

Cranberry Wassail

1/4	teaspoon nutmeg
1/4	teaspoon cinnamon
1/4	teaspoon allspice
3	tablespoons loose tea
2 1/2	cups boiling water
1	16-ounce can whole cranberry sauce
1 1/2	cups water
3/4	cups sugar
1/2	cup orange juice
1/4	cup lemon juice

Yield: 8 to 10 servings

Tie nutmeg, cinnamon, allspice and tea in cheesecloth bag. Combine with boiling water; remove from heat. Steep for 5 minutes. Stir cranberry sauce in saucepan. Add 1 1/2 cups water and sugar. Remove cheesecloth bag from tea. Add tea to cranberry mixture with orange juice and lemon juice. Cook until heated through. Serve hot.

Easy Wassail

2	cups white grape juice
2	cups apple juice
2	cups ginger ale
1/4	cup red hot cinnamon candies

Yield: 9 servings

Combine grape juice, apple juice and ginger ale in electric percolator. Place candies in basket of percolator. Perk through cycle as for strong coffee. Serve in small punch cups.

This is easy to clean up and will not damage your percolator.

Chocolate-Coffee Deluxe

4	cups hot chocolate
1 1/2	cups strong coffee
1	cup rum
1/2	cup whipping cream, whipped
1	teaspoon sugar

Yield: 6 to 8 servings

Combine hot chocolate, coffee and rum in saucepan. Heat to serving temperature. Top each serving with mixture of whipped cream and sugar.

Chocolate Vienna

4	ounces semisweet chocolate
1/3	cup sugar
1/4	teaspoon salt
1 1/3	cups boiling water
4	cups milk, scalded
1	teaspoon vanilla extract
1/2	cup whipping cream, whipped

Yield: 10 to 12 servings

Melt chocolate in double boiler over hot water. Stir in sugar and salt. Blend in boiling water. Add milk. Simmer for several minutes. Add vanilla. Whisk until frothy. Top servings with whipped cream.

Mocha Java

8	ounces sweet cooking chocolate
1	cup strong coffee
1 1/2	quarts milk, scalded

Yield: 8 servings

Melt chocolate in double boiler over hot water. Stir in coffee. Cook over low heat for 1 minute. Stir in milk. Heat to serving temperature. Whisk until frothy. Serve in mugs.

Spiced Tea Mix

1	teaspoon ground cinnamon
1/2	teaspoon ground cloves
1/2	teaspoon ground nutmeg
1 1/2	cups sugar
1/2	cup instant tea
1	cup instant orange breakfast drink mix

Yield: 60 servings

Combine cinnamon, cloves, nutmeg, sugar, tea and drink mix in bowl; mix well. Store in airtight container. Combine 2 teaspoons tea mix with 1 cup boiling water for each serving.

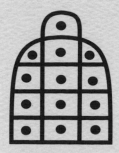

Hopi Corn

Breads

Maize

Maize, or corn, was introduced to Europe by the Spanish. "Corn" is the name given to the primary grain crop of any nation; thus "corn" and "maize" both refer to the same plant here in the Americas. In other countries, however, "corn" may be synonymous with oats, wheat, rye, barley, rice, etc.

Maize is very nutritious and is the most productive food crop per acre known to man. Maize grows easily in soils that receive too much or too little moisture. While rice grows best in semi-tropical zones and wheat flourishes primarily in temperate zones, maize thrives in both.

Corn is grown in such quantities and is used in so many products in the United States that each person consumes corn in some form every day. Livestock and poultry are fed corn. Cornstarch is used to coat frozen meats and fish to prevent freezer burn. Corn dyes color soft drinks. Corn is used to make food containers, soap, MSG, candy, ice cream, vinegar, toothpaste, dog food, cosmetics and charcoal briquettes.

Corn pollen has been discovered in prehistoric sites dating to 80,000 years ago. It is amazingly durable; thousand-year-old corn has been successfully popped. Although most people enjoy the modern, hybrid variety, there are many types, colors and sizes of corn still cultivated by Native peoples.

Popcorn, or more appropriately popped corn, has been enjoyed by Native Americans for the past 5,000 years. Columbus brought necklaces of strung popcorn back to the court of Spain from the Caribbean. Cortés recorded in his journal, dated 1510, that the Aztecs used popcorn in their religious rituals.

The Indians sometimes popped corn by holding the cob over the fire. Another method was to remove the kernels, throw them into the fire and scramble for those that popped. A more dignified method called for placing the kernels in a clay pot with hot sand. It wasn't until 1952 that the agronomist Orville Redenbacher decided to develop a hybrid strain of corn that uniformly contained 14% moisture in every kernel, thus insuring that every kernel would pop.

Mother's Whole Wheat Bread

2	**cups scalded milk or hot potato water**
1/2	**cup molasses, honey or brown sugar**
2	**tablespoons shortening**
1	**teaspoon salt**
1	**envelope dry yeast**
1/4	**cup lukewarm (105 to 115-degree) water**
4	**cups whole wheat flour**
1 1/2	**cups all-purpose flour**

Yield: 2 loaves

Combine hot milk, molasses, shortening and salt in large bowl. Let stand until cooled to lukewarm. Dissolve yeast in warm water. Add to milk mixture. Add flours gradually, mixing until dough pulls from side of bowl. Knead on floured surface for 8 minutes or until smooth and elastic. Place in greased bowl, turning to coat surface. Let rise, covered, until doubled in bulk. Punch dough down. Shape into 2 loaves; place in greased 5x9-inch loaf pans. Let rise, covered, until doubled in bulk. Bake at 350 degrees for 1 hour or until loaf sounds hollow when tapped with knife. Remove from pans to cool on wire rack.

Cheese Bread

2 3/4	**cups milk**
2	**cups shredded Cheddar cheese**
3	**tablespoons sugar**
2	**teaspoons salt**
2	**envelopes dry yeast**
6 1/2	**cups (about) flour**

Yield: 2 loaves

Heat milk and cheese in saucepan over low heat until 125 to 130 degrees; cheese need not melt. Combine sugar, salt, dry yeast and 3 cups flour in large mixer bowl. Add warm milk mixture. Beat at medium speed for 2 minutes. Stir in enough remaining flour to make stiff dough. Let rise, covered, until doubled in bulk. Punch dough down. Shape into 2 loaves; place in greased 5x9-inch loaf pans. Let rise until doubled in bulk. Bake at 375 degrees for 30 to 35 minutes or until loaves test done.

The Major General's Bakery Works

Basic Dough

4	cups lukewarm (105 to 115-degree) milk
1	cup shortening
4	cakes compressed yeast, crumbled
1	cup sugar
4	teaspoons salt
4	eggs, room temperature
10–15	cups flour

Yield: 8 loaves or 16 dozen rolls or doughnuts

Combine milk, shortening and yeast in large bowl; mix well. Mix in sugar, salt and eggs. Add flour about 3 cups at a time, mixing until dough pulls from side of bowl. Knead on floured surface for 10 to 15 minutes or until smooth and elastic. Place in greased bowl, turning to coat surface. Let rise, covered with slightly damp cloth, in warm place for 1^1/2 to 2 hours. Punch dough down; turn over. Let rise, covered, for 30 to 45 minutes. Turn onto floured surface. Divide into 4 portions. Proceed with following recipes as desired. May substitute fast-acting dry yeast for yeast cakes. Rising times will be reduced by half.

Coffee Cakes or Cinnamon Loaves

1	portion Basic Dough (above)
^{1}/4	cup butter, softened
^{1}/2	cup sugar
2	teaspoons cinnamon
^{2}/3	cup finely chopped walnuts
1	tablespoon butter, softened
1	tablespoon hot cream or water
2	cups confectioners' sugar
^{1}/2	teaspoon vanilla extract

Yield: 2 coffee cakes or loaves

Roll 1 portion of dough into 2 rectangles. Spread each with 2 tablespoons butter. Mix sugar and cinnamon. Sprinkle each rectangle with half the cinnamon-sugar and half the walnuts; press filling lightly. **Coffee Cakes:** Cut diagonal strips from outer edge toward center, leaving center ^{1}/3 intact. Fold strips over center area alternately to resemble braid. Place on greased baking sheet. Let rise, covered, for 1 hour. Bake at 400 degrees for 20 minutes or until golden brown. Spread mixture of remaining ingredients over cooled Coffee Cakes. **Cinnamon Loaves:** Roll dough and add filling as above. Roll as for jelly roll; place in greased loaf pans. Let rise and bake as above. Cool. Frost as for Coffee Cakes.

Doughnuts

¹/₂	portion Basic Dough (page 40)
	Oil for deep frying
1	cup confectioners' sugar
¹/₃	cup water
¹/₂	teaspoon vanilla extract

Yield: 2 dozen

Roll dough ¹/₂ inch thick on lightly floured surface; cut with doughnut cutter. Let rise, covered, until doubled in bulk. Blend confectioners' sugar, water and vanilla in bowl. Deep-fry several doughnuts at a time in 375-degree deep oil until brown on both sides, turning once; drain well. Dip hot doughnuts into confectioners' sugar glaze. Cool on wire rack. Freeze doughnuts by arranging in single layer with space between on tray, freezing until firm and placing desired number in plastic bag for storage in freezer.

A "man-sized" recipe—but note how easily it can be cut to your needs! Now retired, Major General Chuck Krevitsky has been using this recipe for years. The coffee cake and doughnuts never fail to win the blue ribbon at the Arizona State Fair. The whole family pitches in to make about 150 of these as gifts at holiday time.

Onion Rolls

1	portion Basic Dough (page 40)
	Chopped onion to taste
1	egg, beaten
	Poppy seeds to taste

Yield: 4 dozen

Divide 1 dough portion into equal portions. Shape each into a ball; place on greased baking sheet. Press to flatten. Place 1 teaspoon chopped onion on top of each. Brush with beaten egg; sprinkle with poppy seeds. Let rise, covered, until doubled in bulk. Bake at 425 degrees for 12 to 15 minutes or until well browned.

Butterhorn Dinner Rolls

1 1/2	cups milk, scalded
1	cup butter or margarine
1/2	cup sugar
1	teaspoon salt
1	envelope dry yeast
3	tablespoons warm (105 to 115-degree) water
5–5 1/2	cups all-purpose or bread flour
3	eggs
1/4	cup butter or margarine, softened
1/2	cup butter or margarine, melted

Yield: 3 dozen

Combine milk, 1 cup butter, sugar and salt in large bowl; mix until sugar dissolves. Let stand until cooled to lukewarm. Mix yeast with warm water. Let stand for 3 to 4 minutes. Add 2 cups flour to milk mixture. Beat in eggs 1 at a time. Stir in yeast. Add enough remaining flour 1 cup at a time to make medium dough. Let rise, covered, in warm place until doubled in bulk. Punch dough down. Refrigerate overnight. Divide dough into 3 portions; roll each into 12-inch circle. Spread with softened butter; cut into 12 wedges. Roll as for jelly roll from wide end; shape into crescent on greased baking sheet. Brush with melted butter. Let rise, covered, for 1 to 2 hours or until light. Bake at 350 degrees for 10 to 15 minutes or until golden brown.

Easy Butterscotch Rolls

1	cup chopped nuts
18	frozen rolls
1/2	cup packed brown sugar
1/2	4-ounce package butterscotch pudding and pie filling mix
1/2	cup melted butter or margarine

Yield: 8 to 10 servings

Spray bundt pan with nonstick cooking spray. Layer nuts, rolls, brown sugar and pudding mix in prepared pan. Drizzle melted butter over top. Let stand, covered with foil, at room temperature overnight to rise. Bake at 375 degrees for 30 minutes. Let stand in pan for 5 minutes. Invert onto serving plate. Do not use instant pudding mix.

Overnight Caramel-Pecan Rolls

2	cups milk, scalded
2	envelopes dry yeast
1/2	cup lukewarm (105 to 115-degree) water
1/3	cup sugar
1/3	cup vegetable oil
1	tablespoon baking powder
2	teaspoons salt
1	egg
7 1/2	cups (or less) flour
	Caramel Topping
2	cups pecan halves
1/4	cup butter or margarine, softened
1/2	cup sugar
4 1/2	teaspoons ground cinnamon

Yield: 2 dozen

Cool milk to lukewarm. Dissolve yeast in warm water in large bowl. Add milk, sugar, oil, baking powder, salt, egg and 3 cups flour; beat until smooth. Add remaining 3 1/2 cups flour; mix well. Add up to 1 additional cup flour or enough to make easy-to-handle dough. Knead on floured surface for 8 to 10 minutes or until smooth and elastic. Place in greased bowl, turning to coat surface. Let rise, covered, in warm place for 1 1/2 hours or until doubled in bulk. Divide Caramel Topping between two 9x13-inch baking pans. Sprinkle each with 1 cup pecans. Punch dough down. Divide into 2 portions. Roll each portion into 10x12-inch rectangle. Spread with butter; sprinkle with mixture of sugar and cinnamon. Roll as for jelly roll from 12-inch side. Cut each into 12 slices; arrange in prepared pans. Refrigerate, covered with foil, for 12 to 48 hours. Bake, uncovered, at 350 degrees for 30 to 35 minutes or until golden brown. Invert onto heatproof serving platter immediately. Let stand for 1 minute before removing pan to allow caramel to drizzle over rolls.

Caramel Topping

2	cups packed brown sugar
1	cup butter or margarine
1/4	cup light corn syrup

Heat brown sugar and butter in saucepan over low heat until butter melts, stirring contantly; remove from heat. Blend in corn syrup.

Avocado Bread

2	cups flour
1/2	teaspoon baking soda
1	teaspoon baking powder
1/4	teaspoon salt
1/2	cup butter or margarine, softened
3/4	cup sugar
2	eggs
3/4	cup mashed ripe avocado
1	tablespoon fresh lemon juice
1/3	cup milk
1/2	cup sliced almonds

Yield: 1 loaf

Sift flour, baking soda, baking powder and salt together; set aside. Cream butter and sugar in large bowl until light and fluffy. Add eggs and avocado; mix until smooth. Mix lemon juice and milk; milk will curdle. Add milk mixture and flour mixture alternately to avocado mixture, mixing well after each addition. Stir in almonds. Pour into greased 5x9-inch loaf pan. Bake at 350 degrees for 1 hour.

Bread is best when allowed to mellow for a day before slicing.

Mano and Metate ∼

The term "metate" is used in the Southwest to refer to a shallow, trough-shaped stone that is used to grind corn. The corn is placed in the metate and the hand-held "mano," a smaller flat stone, is rubbed back and forth on the corn until the desired consistency is reached.

A number of manos and metates have been placed around the Courtyard of The Heard Museum so visitors may grind a handful of corn to get an idea of the amount of work required to grind enough corn to make a batch of corn bread.

Although manos and metates are still used, food grinders or blenders have replaced them in many of today's Native American kitchens.

Cheddar-Nut Bread

3³/₄	cups buttermilk baking mix
1¹/₂	cups shredded sharp Cheddar cheese
1	cup evaporated milk
¹/₂	cup water
¹/₂	cup chopped nuts
1	egg, slightly beaten

Yield: 1 loaf

Combine baking mix, cheese, evaporated milk, water, nuts and egg in bowl. Beat vigorously for 30 seconds. Spoon into greased 5x9-inch loaf pan. Bake at 350 degrees for 40 to 50 minutes or until wooden pick inserted in center comes out clean. Serve warm or cold.

Chutney Bread

2¹/₂	cups flour
3¹/₂	teaspoons baking powder
1	teaspoon salt
¹/₂	cup sugar
¹/₂	cup packed brown sugar
1	tablespoon grated orange rind
1¹/₄	cups milk
1	egg
3	tablespoons vegetable oil
1	9 or 10-ounce jar mango chutney
1	cup chopped walnuts
8	ounces cream cheese, softened
¹/₂	cup confectioners' sugar
1–2	tablespoons curry powder

Yield: 1 loaf

Mix flour, baking powder and salt; set aside. Combine sugar, brown sugar, orange rind, milk, egg and oil in large bowl; mix until smooth. Add flour mixture; mix well. Stir in chutney and walnuts. Pour into greased and floured 5x9-inch loaf pan. Bake at 350 degrees for 65 to 75 minutes or until wooden pick inserted in center comes out clean. Cool in pan for 10 minutes. Remove to wire rack to cool completely. Combine cream cheese, confectioners' sugar and curry powder in bowl; beat until smooth. Serve on thinly sliced bread.

Chutney Bread with the curried cheese spread is great served as an appetizer, or with a luncheon main dish chicken or fruit salad. Chutney Bread is a tasty snack served with Cheddar or Havarti cheese.

Crackling Coconut Bread

3	cups flour
1/2	teaspoon baking soda
1/2	teaspoon baking powder
1/2	teaspoon salt
4	eggs
2	cups sugar
1	cup vegetable oil
2	teaspoons coconut extract
1	cup buttermilk
1	cup coconut
1	cup chopped pecans
	Coconut Glaze

Yield: 2 loaves

Combine flour, baking soda, baking powder and salt; set aside. Combine eggs, sugar, oil and coconut extract in bowl; mix well. Add flour mixture alternately with buttermilk, mixing well after each addition. Stir in coconut and pecans. Pour into 2 greased 5x9-inch loaf pans. Bake at 325 degrees for 1 hour or until loaves test done. Pour Coconut Glaze over hot loaves. Let stand in pans for 10 minutes. Remove to wire rack to cool.

Coconut Glaze

1 1/2	cups sugar
3/4	cup water
3	tablespoons butter
1	teaspoon coconut extract

Combine sugar, water and butter in saucepan. Boil for 5 minutes. Stir in coconut extract.

Freezes well.

Pima Wheat ∼

Traditionally the Pima grew summer crops of corn, beans and squash on land irrigated by the Gila River. In the late 1600s, Father Kino introduced wheat to the Pima which could be grown in winter months. By the mid-19th century the Pima had surplus wheat which they sold to pioneers and to military personnel who came through the Arizona territory.

Lemon Loaf

1¹/₂	**cups flour**
1	**teaspoon baking powder**
¹/₂	**teaspoon salt**
6	**tablespoons butter, softened**
1	**cup sugar**
2	**eggs**
2	**teaspoons grated lemon rind**
¹/₂	**cup milk**
¹/₂	**cup chopped nuts**
	Juice of 1 lemon
¹/₂	**cup sugar**

Yield: 1 loaf

Sift flour, baking powder and salt together; set aside. Cream butter and 1 cup sugar in mixer bowl. Add eggs and lemon rind; beat until fluffy. Add flour mixture alternately with milk, mixing well after each addition. Stir in nuts. Pour into greased 5x9-inch loaf pan lined with waxed paper. Bake at 350 degrees for 1 hour or until loaf tests done. Heat lemon juice and ¹/₂ cup sugar in saucepan, stirring until sugar dissolves. Pour hot mixture over hot loaf. Let stand in pan for 30 minutes. Remove to wire rack to cool. Remove waxed paper.

Wrap loaf in foil and let stand overnight before cutting.

Pineapple-Date-Nut Loaf

2³/₄	**cups flour**
1	**tablespoon baking powder**
¹/₂	**teaspoon baking soda**
¹/₄	**teaspoon salt**
³/₄	**cup sugar**
¹/₃	**cup melted butter**
1	**egg, beaten**
1	**16-ounce can crushed pineapple**
1	**8-ounce package pitted dates, chopped**
1	**cup chopped nuts**

Yield: 1 loaf

Sift flour, baking powder, baking soda and salt together; set aside. Combine sugar, butter and egg in bowl; beat until light. Add undrained pineapple, dates and nuts; mix well. Add flour mixture; mix well. Pour into greased and floured 5x9-inch loaf pan. Bake at 350 degrees for 1¹/₄ hours or until loaf tests done.

Olive-Nut Bread

1¹/₂   **cups all-purpose flour**
4   **teaspoons baking powder**
¹/₂   **teaspoon salt**
1   **cup whole wheat flour**
1   **egg, beaten**
1   **cup milk**
2   **tablespoons melted butter**
1   **cup sliced stuffed green olives**
³/₄   **cup chopped nuts**

Yield: 1 loaf

Sift all-purpose flour, baking powder and salt into bowl. Mix in whole wheat flour. Combine egg, milk and butter; mix well. Add to flour mixture; mix with several swift strokes. Fold in olives and nuts. Batter will be stiff. Pour into greased 5x9-inch loaf pan. Bake at 350 degrees for 45 minutes or until loaf tests done. Remove from pan to cool on wire rack.

Thinly sliced bread makes a good canapé or sandwich base.

Banana-Bran Muffins

1¹/₂   **cups flour**
¹/₂   **cup packed brown sugar**
2¹/₂   **teaspoons baking powder**
¹/₂   **teaspoon cloves**
    Dash of salt
³/₄   **cup mashed bananas**
1   **cup whole bran cereal**
²/₃   **cup milk**
1   **egg, beaten**
¹/₄   **cup vegetable oil**
¹/₂   **cup chopped nuts**
¹/₂   **cup raisins**

Yield: 1 dozen

Mix flour, brown sugar, baking powder, cloves and salt together; set aside. Combine bananas, cereal and milk in bowl. Let stand for 2 minutes or until cereal is soft. Add egg and oil; mix well. Add flour mixture; mix just until moistened. Stir in nuts and raisins. Fill greased or paper-lined muffin cups ³/₄ full. Bake at 375 degrees for 25 to 30 minutes or until rich golden brown.

May freeze muffins and reheat by wrapping in paper towel sprinkled with water and microwaving for 45 seconds.

Chocolate-Zucchini Muffins

3	eggs
2	cups sugar
3/4	cup corn oil
1/4	cup butter, softened
1	teaspoon vanilla extract
2	teaspoons almond extract
2 1/4	cups flour
1	teaspoon baking soda
1	teaspoon baking powder
1/2	teaspoon salt
1	tablespoon cinnamon
1/4	cup baking cocoa
2	cups grated zucchini
1	cup chopped walnuts
1	cup miniature chocolate chips

Yield: 2 dozen

Beat eggs in mixer bowl until frothy. Add sugar; beat until thickened. Add corn oil, butter and vanilla and almond extracts; beat until well blended. Sift in dry ingredients. Beat for 2 minutes. Scrape bowl. Beat for 2 minutes longer. Stir in zucchini, walnuts and chocolate chips. Fill greased or paper-lined muffin cups 3/4 full. Bake at 350 degrees for 25 to 30 minutes or until muffins test done. Garnish with dusting of confectioners' sugar.

Muffins freeze well.

Fruitful Muffins

1	cup uncooked rolled oats
1	cup flour
1	tablespoon baking powder
1/2	teaspoon cinnamon
1	cup skim milk
1/2	cup mashed banana
1/2	cup raisins
1/4	cup vegetable oil
1/4	cup packed brown sugar
2	egg whites

Yield: 1 dozen

Combine oats, flour, baking powder and cinnamon in bowl. Combine skim milk, banana, raisins, oil, brown sugar and egg whites in medium bowl; mix well. Add to dry ingredients; mix just until moistened. Fill greased or paper-lined muffin cups 3/4 full. Bake at 400 degrees for 20 to 25 minutes or until golden brown.

May substitute 1/2 cup chopped apricots, dates or prunes for raisins if desired.

Blueberry-Sour Cream Muffins

1¹/₄	cups flour
¹/₂	teaspoon baking soda
¹/₂	teaspoon baking powder
¹/₄	teaspoon salt
¹/₄	cup butter, softened
³/₄	cup sugar
2	eggs
1	teaspoon grated lemon rind
¹/₂	cup sour cream
1	cup fresh or frozen blueberries
¹/₄	cup sugar
2	tablespoons flour
¹/₄	teaspoon nutmeg
1	tablespoon cold butter

Yield: 1 dozen

Sift 1¹/₄ cups flour, baking soda, baking powder and salt together; set aside. Cream ¹/₄ cup butter and ³/₄ cup sugar in mixer bowl until light and fluffy. Add eggs and lemon rind; beat until fluffy. Add sifted dry ingredients alternately with sour cream, mixing well after each addition. Fold in blueberries. Fill greased or paper-lined muffin cups ³/₄ full. Mix ¹/₄ cup sugar, 2 tablespoons flour and nutmeg in small bowl. Cut in 1 tablespoon butter until crumbly. Sprinkle over muffin batter. Bake at 400 degrees for 18 to 20 minutes or until brown.

Muffins freeze well.

Corn Muffins

1²/₃	cups flour
1²/₃	cups yellow cornmeal
4	teaspoons baking powder
¹/₂	teaspoon salt
³/₄	cup butter or margarine, softened
³/₄	cup sugar
3	eggs
2	cups milk
1	11-ounce can whole kernel corn, drained

Yield: 2 dozen

Combine flour, cornmeal, baking powder and salt; set aside. Cream butter and sugar in bowl until light and fluffy. Add eggs 1 at a time, beating well after each addition. Add cornmeal mixture alternately with milk, mixing well after each addition. Stir in corn. Spoon into greased muffin cups. Bake at 425 degrees for 20 to 25 minutes or until golden brown.

Anne's Corn Muffins

1	cup cornmeal
1	cup boiling water
1	tablespoon margarine, softened
1	egg
1/2	cup milk
1/2	teaspoon salt
1	tablespoon sugar
2	teaspoons baking powder

Yield: 1 dozen

Combine cornmeal and boiling water in bowl. Stir in margarine. Add egg, milk, salt, sugar and baking powder; beat until smooth. Spoon into greased muffin cups. Bake at 475 degrees for 25 to 30 minutes or until golden brown.

There is no flour in this recipe.

Cranberry Streusel Muffins

1	cup flour
1	cup packed brown sugar
1/2	cup butter
3	tablespoons finely chopped walnuts
1	cup flour
2	teaspoons baking powder
1/2	teaspoon baking soda
1/2	teaspoon salt
1	teaspoon nutmeg
1/2	teaspoon grated orange rind
2	eggs, beaten
3/4	cup buttermilk
1	cup chopped fresh cranberries
1/2	cup chopped walnuts

Yield: 1 1/2 dozen

Mix 1 cup flour and brown sugar in bowl. Cut in butter until crumbly. Reserve 1/2 cup mixture. Mix finely chopped walnuts into reserved crumb mixture; set aside. Add 1 cup flour, baking powder, baking soda, salt, nutmeg and orange rind to remaining crumb mixture. Beat eggs with buttermilk. Add to flour mixture; mix just until moistened. Stir in cranberries and walnuts. Fill 18 greased muffin cups half full. Sprinkle with reserved crumb mixture. Bake at 375 degrees for 20 to 25 minutes or until golden brown.

Muffins freeze well.

Orange-Date Muffins

1³/4	cups flour
3/4	cup sugar
1	teaspoon baking powder
1	teaspoon baking soda
1	orange
1/2	cup orange juice
1/2	cup chopped dates
1	egg
1/2	cup butter or margarine, softened

Yield: 16 muffins

Sift flour, sugar, baking powder and baking soda together; set aside. Cut orange into 7 or 8 pieces; discard seeds. Combine orange pieces and orange juice in blender container. Process until puréed. Add dates, egg and butter to blender container. Process until well mixed. Pour into bowl. Add flour mixture; mix just until moistened. Fill greased muffin cups 3/4 full. Bake at 400 degrees for 20 minutes.

Banana Brunch Coffee Cake

1	2-layer package yellow cake mix
1	small package vanilla instant pudding mix
1/2	cup vegetable oil
4	eggs or 1 cup egg substitute
1	teaspoon vanilla extract
1	cup mashed ripe bananas
1/2	cup chopped nuts
2/3	cup packed brown sugar
1	teaspoon cinnamon
1	teaspoon nutmeg

Yield: 12 servings

Combine cake mix, pudding mix, oil, eggs, vanilla and bananas in mixer bowl. Beat at medium speed for 8 minutes, scraping side of bowl frequently. Combine nuts, brown sugar, cinnamon and nutmeg in small bowl; mix well. Pour half the batter into greased 3-quart bundt pan. Sprinkle with brown sugar mixture. Add remaining batter. Swirl through layers with knife in figure-8 pattern. Bake at 300 degrees for 55 minutes. Cool in pan for 10 to 15 minutes. Invert onto serving plate.

May dust coffee cake with confectioners' sugar before serving.

Warm Plum Coffee Cake

1¹/₂	cups flour
¹/₂	cup sugar
2	teaspoons baking powder
1	teaspoon salt
1	egg
¹/₂	cup milk
¹/₃	cup vegetable oil
2	pounds fresh plums
¹/₃	cup butter
¹/₂	cup flour
¹/₃	cup sugar
¹/₂	teaspoon cinnamon

Yield: 1 coffee cake

Combine 1¹/₂ cups flour, ¹/₂ cup sugar, baking powder and salt in large bowl. Beat egg with milk and oil. Add to flour mixture; stir until well mixed. Spread batter evenly in greased 9x13-inch baking pan. Cut plums into halves, discarding pits. Arrange plums cut side up over batter. Combine butter, ¹/₂ cup flour, ¹/₃ cup sugar and cinnamon in small bowl; mix until crumbly. Sprinkle over plums. Bake at 425 degrees for 25 minutes or until golden brown. Serve slightly warm.

May substitute other fruit such as peaches, nectarines, or fresh berries or canned cherry pie filling for plums.

Cornmeal Waffles

1	egg
³/₄	cup milk
¹/₄	cup vegetable oil
1	cup flour
2	tablespoons cornmeal
2	teaspoons baking powder
2	teaspoons sugar
¹/₄	teaspoon salt

Yield: 6 (6¹/₂-inch) waffles

Preheat waffle iron. If your waffle iron is not nonstick, spray both top and bottom grids lightly with nonstick cooking spray. Combine egg, milk, oil, flour, cornmeal, baking powder, sugar and salt in blender container. Process just until ingredients are moistened; do not overmix. Pour ¹/₂ cup batter onto hot waffle grid; close top. Bake for 3 minutes or until golden brown. Serve piping hot with warmed syrup, sour cream and fruit, warmed preserves or marmalade, whipped cream or ice cream.

Gingerbread Waffles

1	cup all-purpose flour
3/4	cup whole wheat or oat bran flour
1	tablespoon baking powder
1/4	teaspoon salt
1/2	teaspoon ginger
1/4	teaspoon cloves
2	eggs
11/3	cups milk
1/2	cup vegetable oil
1/3	cup molasses

Yield: 10 to 12 (4-inch) waffles

Preheat waffle iron. If your waffle iron is not nonstick, spray both top and bottom grids lightly with nonstick cooking spray. Combine all-purpose flour, whole wheat flour, baking powder, salt, ginger and cloves; set aside. Combine eggs, milk, oil and molasses in medium bowl; whisk until blended. Add flour mixture; mix just until moistened. Batter will be lumpy. Ladle onto hot waffle grid; close top. Bake using manufacturer's instructions. Serve warm with syrup or apricot jam.

Waffles freeze well.

Corn Sticks

11/4	cups yellow cornmeal
1/2	cup flour
1	tablespoon baking powder
1	teaspoon salt
2	teaspoons sugar
1	egg
1	cup minus 1 tablespoon milk
3	tablespoons melted margarine

Yield: 14 servings

Combine cornmeal, flour, baking powder, salt and sugar in medium bowl. Beat egg with milk and melted margarine. Add to cornmeal mixture; stir just until mixed. Spoon into 2 oiled 7-corn stick pans or 1 greased 8x8-inch baking pan. Bake at 425 degrees for 20 minutes or until brown. Serve hot.

Zuni Frog

Soups
& Sandwiches

Peanuts

Peanuts, called groundnuts by the Spanish explorers, were first encountered in what is today Haiti. The peanut, however, had a wide distribution in Native America, and it was also an important cultivated crop of the Inca. High in protein, the peanut was an important food crop for an empire that stretched from southern Colombia to central Chile, and included 15 million people. The Spanish, however, considered the peanut odd. They were familiar with nuts that grew on trees, but were unprepared for nuts that grew underground. Because of this, they labeled the plant "groundnut" and were slow to adopt it into their diet.

Peanuts were more readily accepted in Southeast Asia, and currently they are a part of Thai, Vietnamese, Chinese and Indonesian cuisines. Peanuts also became an important part of the African diet.

In the United States, an unknown St. Louis physician popularized peanut butter as a health food, and the craze for peanut butter and jelly sandwiches was launched. Although the Native Americans of the New England area had long dipped popped corn and peanuts into maple syrup to make a snack, it wasn't until the Chicago World's Fair in 1893 that Cracker Jack snacks became popular.

Cream of Asparagus Soup

1	large yellow onion, coarsely chopped
4	cloves of garlic, minced
2	large leeks with green part, coarsely chopped
1/4	cup unsalted butter
2	14-ounce cans chicken broth
3	pounds fresh asparagus
1/4	cup chopped fresh parsley
1	teaspoon dried tarragon
1/4	teaspoon basil
1	teaspoon salt
1	teaspoon freshly ground black pepper
	Cayenne pepper to taste
1	cup half and half
1	cup sour cream

Yield: 6 to 8 servings

Sauté onion, garlic and leeks in butter in saucepan for 10 to 15 minutes or until tender. Add chicken broth. Bring to a boil. Discard woody ends of asparagus and peel stems; cut into 1-inch pieces. Reserve asparagus tips; add remaining asparagus to soup with parsley, tarragon, basil, salt, black pepper and cayenne pepper. Simmer, covered, for 45 minutes. Cool slightly. Process in several batches in blender until smooth. Strain through medium sieve into saucepan. Add reserved asparagus tips. Simmer over medium heat for 10 minutes or until tender. Stir in half and half. Chill, covered, for 4 hours to several days. Reheat to serve. Ladle into soup bowls. Top each serving with sour cream.

Flavor improves with longer chilling time.

Avocado Soup

1	large avocado, peeled, sliced
1 1/2	cups chicken broth
1	clove of garlic
	Cayenne pepper or hot pepper sauce to taste
1	cup sour cream
1	cup half and half or milk
	Salt to taste

Yield: 4 to 6 servings

Combine avocado, chicken broth, garlic and cayenne pepper in blender container; process at high speed for 15 seconds, scraping down side. Add sour cream, half and half and salt; process for 10 seconds or until smooth. Chill until serving time. Pour into soup bowls. Garnish each serving with chopped chives or parsley.

Orange and Carrot Soup

¹/₂	teaspoon minced ginger
1	pound carrots, sliced
¹/₂	cup chopped onion
2	tablespoons margarine
3	cups chicken broth
1¹/₂	cups orange juice

Yield: 6 to 8 servings

Sauté ginger, carrots and onion in margarine in saucepan. Add chicken broth. Simmer, covered, for 30 to 40 minutes or until of desired consistency. Add orange juice. Process in blender until smooth. Cool to room temperature. Chill until serving time. Ladle into soup bowls.

Gazpacho

1	46-ounce can tomato juice
1	clove of garlic, crushed
1	tablespoon sugar
¹/₄	cup olive oil
2	tablespoons fresh lemon juice
1	teaspoon Worcestershire sauce
3	tomatoes, chopped
1	cucumber, chopped
1	green bell pepper, chopped
1	cup shredded carrot
1	cup thinly sliced celery
¹/₄	cup sliced scallions

Yield: 10 to 14 servings

Combine tomato juice, garlic, sugar, olive oil, lemon juice and Worcestershire sauce in large bowl; mix well. Add tomatoes, cucumber, green pepper, carrot, celery and scallions; mix well. Chill for 4 hours to overnight. Ladle into soup bowls.

This cold soup may be served as an appetizer or as a light supper with hard rolls and a good cheese.

Saltbush ～

Saltbush is a common southwestern shrub. The leaves and young shoots are gathered in spring and added to soups and stews. The four-winged seeds are collected in summer and autumn and ground into meal. The Hopi use ashes of the leaves to enrich the color of Piki Bread.

Cream of Leek Soup

1¹/₂	cups minced leeks with tops
¹/₂	cup minced onion
1	clove of garlic, minced
¹/₄	cup butter
1	quart chicken broth
1¹/₂	cups chopped peeled potatoes
1	cup whipping cream
	Salt and pepper to taste

Yield: 8 to 10 servings

Sauté minced leeks, onion and garlic in butter in saucepan until tender. Add chicken broth and potatoes. Simmer, covered, for 15 minutes. Process in food processor until smooth. Combine with cream, salt and pepper in bowl or saucepan. Ladle into soup bowls. Serve cold or heat to serving temperature. Garnish servings with chopped chives.

To prepare leeks, slice lengthwise almost to bottom. Rinse well under running water, spreading layers to remove all sand.

Cold One-of-Each Soup

1	medium potato, peeled, chopped
1	medium onion, chopped
¹/₂	banana, chopped
1	stalk celery heart with leaves, chopped
1	apple, chopped
3	cups chicken broth
1	tablespoon melted butter
1	cup cream
1	teaspoon salt
1	teaspoon (heaping) curry powder

Yield: 6 servings

Combine chopped potato, onion, banana, celery, apple and chicken broth in saucepan. Simmer until tender. Process in food processor until smooth. Combine with melted butter, cream, salt and curry powder in bowl; mix well. Chill until serving time. Ladle into soup bowls. Garnish servings with chopped chives.

Chilled Orange Soup

1½	tablespoons unflavored gelatin
½	cup cold water
1	cup strained orange juice
1	cup sugar
3	cups strained orange juice
2	tablespoons lime juice
	Juice and grated rind of 1 lemon
	Juice and pulp of 6 oranges

Yield: 8 to 12 servings

Soften gelatin in cold water in saucepan. Heat over low heat until gelatin dissolves. Add 1 cup strained orange juice and sugar. Cook until sugar dissolves; remove from heat. Add 3 cups strained orange juice, lime juice, lemon juice and lemon rind; mix well. Chill until partially set. Beat until frothy. Add juice and pulp of 6 oranges; mix well. Chill until serving time, beating occasionally. Beat just before serving. Spoon into chilled glasses; garnish with mint sprigs.

Chilled Red Bell Pepper Soup

4	cups chopped seeded red bell peppers
2	cups sliced leeks with green parts
⅓	cup butter
1½	cups chicken stock
4	cups buttermilk
	Salt and white pepper to taste
	Hot pepper sauce to taste
1	bunch chives, finely chopped

Yield: 6 to 8 servings

Sauté bell peppers and leeks in butter in 3-quart aluminum saucepan until tender but not brown. Add chicken stock. Bring to a boil; reduce heat. Simmer, covered, for 30 minutes. Cool for 15 minutes. Process in blender until smooth. Add buttermilk, salt, white pepper and hot sauce. Chill for 3 to 24 hours. Pour into soup bowls. Top servings with chives.

This soup improves in flavor if allowed to mellow 24 hours.

Cheese and Potato Soup

3	cups chopped potatoes
1	cup chopped celery
1	cup chopped carrot
1	cup chopped onion
1	cup water
1¹/₂	cups chicken broth
2	tablespoons flour
8	ounces shredded American cheese
1	tablespoon chopped parsley
¹/₂	teaspoon salt
¹/₂	teaspoon pepper

Yield: 4 to 6 servings

Combine potatoes, celery, carrot, onion and water in saucepan. Bring to a boil; reduce heat. Simmer for 15 minutes or until vegetables are tender, stirring occasionally. Blend chicken broth and flour in small bowl. Add to soup. Cook until thickened, stirring constantly. Add cheese, stirring until melted. Add parsley, salt and pepper. Cook until heated through. Ladle into soup bowls.

When broccoli is in season, chop 1 to 2 cups and add to soup at end of cooking time for flavor and color.

Many Bean Soup

2	cups mixed dried Anasazi, Great Northern, navy, black, garbanzo, pinto and red beans
2	tablespoons salt
2	quarts water
2	cups chopped cooked ham or sliced smoked sausage
1	large onion, chopped
1	clove of garlic, minced
1	teaspoon pepper
1	28-ounce can tomatoes, chopped
1–2	tablespoons fresh lemon juice

Yield: 2 quarts

Sort and rinse beans. Combine with salt and water to cover in bowl. Soak overnight; drain. Combine with 2 quarts water and ham in large saucepan. Simmer for 2¹/₂ to 3 hours. Add onion, garlic, pepper, tomatoes and lemon juice. Simmer for 45 minutes longer. Adjust salt if necessary. Ladle into soup bowls.

Cream of Zucchini Soup

2	tablespoons finely chopped shallots
1	clove of garlic, minced
1	pound young zucchini, thinly sliced
2	tablespoons butter
1	teaspoon curry powder
1/2	teaspoon salt
1/2	cup whipping cream or milk
1³/4	cups chicken broth

Yield: 4 servings

Cook shallots, garlic and zucchini in hot butter in covered skillet over low heat for 10 minutes or until tender but not brown. Process in blender or food processor until smooth. Combine with curry powder, salt, cream and chicken broth in bowl; mix well. Chill until serving time. Ladle into soup bowls.

Chili

1	pound lean ground beef
1	clove of garlic, minced
1	large onion, finely chopped
1	medium green bell pepper, finely chopped
1/4	cup chili powder
1	tablespoon cider vinegar
1/4	teaspoon allspice
1/4	teaspoon coriander
1	teaspoon cumin
1/2	teaspoon salt
1/2	cup water
1	16-ounce can crushed tomatoes
1	16-ounce can red kidney beans

Yield: 8 servings

Brown ground beef with garlic, onion and green pepper in heavy saucepan over high heat, stirring until ground beef is crumbly; drain. Add chili powder, vinegar, allspice, coriander, cumin, salt, water, tomatoes and undrained beans; mix well. Bring to a boil; reduce heat. Simmer, covered, for 45 minutes, stirring frequently. Ladle into soup bowls.
Beanless Chili: Omit beans and use 2 pounds ground beef; increase salt to ³/4 teaspoon.
Meatless Chili: Omit ground beef and water. Sauté vegetables in 1 tablespoon vegetable oil until tender-crisp and add one 16-ounce can each garbanzo beans and pinto beans.

May add cayenne pepper or hot pepper sauce. May add masa for thicker consistency.

Easy Killer Chili

1	pound lean ground beef
1	onion, chopped
2	cloves of garlic, minced
1	tablespoon chili powder
1	28-ounce can tomatoes, chopped
	Salt and pepper to taste
1	4-ounce can chopped green chiles
2	28-ounce cans ranch-style pinto beans

Yield: 4 to 6 servings

Brown ground beef with onion in 4 to 5-quart saucepan, stirring until ground beef is crumbly; drain. Add garlic, chili powder, undrained tomatoes, salt, pepper and green chiles. Simmer, covered, for 1 hour. Add beans. Cook until heated through. Ladle into soup bowls. Serve with corn bread or Indian fry bread and with hot pepper sauce for those who want it hotter.

This recipe was contributed by Margaret Wood, a Native American exhibitor at the Heard Museum Guild Indian Fair each year.

Crab Chowder Supreme

1/2	cup chopped onion
1/2	cup chopped celery
3	tablespoons butter or margarine
3	cups milk
1	10-ounce can potato soup
1	7-ounce can crab meat, drained, flaked
1	8-ounce can cream-style corn
2	tablespoons chopped pimento
1/4	teaspoon salt
1/4	teaspoon dried thyme, crushed
1	bay leaf
1/4	cup dry sherry
1/4	cup chopped parsley

Yield: 6 servings

Sauté onion and celery in butter in large saucepan until tender. Add milk, soup, crab meat, corn, pimento, salt, thyme and bay leaf. Cook for 15 minutes or until heated through, stirring frequently. Stir in sherry. Simmer for 2 minutes longer; discard bay leaf. Ladle into soup bowls. Top servings with parsley.

Pasta and Bean Stew

1/2	cup chopped onion
1/2	cup chopped green bell pepper
2	cloves of garlic, minced
2	teaspoons vegetable oil
1	16-ounce can tomatoes, chopped or crushed
4	ounces uncooked small pasta shells
1	cup water
1/2	teaspoon oregano, crushed
1/4	teaspoon basil, crushed
1/8	teaspoon pepper
1	16-ounce can garbanzo beans, drained
1	8-ounce can kidney beans
1	tablespoon grated Parmesan cheese

Yield: 6 servings

Sauté onion, green pepper and garlic in oil in 6-quart saucepan over medium heat until tender. Add tomatoes. Bring to a boil. Add pasta, water, oregano, basil and pepper; reduce heat. Simmer, covered, for 10 minutes, stirring occasionally. Add drained garbanzo beans and undrained kidney beans. Simmer for 5 minutes or until heated through, stirring frequently. Add Parmesan cheese just before serving. Ladle into soup bowls.

Spinach Stracciatella Soup

1	pound fresh spinach
6	cups chicken broth
3	eggs, beaten
5	tablespoons grated Parmesan cheese
1/4	teaspoon salt
1/4	teaspoon white pepper
	Nutmeg to taste
1	lemon, thinly sliced

Yield: 6 servings

Wash spinach, discarding stems; chop fine. Add to boiling chicken broth in 3-quart saucepan. Cook for 1 minute or just until wilted. Beat eggs with Parmesan cheese, salt, pepper and nutmeg in bowl. Add to soup gradually, whisking constantly. Simmer for 1 minute; adjust seasonings. Ladle into soup bowls. Top servings with slice of lemon.

Pistou Soup with Sausage

4	large leeks
8	ounces linguiça sausage, sliced ¹/₂ inch thick
1	large carrot, chopped
1	cup chopped thin-skinned potatoes
6	cups chicken broth
6	cups water
¹/₂	cup dried split peas
4	ounces green beans, cut into 1-inch pieces
²/₃	cup uncooked spaghetti or linguine, broken into 2-inch pieces
	Pistou

Yield: 6 to 8 servings

Discard all but 2 inches green stems from leeks. Split leeks lengthwise, rinse well and slice. Brown sausage in 8-quart saucepan over medium heat, stirring frequently. Add leeks and carrot. Sauté for 6 to 8 minutes or until leeks are tender. Add potatoes, chicken broth, water and peas. Simmer, covered, for 1 hour. Add beans, pasta and Pistou. Simmer for 6 minutes or until pasta is cooked *al dente*. Ladle into soup bowls. Serve with green salad and crusty bread.

Pistou

4	cloves of garlic, pressed
1	6-ounce can tomato paste
³/₄	cup grated Parmesan cheese
¹/₄	cup minced parsley
1¹/₂	tablespoons chopped fresh basil
¹/₄	cup olive oil

Combine garlic, tomato paste, Parmesan cheese, parsley, basil and olive oil in bowl; mix until smooth.

Taco-in-a-Bowl

1¹/₂	pounds lean ground beef
1	large onion, chopped
1	28-ounce can crushed tomatoes in purée
1	15-ounce can kidney beans
1	envelope taco seasoning mix
1	8-ounce can corn
1	small avocado, chopped
¹/₄	cup sliced black olives

Yield: 4 to 6 servings

Brown ground beef with onion in saucepan, stirring frequently; drain. Add tomatoes, undrained beans, seasoning mix and undrained corn; mix well. Simmer for 15 minutes, adding tomato juice if necessary for desired consistency. Add avocado and olives. Cook just until heated through. Ladle into soup bowls. Garnish servings with sour cream. Serve with shredded Cheddar cheese and tortilla chips.

Cream of Mushroom Soup

1	pound fresh mushrooms, sliced
5	tablespoons butter or margarine
2	tablespoons flour
1	10-ounce can condensed beef broth
1	onion, sliced 1/2 inch thick
2	small bay leaves
1/2	teaspoon basil, crumbled
1/4	teaspoon salt
1/8	teaspoon white pepper
3	cups milk or light cream

Yield: 6 servings

Sauté mushrooms in 4 tablespoons butter in saucepan over high heat until light brown; remove to bowl. Add remaining 1 tablespoon butter and flour to saucepan; mix well. Cook until bubbly. Add broth gradually, stirring constantly. Add onion and seasonings. Cook until thickened, stirring constantly. Stir in milk. Cook over low heat for 8 minutes, stirring occasionally; do not boil. Remove and discard onion and bay leaves. Add mushrooms. Cook until heated through. Ladle into soup bowls. Serve with crackers.

May substitute 2% milk for whole milk or cream.

Roquefort and Onion Soup

6	large onions, thinly sliced
3	cloves of garlic, pressed
1	tablespoon olive oil
1	tablespoon butter or margarine
6	cups chicken stock
1 1/2	cups dry white wine
1/2	teaspoon dried thyme
2	cups chicken stock
2	teaspoons fresh lemon juice
1/2	teaspoon salt
	Cayenne pepper to taste
	Freshly ground black pepper to taste
4	ounces Roquefort cheese, crumbled
2	tablespoons finely chopped parsley

Yield: 8 servings

Sauté onions and garlic in mixture of olive oil and butter in heavy saucepan over medium heat for 30 to 35 minutes or until onions are a rich brown, stirring frequently. Add 6 cups stock, wine and thyme. Bring to a boil; reduce heat. Simmer for 25 to 30 minutes or until mixture is reduced by 1/3. Remove 1 1/2 cups onions with slotted spoon; set aside. Process remaining mixture in blender until smooth. Combine with reserved onions and next 5 ingredients in saucepan. Cook over medium heat until heated through. Ladle into soup bowls. Sprinkle servings with mixture of cheese and parsley. Serve as a first course or as a meal with a green salad and crusty rolls.

Spicy Pumpkin Soup

8	ounces onions, chopped
3	shallots with green tops, chopped
1/2	bunch green onions with tops, chopped
4	whole cloves
1/2	teaspoon cumin
1/2	teaspoon oregano
1/2	teaspoon chili powder
1/2	teaspoon cayenne pepper
2	ounces butter or olive oil
1/4	cup flour
4	cups hot chicken broth
1	pound pumpkin, peeled, chopped
1/2	bunch cilantro, finely chopped
1/4	cup milk or half and half

Yield: 4 servings

Sauté onions, shallots, green onions, cloves, cumin, oregano, chili powder and cayenne pepper in butter in large saucepan until onions are tender. Stir in flour. Cook for 12 minutes, stirring constantly. Add hot chicken broth, pumpkin and cilantro. Cook until pumpkin is tender. Discard cloves. Process in food processor or blender until smooth. Combine with milk in saucepan. Cook until heated through. Ladle into soup bowls. Garnish servings with sour cream and tortilla chips.

May substitute acorn squash, banana squash or any hard yellow squash for pumpkin.

Lemon and Rice Soup

1	egg yolk
1	tablespoon fresh lemon juice
1/4	cup grated Parmesan cheese
4	cups chicken stock
3/4	cup cooked rice

Yield: 4 servings

Combine egg yolk, lemon juice and Parmesan cheese in bowl; mix well. Bring chicken stock to a boil in saucepan. Stir egg mixture gradually into boiling stock with fork. Add cooked rice. Cook just until heated through. Ladle into soup bowls.

Juniper Berries ⌁

Juniper trees grow wild above 3,000 feet near piñon pine trees. Some varieties of the juniper berries are dried for use in cooking. Mature berries are reddish or purple in color and spicy-sweet in flavor. A well known use of juniper berries is to flavor gin.

Microwave Minestrone

1	tablespoon olive oil
1	small onion, chopped
1	cup each sliced carrot, celery and zucchini
1/2	cup chopped yellow bell pepper
1	14-ounce can beef broth
1	14-ounce can whole peeled tomatoes, chopped
1	cup cooked medium pasta shells
1	10-ounce can white kidney beans
1/2	teaspoon basil
	Salt and pepper to taste

Yield: 4 servings

Combine olive oil, onion, carrot, celery, zucchini and bell pepper in 2 to 3-quart glass dish. Microwave, loosely covered with heavy-duty plastic wrap, on High for 5 minutes. Add beef broth, undrained tomatoes, pasta, beans, basil, salt and pepper; mix well. Microwave on High for 15 minutes. Ladle into soup bowls.

May omit bell pepper if preferred.

Fresh Tomato Bisque

1	medium onion, thinly sliced
1	tablespoon butter
2	pounds ripe tomatoes, peeled, seeded, chopped
1	bay leaf
1 1/2	tablespoons brown sugar
2	teaspoons chopped fresh basil
2	whole cloves
1	teaspoon salt
1/2	teaspoon freshly ground pepper
2	cups half and half
1	cup milk

Yield: 6 servings

Sauté onion in butter in saucepan until tender. Add tomatoes, bay leaf, brown sugar, basil, cloves, salt and pepper; mix well. Simmer for 30 minutes or until tomatoes are tender. Discard bay leaf and cloves. Process soup in blender or food processor until smooth. Combine with half and half and milk in saucepan. Cook just until heated through. Ladle into soup bowls. Garnish servings with buttered croutons and chopped chives.

Broiled Crab and Tomato Sandwiches

3	ounces cream cheese, softened
1	cup shredded crab meat
1	teaspoon fresh lemon juice
1	egg, slightly beaten
3	tablespoons mayonnaise
2	teaspoons minced parsley
2	tablespoons grated Parmesan cheese
	Cayenne pepper to taste
2	large tomatoes, thickly sliced
3	English muffins, split

Yield: 6 servings

Combine cream cheese, crab meat, lemon juice, egg, mayonnaise, parsley, Parmesan cheese and cayenne pepper in bowl; mix well. Place 1 slice tomato on each muffin half; spread with crab mixture. Place on baking sheet. Broil 5 inches from heat source in preheated oven until sandwiches are puffed and brown.

Egg and Bacon Sandwich Filling

8	hard-cooked eggs, finely chopped
6	slices bacon, crisp-fried, crumbled
1/2	cup minced sweet pickle
1/2	cup mayonnaise

Yield: 4 to 5 servings

Combine eggs, bacon, pickle and mayonnaise in bowl; mix well. Use as sandwich filling on bread or rolls or in pita pockets.

Ham and Egg Salad Sandwich Filling

6	hard-cooked eggs, finely chopped
1	cup chopped cooked ham
6	sweet pickles, chopped
1	cup finely chopped celery
10	stuffed green olives, finely chopped
3/4	cup mayonnaise

Yield: 6 to 8 servings

Combine eggs, ham, pickles, celery, olives and mayonnaise in bowl; mix well. Chill in refrigerator. Use as sandwich filling on bread or rolls or in pita pockets.

Greek Pocket Sandwiches

12	ounces ground beef or lamb
1	medium onion, chopped
3/4	cup water
2	tablespoons flour
1	teaspoon salt
3/4	teaspoon oregano leaves
1/4	teaspoon pepper
1	medium tomato, chopped
1	4-ounce can sliced black olives, drained
2	tablespoons wine vinegar
4	ounces feta cheese, crumbled
4	oatbran pita bread rounds

Yield: 4 servings

Brown ground beef with onion in large skillet over high heat, stirring until ground beef is crumbly; drain. Blend water and flour in cup. Add to skillet with salt, oregano and pepper; mix well. Bring to a boil, stirring constantly; reduce heat. Cook until thickened, stirring constantly; remove from heat. Stir in tomato, olives and vinegar. Cool slightly. Stir in cheese. Cut pita rounds into halves to form pockets. Spoon filling into pockets.

Salmon Salad Sandwich Filling

1	15-ounce can red sockeye salmon
1/2	cup finely chopped celery
1/4	cup sweet pickle relish
2	tablespoons finely chopped red bell pepper
1	tablespoon fresh lemon juice
1/3	cup mayonnaise or mayonnaise-type salad dressing

Yield: 4 servings

Drain and flake salmon, discarding skin and bones. Combine with celery, relish and bell pepper in bowl. Blend lemon juice and mayonnaise in small bowl. Add to salmon mixture; mix well. Chill in refrigerator. Use as sandwich filling.

Shrimp and Caper Sandwich Filling

1	pound cooked shrimp, chopped
1	medium red onion, thinly sliced
1	3-ounce jar capers, drained
1/2	cup mayonnaise or mayonnaise-type salad dressing

Yield: 8 to 10 servings

Combine shrimp, onion, capers and mayonnaise in bowl; mix well. Chill for 4 hours or longer. Use as sandwich filling.

May also serve as salad in lettuce cups.

Hot Pepperoni Sandwiches

1   **10-ounce can pizza dough**
8   **ounces pepperoni, thinly sliced**
8   **slices mozzarella cheese**
      Garlic powder and oregano to taste
2   **tablespoons melted butter or margarine**

Yield: 4 servings

Spread pizza dough on baking sheet, rolling until smooth. Arrange pepperoni slices in overlapping layer on dough, covering completely. Top with cheese; sprinkle with garlic powder and oregano. Fold dough over into thirds; seal edges. Place seam side down on baking sheet; brush with butter. Bake at 325 degrees for 25 minutes. Cool slightly. Cut into 4 portions. Serve with green salad.

May cut into 16 to 20 pieces to serve as appetizers.

Grilled Green Chile and Tuna Sandwiches

1   **7-ounce can tuna, drained**
1/2 **cup chopped green chiles**
2   **tablespoons finely chopped onion**
1/2 **cup sour cream**
1/2 **cup shredded sharp Cheddar cheese**
      Salt and pepper to taste
8   **sourdough English muffins, split**
      Butter or margarine, softened

Yield: 8 servings

Combine tuna, green chiles, onion, sour cream, cheese, salt and pepper in bowl; mix well. Spread uncut sides of English muffins with butter; fill halves with tuna filling. Cook on griddle over medium heat for 4 minutes on each side or until filling is heated through. Serve hot.

May substitute 16 slices sourdough bread for English muffins.

Seven-Layer Taco Sandwiches

	Taco Sandwich Dressing
4	large French bread slices
1	large tomato, sliced
8	ounces sliced turkey
1	avocado, sliced
3/4	cup shredded mixed Cheddar and Monterey Jack cheese
4	lettuce leaves

Yield: 4 servings

Spread half the Taco Sandwich Dressing on bread slices. Layer tomato slices and turkey slices on bread; spread with remaining dressing. Layer avocado and cheese over top; place on baking sheet. Bake at 350 degrees for 20 minutes. Place on lettuce-lined serving plates; serve with salsa.

May prepare sandwiches in advance and chill until time to bake.

Taco Sandwich Dressing

1/2	cup chopped black olives
1/2	cup sliced green olives
1/2	teaspoon chili powder
1/2	teaspoon cumin
1/4	teaspoon salt
1/2	cup mayonnaise
1/2	cup sour cream

Yield: 2 cups

Combine olives, chili powder, cumin, salt, mayonnaise and sour cream in bowl; mix well.

Mesquite ⌁

The mesquite tree is known as the "tree of life" to the Native peoples of the Sonoran Desert because it is a source of food, medicine, dye, fiber, fuel and timber. A water-indicating plant, its long roots sometimes penetrate 50 to 60 feet into the ground seeking moisture. More wood is below ground than above.

The long bean-like seedpods are collected in the late summer and ground into flour for making bread, a beverage and a gruel (atole). The pods, rich in protein, carbohydrate and calcium, have a sweet flavor. The catkin-like yellow blossoms are picked in early spring and eaten as a delicacy. Bees make a delicious mesquite honey from the fragrant blossoms.

Navajo Sun

Salads
& Salad Dressings

Tomato

The tomato was, at first, a confusing food to the Europeans. It resembled a fruit, but it was much too acidic to be used that way. It might be a vegetable, but it was unlike any they had seen. Introduced into England in 1596, the tomato was initially known as *pomodoro* (Italian) or *pomme d'amour* (French), probably because the tomato was thought to be related botanically to the eggplant (*pomme des mours,* or fruit of the Moors). The name used today, tomato, comes from the Aztec *tomatl.* Tomatoes apparently made their first appearance as weeds in Mexican maize fields. Careful cultivation increased their yield and by the time the Spanish arrived, the Aztecs were using the tomato in a variety of dishes and sauces.

After 1590, several cookbooks were published in Spain indicating that tomatoes could be used in sauces. The information was based upon reports of Aztec use and not upon direct experience. The Italians considered the tomato a luxury until the late 1700s because there was no way of preserving it. This changed with the invention of the canning process in 1812 and was made practical in 1868 by the invention of a machine to make the tin can. In England, the tomato was slow to be adopted and was not used in the English diet until the end of the 1800s. The tomato, as well as the potato, was rapidly adopted by the Hindu and Buddhist peoples of Southeast Asia. Since these people did not eat meat, they were quick to integrate new vegetable foods from the Americas into their cuisines.

Tomatoes are today a favored ingredient in salads and mixed dishes throughout the world. In Spain, the tomato joined the onion to create the most typical of Spanish culinary preparations, the *sofrito,* a flavoring added to countless dishes in Spain and Latin America. The American condiment, ketchup or catsup, began its history in China as *katsup,* a pickled fish sauce. American cooks omitted the fish and added the tomato.

Taffy Apple Salad

1	8-ounce can crushed pineapple
1	tablespoon flour
1/2	cup sugar
1	egg, beaten
2	tablespoons cider vinegar
5	cups chopped unpeeled red Delicious apples
1	cup salted peanuts
8	ounces whipped topping

Yield: 10 servings

Drain pineapple, reserving juice. Mix flour and sugar in saucepan. Add egg and mixture of vinegar and reserved pineapple juice; mix well. Cook over low heat until thickened, stirring constantly. Cool to room temperature. Combine apples, pineapple and peanuts in bowl; mix well. Add cooled dressing; mix well. Fold in whipped topping. Garnish with additional peanuts.

Layered Overnight Fruit Salad

2	cups shredded lettuce
2	medium golden Delicious apples, thinly sliced
2	navel oranges
2	cups seedless green grapes
1/3	cup mayonnaise
1/3	cup sour cream
1	cup shredded Cheddar cheese

Yield: 6 servings

Layer lettuce and apples in 2-quart serving dish. Peel and section oranges. Layer sections over apple; squeeze juice from rind and membranes over oranges. Layer grapes over top. Combine mayonnaise and sour cream in bowl; mix well. Spread over fruit; sprinkle with cheese. Chill, tightly covered with plastic wrap, overnight. Spoon through layers to serve.

Piquant Fruit Salad with Jicama and Cucumber

12	ounces jicama, peeled, chopped
1	small cucumber, peeled, seeded, chopped
1/2	medium cantaloupe, peeled, seeded, chopped
1/4	medium pineapple, peeled, cored, cubed
3	tablespoons chopped mint
	Piquant Dressing

Yield: 4 to 6 servings

Combine jicama, cucumber, cantaloupe and pineapple in large serving bowl; mix well. Add Piquant Dressing; toss to coat well. Chill for 1 to 2 hours. Sprinkle with mint at serving time.

This is a good side dish for grilled meats or fish and travels well.

Piquant Dressing

1	teaspoon grated lime zest
1	tablespoon honey
4	whole cloves
1	large clove of garlic, cut into quarters
1/3	cup rice wine vinegar
1/4	teaspoon cayenne pepper
1/2	teaspoon salt
3	tablespoons fresh lime juice

Yield: 1/2 cup

Combine lime zest, honey, cloves, garlic, vinegar, cayenne pepper and salt in small nonreactive saucepan. Bring to a boil. Cool to room temperature. Remove garlic and whole cloves. Stir in lime juice.

Molded Spiced Peaches

1	29-ounce can sliced peaches
2–4	teaspoons vinegar
1	teaspoon whole cloves
2	2-inch cinnamon sticks
	Water
1	3-ounce package orange gelatin
1	cup chopped walnuts
	Mayonnaise
	Whole walnuts

Yield: 6 servings

Bring first 4 ingredients to a boil in saucepan. Remove from heat. Let stand, covered, for 5 minutes. Remove peaches; chill in refrigerator. Strain hot liquid into glass measure. Add enough water to measure 2 cups. Dissolve gelatin in hot liquid. Stir in chopped walnuts. Arrange 5 or 6 peach slices in 6 individual molds. Add gelatin mixture. Chill until set. Invert onto lettuce-lined salad plates. Garnish with remaining peaches, mayonnaise and whole walnuts. May serve spiced peaches without the gelatin as a meat accompaniment.

Supreme Peach Salad

1   16-ounce can peach slices
1   3-ounce package cherry gelatin
1   cup boiling water
1   3-ounce package lemon gelatin
1   cup boiling water
3/4 cup cold water
1   8-ounce package cream cheese,
       softened

Yield: 8 servings

Drain peaches, reserving syrup. Add enough cold water to reserved syrup to measure 1 cup. Dissolve cherry gelatin in 1 cup boiling water in bowl. Add reserved syrup. Chill until partially set. Arrange peach slices in bottom of 9-inch springform pan fitted with ring insert. Spoon gelatin-syrup mixture over peach slices. Chill until almost set. Dissolve lemon gelatin in 1 cup boiling water in bowl. Add cold water. Blend into cream cheese gradually. Pour over congealed layer. Chill until firm. Unmold onto serving platter.

Sangria Fruit Salad with Jicama

1   medium jicama
     Sections of 3 large oranges
     Sections of 2 red grapefruit
     Wine Dressing

Yield: 6 servings

Peel jicama and cut into 1/2-inch cubes. Combine with oranges and grapefruit in salad bowl. Add Wine Dressing; toss to coat well.

Wine Dressing

1/4 cup vegetable oil
1/4 cup dry red wine
2   tablespoons honey
2   tablespoons orange juice

Yield: 3/4 cup

Combine oil, wine, honey and orange juice in jar with cover; shake to mix well.

May use this dressing on other fruit salads. To make without oil, just increase the amounts of the other ingredients to replace the oil.

Cheese-Filled Pears with Glazed Cranberries

6   pears
     Grated zest and juice of 1 lemon
2–3 tablespoons sugar
4   ounces ricotta cheese
4   ounces cream cheese, softened
1   tablespoon sugar
2–3 tablespoons light cream or milk
     Glazed Cranberries

Yield: 12 servings

Peel pears, cut into halves and discard cores. Combine with water to cover, lemon zest, lemon juice and 2 to 3 tablespoons sugar in saucepan. Poach until tender; drain. Cool to room temperature. Chill in refrigerator. Combine ricotta cheese, cream cheese, 1 tablespoon sugar and cream in bowl; mix well. Chill in refrigerator. Arrange pears with rounded end toward edge on lettuce-lined 10 or 12-inch plate. Fill each with a portion of the cheese mixture. Mound remaining cheese mixture in center of plate; spoon Glazed Cranberries over cheese.

May also serve on individual luncheon plates with nut bread or muffins and rolled flutes of thinly sliced ham or turkey. May serve Glazed Cranberries as relish with meats and sandwiches.

Glazed Cranberries

2   cups fresh cranberries
2/3 cup sugar
2   teaspoons grated orange zest
1   1-inch cinnamon stick

Yield: 2 cups

Combine cranberries, sugar, orange zest and cinnamon stick in 9-inch skillet. Cook, covered, over very low heat for 30 to 40 minutes or until sugar is dissolved and cranberries are glazed. Discard cinnamon stick. Chill until serving time.

Frosty Cranberry Salad

1   16-ounce can whole cranberry sauce
1   8-ounce can crushed pineapple,
         drained
1   cup sour cream
1/4   cup confectioners' sugar

Yield: 6 servings

Combine cranberry sauce and pineapple in bowl; mix well. Add mixture of sour cream and confectioners' sugar; mix well. Spoon into 8x8-inch pan or freezer tray. Freeze until firm. Cut into wedges and garnish with 1/2 pineapple slice.

Frozen Fruit Salad

3   10-ounce packages frozen
         strawberries, partially thawed
1   20-ounce can crushed pineapple,
         drained
1   28-ounce can apricots, drained,
         chopped
3–4   bananas, chopped
1   cup water
1   cup sugar
2   ounces thawed frozen orange juice
         concentrate
       Juice of 2 lemons

Yield: 24 servings

Combine undrained strawberries, pineapple, apricots and bananas in bowl. Combine water and sugar in saucepan. Boil for several minutes, stirring to dissolve sugar. Add orange juice concentrate and lemon juice. Pour over fruits; mix gently. Spoon into paper-lined muffin cups. Freeze until firm. Remove from muffin tins and discard paper. Store in plastic bags in freezer. Let stand at room temperature for 20 minutes or longer before serving.

These frozen salads are especially good for a brunch or luncheon.

Crunchy Cabbage Slaw

1/2	large head cabbage, shredded
1/2	cup toasted sesame seeds
1/2	cup chopped green onions
	Slaw Dressing
1/2	cup pine nuts
1/2	cup slivered almonds
2	3-ounce packages ramen noodles, broken
1	small pimento, chopped

Yield: 12 to 16 servings

Combine cabbage, sesame seeds and green onions in bowl. Add Slaw Dressing; mix well. Chill in refrigerator overnight. Add pine nuts, almonds, noodles and pimento at serving time; mix gently.

Slaw Dressing

1/4	cup sugar
1/4	cup rice wine vinegar
1	cup salad oil
1	teaspoon salt
	Pepper to taste

Yield: 1 1/2 cups

Combine sugar, vinegar, oil, salt and pepper in bowl. Whisk until sugar is dissolved and mixture thickens.

Molded Chicken Salad

1	3-ounce package lemon gelatin
1	cup boiling water
1	10-ounce can cream of chicken soup
1	cup chopped celery
1/4	cup sliced black olives
1/4	cup chopped green bell pepper
1	tablespoon minced onion
1	medium carrot, shredded
1	cup chopped cooked chicken

Yield: 8 to 10 servings

Dissolve gelatin in boiling water in bowl. Cool to room temperature. Add soup, celery, olives, green pepper, minced onion, carrot and chicken; mix well. Spoon into oiled 5 or 6-cup mold. Chill until set. Unmold onto lettuce-lined serving plate.

Chinese Chicken Salad

5	cups chopped cooked chicken
1	cup sliced water chestnuts
2	cups pineapple tidbits
2	cups mandarin oranges
1	cup chopped celery
1/2	cup sliced green onions
1/2	cup slivered almonds
	Chicken Salad Dressing
2	3-ounce cans Chinese noodles

Yield: 10 to 12 servings

Combine chicken, water chestnuts, pineapple, mandarin oranges, celery, green onions and almonds in bowl. Add Chicken Salad Dressing; mix well. Chill until serving time. Add noodles just before serving.

Chicken Salad Dressing

1/4	cup chutney
1	cup sour cream
1	cup mayonnaise
1	teaspoon (scant) curry powder

Yield: 2¹/₄ cups

Combine chutney, sour cream, mayonnaise and curry powder in bowl; mix well. Chill in refrigerator until needed.

Oriental Chicken Salad

6	cups finely shredded cabbage
3	green onions, thinly sliced
3	cups chopped cooked chicken breast
2	tablespoons sugar
1/3	cup vegetable oil
1/4	cup white vinegar
1/4	cup soy sauce
1/4	teaspoon pepper
	Garlic powder to taste
1	3-ounce package chicken-flavor ramen noodles, crushed
1/3	cup sliced almonds, toasted
3	tablespoons sesame seeds, toasted

Yield: 6 to 8 servings

Combine cabbage, green onions and chicken in large serving bowl. Combine sugar, oil, vinegar, soy sauce, pepper and garlic powder with seasoning packet from noodles in bowl; mix well. Add to salad; mix well. Chill for up to 2 hours. Add noodles, almonds and sesame seeds at serving time; toss to mix well.

Far East Salad

2	cups cooked brown rice
1	8-ounce bottle of sweet and sour salad dressing
2	cups chopped cooked chicken
1	cup chopped celery
1/4	cup minced onion
1/2	cup chopped water chestnuts
1/4	cup chopped green bell pepper
1	cup drained pineapple chunks
1/2	cup chopped cashews

Yield: 8 servings

Combine rice with half the salad dressing in bowl; mix well. Marinate for several hours; drain. Add chicken and next 5 ingredients; mix well. Chill until serving time. Add cashews and remaining salad dressing at serving time; mix well. Serve with chutney.

May substitute tuna or shrimp for chicken.

Shrimp Salad with Sesame Vinaigrette

2	pounds medium shrimp, peeled, deveined
1/2–3/4	cup cold-pressed peanut oil
3	cloves of garlic, minced
1/3	ounce fresh gingerroot, peeled, minced
8	medium scallions, trimmed, thinly sliced
	Sesame Vinaigrette
3	cups shredded lettuce
12	medium mushrooms, sliced

Yield: 6 to 8 servings

Rinse shrimp and pat dry. Stir-fry half the shrimp in half the peanut oil in wok for 3 minutes or until cooked through. Add half the garlic, gingerroot and scallions; toss to mix well. Stir-fry for 30 seconds. Remove to bowl. Repeat process. Add to first shrimp mixture with half the Sesame Vinaigrette; toss to coat well. Combine remaining Sesame Vinaigrette with lettuce and mushrooms in bowl; toss to mix well. Spoon onto serving platter. Top with shrimp mixture.

Sesame Vinaigrette

1	clove of garlic, minced
1	teaspoon Dijon mustard
1/2	beaten egg yolk
2	tablespoons wine vinegar
3	tablespoons dark soy sauce
2	cups cold-pressed peanut oil
1/2	cup sesame oil

Yield: 2 3/4 cups

Combine garlic, mustard, egg yolk, vinegar and soy sauce in mixer bowl; mix well. Add peanut oil and sesame oil in a fine stream, beating until smooth.

Seafood and Pecan Salad with Vanilla Mayonnaise

1¹/₂	pounds shrimp, crab meat or lobster, cooked
3	green onions, finely chopped
1	cup thinly sliced celery
	Vanilla Mayonnaise
1	head Boston lettuce, torn
1	cup sliced fresh mushrooms
1	avocado, sliced
1	8-ounce can artichoke hearts, drained
¹/₂	cup slivered pecan halves, lightly toasted

Yield: 4 to 6 servings

Combine shrimp, green onions and celery in bowl. Add enough Vanilla Mayonnaise to bind mixture. Add lettuce; toss to mix well. Top with mushrooms, avocado, artichoke hearts and toasted pecans.

Vanilla Mayonnaise

1	egg
¹/₂	teaspoon Dijon mustard
¹/₂	teaspoon sugar
1	tablespoon fresh lemon juice
1	tablespoon fruit vinegar
1	cup vegetable oil
1	teaspoon vanilla extract

Yield: 1¹/₂ cups

Combine egg, mustard, sugar, lemon juice and vinegar in blender or food processor container; process until smooth. Add a few drops of oil, processing constantly. Add remaining oil in fine stream, processing constantly. Stir in vanilla. May whisk in a small amount of additional oil and vinegar if needed for desired consistency.

Jojoba ~

The jojoba bush is a desert plant with waxy, oval grayish-green leaves. Mature, acorn-like, jojoba nuts are about an inch long. Jojoba nuts were an important food item for Native Americans and early settlers. They taste like hazelnuts. Recently the nuts were explored for commercial value because they yield a liquid wax similar to sperm whale oil which is suitable for high-temperature applications. Jojoba remained unexploited in the United States until 1972 when sperm whale by-products were prohibited. Sperm whales are an endangered species. Attempts to produce the nut in commercial quantities have not been successful.

Ojibway Wild Rice and Chicken Salad

1/3	cup uncooked wild rice
2	cups water
2	teaspoons salt
1/2	cup mayonnaise
1/3	cup milk
1/3	cup fresh lemon juice
1/2	small onion, minced
2 1/2	cups chopped cooked chicken
1	8-ounce can sliced water chestnuts, drained
8	ounces seedless green grapes, cut into halves
1	cup cashews
	Salt and pepper to taste

Yield: 6 servings

Rinse rice and drain well. Combine with water and 2 teaspoons salt in saucepan. Cook over low heat for 45 to 60 minutes or until rice is tender. Combine mayonnaise, milk, lemon juice and onion in large bowl. Stir in rice, chicken and water chestnuts. Chill in refrigerator. Fold in grapes and cashews at serving time. Season with salt and pepper to taste. Spoon onto lettuce-lined serving plate; garnish with lemon slices.

Molded Asparagus Salad

1	10-ounce can cream of asparagus soup
1	8-ounce package cream cheese
1/2	cup water
1	3-ounce package lime gelatin
1	cup mayonnaise
2–3	drops of hot pepper sauce
3/4	cup chopped celery
1	tablespoon chopped green onion
1/2	cup chopped green bell pepper
1/2	cup chopped pecans

Yield: 6 to 8 servings

Combine soup, cream cheese and water in medium saucepan. Heat until cream cheese melts, stirring to mix well. Add gelatin, stirring until dissolved. Cool slightly. Add mayonnaise and pepper sauce; mix well. Chill until partially set. Stir in celery, green onion, green pepper and pecans. Spoon into oiled 1 1/2-quart mold. Chill until set. Unmold onto lettuce-lined plate.

Piquant Molded Beet Salad

1	20-ounce can crushed pineapple
2	16-ounce cans julienned beets
6	tablespoons fresh lemon juice
1/2	cup red wine vinegar
1	6-ounce package raspberry gelatin
1	cup chopped celery
1	cup sliced green onions

Yield: 12 servings

Drain pineapple and beets, reserving liquid. Combine reserved liquid with lemon juice, vinegar and enough water to measure 1³/₄ cups. Bring to a boil in saucepan. Add gelatin, stirring until dissolved. Chill, covered, until partially set. Stir in pineapple, beets, celery and green onions. Spoon into oiled 9-cup mold. Chill, covered, for 6 hours to overnight. Unmold onto serving plate.

May add nuts if desired or 2 teaspoons horseradish for zip.

Cranberry and Wine Molded Salad

2	3-ounce packages raspberry gelatin
1¹/₄	cups boiling water
1	16-ounce can whole cranberry sauce
1	20-ounce can crushed pineapple
1/2	cup Port
1	cup chopped walnuts

Yield: 12 servings

Dissolve gelatin in boiling water in bowl. Cool to room temperature. Add cranberry sauce, undrained pineapple, wine and walnuts; mix well. Spoon into 9x9-inch dish or large mold. Chill until set. Cut into servings or unmold onto serving plate.

Frosted Lemon and Pineapple Salad

1	6-ounce package lemon gelatin
1¹/₂	cups boiling water
2	cups lemon-lime soda
1	20-ounce can crushed pineapple
1	cup miniature marshmallows
2	large bananas, sliced
¹/₂	cup sugar
2	tablespoons flour
1	egg, slightly beaten
2	tablespoons butter or margarine
2	cups whipped topping
¹/₄	cup shredded Cheddar cheese

Yield: 10 to 12 servings

Dissolve gelatin in boiling water in bowl. Stir in lemon-lime soda. Chill until partially set. Drain pineapple, reserving 1 cup juice. Fold pineapple, marshmallows and bananas into gelatin mixture. Spoon into 7x12-inch dish. Chill until firm. Combine reserved pineapple juice with sugar, flour and egg in saucepan. Cook over low heat until thickened, stirring constantly; remove from heat. Stir in butter. Chill in refrigerator. Fold in whipped topping. Spread over congealed layer; sprinkle with cheese. Chill for several hours to overnight.

Pistachio-Fruit Salad

1	4-ounce package whipped topping mix
1	4-ounce package pistachio instant pudding mix
1	cup drained pineapple tidbits
1	cup drained fruit cocktail
1	cup miniature marshmallows
1	cup chopped pecans

Yield: 6 to 8 servings

Prepare whipped topping mix using package directions. Fold in dry pudding mix, pineapple tidbits, fruit cocktail, marshmallows and pecans. Chill overnight.

Tomato Aspic

2	envelopes unflavored gelatin
4	cups mixed vegetable juice
1	small bay leaf
1/4	teaspoon each crumbled basil and oregano
1	tablespoon fresh lemon juice
1/2	teaspoon sugar
1	tablespoon Worcestershire sauce
1/2	teaspoon hot pepper sauce
4	black peppercorns
10	pimento-stuffed green olives, sliced
1	4-ounce can tiny shrimp, rinsed, drained
1	cup finely chopped celery
1	14 to 16-ounce can cut asparagus, drained

Yield: 8 to 12 servings

Soften gelatin in 1 cup vegetable juice in small bowl. Combine remaining vegetable juice with bay leaf, basil, oregano, lemon juice, sugar, Worcestershire sauce, pepper sauce and peppercorns in saucepan. Cook over low heat until bubbly; remove from heat. Add gelatin, stirring until dissolved; strain. Spray 6-cup mold with nonstick cooking spray. Add enough gelatin mixture to measure 1/2 inch. Chill until partially set. Arrange olive slices in decorative pattern on gelatin. Chill until set. Add half the remaining gelatin. Chill until set. Spread mixture of shrimp and celery over top. Add remaining gelatin. Arrange asparagus over gelatin. Chill until set. Run sharp knife around edge of mold or place moist hot towel on mold; unmold onto serving plate. Garnish with parsley and additional olives or asparagus.

This recipe has turned many an aspic-hater into an aspic-lover.

Broccoli and Cauliflower Salad

1	bunch broccoli
1	head cauliflower
1	bunch green onions, sliced
8	ounces Monterey Jack cheese, cubed
8	ounces bacon, crisp-fried, crumbled
2	tablespoons vinegar
1/4	cup sugar
2	cups mayonnaise

Yield: 8 to 10 servings

Chop or break broccoli and cauliflower into bite-sized pieces. Combine with green onions, cheese and bacon in large bowl. Mix vinegar, sugar and mayonnaise in small bowl. Add to salad; mix lightly. Chill until serving time.

To serve as a hot vegetable, spoon into baking dish and bake at 350 degrees for 25 to 30 minutes or until heated through.

Black Bean Salad with Corn and Peppers

1	cup dried black beans
1	10-ounce package frozen corn, thawed
1	green bell pepper, chopped
1	red bell pepper, chopped
1/3	cup sliced green onions
2	tablespoons minced cilantro or parsley
2	tablespoons olive oil
3	tablespoons fresh lime juice
1/8	teaspoon salt

Yield: 6 to 8 servings

Sort and rinse dried beans. Soak in water to cover in bowl overnight; drain. Combine with fresh water to cover in saucepan. Cook for 1 hour or until tender. Drain and cool. Combine with corn, bell pepper, green onions, cilantro, olive oil, lime juice and salt in bowl; mix well. Chill until serving time.

May substitute two 15-ounce cans drained and rinsed black beans for dried beans.

Coleslaw à la Jacques Pepin

1	2-ounce can anchovies, drained, mashed
5	cloves of garlic, minced
1	tablespoon wine vinegar
1/2	cup vegetable oil
	Salt to taste
1/2	teaspoon pepper
1	head cabbage, shredded

Yield: 10 to 12 servings

Combine anchovies, garlic, vinegar, oil, salt and pepper in bowl; mix well. Add cabbage; mix well. Chill until serving time.

Don't be discouraged by the amounts of anchovies and garlic; the end result is delicious.

Cobb Salad

6	cups shredded lettuce
3	cups chopped cooked chicken
3	hard-cooked eggs, chopped
2	medium tomatoes, seeded, chopped
3/4	cup crumbled bleu cheese
6	slices bacon, crisp-fried, crumbled
1	medium avocado, cut into wedges
1	small head Belgian endive (optional)
	Brown Derby French Salad Dressing

Yield: 6 servings

Place lettuce on 6 salad plates. Arrange chicken, eggs, tomatoes, cheese and bacon in rows across lettuce. Arrange avocado and endive leaves to 1 side. Serve with Brown Derby French Salad Dressing.

Brown Derby French Salad Dressing

1/3	cup red wine vinegar
1	tablespoon fresh lemon juice
1	teaspoon Worcestershire sauce
1/2	teaspoon sugar
1/2	teaspoon dry mustard
1	clove of garlic
1/2	teaspoon pepper
1/2	cup olive oil or vegetable oil

Yield: 1 cup

Combine vinegar, lemon juice, Worcestershire sauce, sugar, dry mustard, garlic and pepper in jar with lid. Shake to mix well. Add oil. Shake well. Chill until serving time. Discard garlic to serve.

Cucumber and Sour Cream Salad

2	cucumbers, thinly sliced
1	cup sour cream
1–1½	tablespoons vinegar
2	tablespoons sugar
2–3	slices Bermuda onion, chopped
	Paprika, salt and pepper to taste

Yield: 4 to 6 servings

Blot cucumbers with paper towels to remove excess moisture. Combine sour cream, vinegar, sugar, onion, paprika, salt and pepper in bowl; mix well. Add cucumbers; mix gently. Chill until serving time.

Sesame Cucumbers

2	tablespoons sesame seeds
1	tablespoon sugar
2	teaspoons cornstarch
¼	teaspoon salt
1	tablespoon water
½	cup vinegar
2	medium unpeeled cucumbers, very thinly sliced
½	cup finely chopped celery

Yield: 4 servings

Spread sesame seeds on baking sheet. Toast at 350 degrees for 5 minutes. Combine sugar, cornstarch and salt in saucepan. Stir in water and vinegar. Bring to a boil, stirring constantly. Cook for 1 minute. Stir in sesame seeds. Chill in refrigerator. Combine cucumbers, celery and dressing in serving bowl; mix well. Chill for 6 to 8 hours.

This is good with Chinese dishes.

Six-Pepper Slaw

1	each green, red, yellow, purple and orange bell pepper, julienned
1	red onion, cut into thin strips
1	jalapeño pepper, minced
2	tablespoons tarragon vinegar
1	tablespoon Dijon mustard
2	teaspoons sugar
1/4	teaspoon hot pepper sauce
1	teaspoon salt
	Freshly ground pepper to taste
1/4	cup vegetable oil
2	tablespoons peanut oil
1	tablespoon caraway seeds, crushed
2	teaspoons grated lime zest

Yield: 6 servings

Combine bell peppers with onion in large bowl. Combine jalapeño pepper, vinegar, mustard, sugar, pepper sauce, salt and pepper in bowl. Whisk in oils until thick. Add to vegetables; toss to mix well. Stir in caraway seeds and lime zest. Chill, covered, for 3 hours.

If purple and orange bell peppers are not available, substitute green and yellow peppers.

Prickly Pear Cactus 〜

The young tender pads of the prickly pear cactus are gathered in the spring. These young pads, called nopalitos, are fat free, low in calories and high in vitamins and minerals. The pads are diced and boiled until tender. Cooking and rinsing in lots of water reduces the mucilaginous texture. The flavor of the cooked pads is similar to tart green beans.

The fruit of the prickly pear is gathered in the summer. It is juicy, mildly sweet and a good source of Vitamin C. The ripe fruit is usually made into jam, jelly or syrup.

Green Beans with Minted Yogurt Dressing

1	pound fresh green beans, trimmed
1/2	teaspoon salt
1 1/2	teaspoons dry mustard
2	tablespoons lemon juice
1	tablespoon grated lemon zest
1	tablespoon finely chopped fresh mint
1	clove of garlic, pressed
1/2	teaspoon sugar
	Freshly ground pepper to taste
1/3	cup plain low-fat yogurt
3	Roma tomatoes, sliced

Yield: 6 servings

Steam beans in steamer for 5 to 6 minutes or just until tender; rinse in cold water and drain. Combine with salt in bowl; toss to mix well. Combine dry mustard, lemon juice and lemon zest in large bowl; mix to form paste. Add mint, garlic, sugar, pepper and yogurt; mix well. Add beans; mix to coat well. Chill for 2 hours. Top with tomatoes at serving time.

Green Beans and Walnuts in Basil Vinaigrette

1 1/2	pounds crisp young green beans, trimmed
	Basil Vinaigrette
2	green onions, thinly sliced
1/4	cup chopped walnuts

Yield: 6 servings

Bring enough water to cover beans to a boil in saucepan. Add beans. Cook just until tender-crisp; do not overcook. Rinse in ice water and drain. Add Basil Vinaigrette; toss to mix well. Spoon into serving bowl lined with curly lettuce. Top with green onions and walnuts.

Basil Vinaigrette

1	teaspoon pressed garlic
15	basil leaves
1/2	teaspoon salt
1/2	teaspoon freshly ground pepper
2	teaspoons Dijon mustard
1/4	cup wine vinegar
1/2	cup olive oil

Yield: 1 cup

Combine garlic, basil, salt and pepper in blender container; process for 1 second. Add mustard and vinegar; process until smooth. Add olive oil in thin stream, processing constantly until smooth.

Peas and Bacon in Sour Cream

2   **16-ounce packages frozen tiny peas,**
        thawed
2   **green onions, chopped**
6   **slices bacon, crisp-fried, crumbled**
1   **cup sour cream**
1/2   **teaspoon salt**
        Freshly ground pepper to taste

Yield: 10 to 12 servings

Combine peas, green onions and bacon in bowl. Add sour cream, salt and pepper; mix gently. Chill until serving time.

If you mix this before the peas are completely thawed, the dish will travel well.

Dilled Pea Salad

1   **10-ounce package frozen peas**
1/4   **cup plain yogurt**
1   **tablespoon reduced-calorie**
        mayonnaise or mayonnaise-type
        salad dressing
3/4   **teaspoon dried dillweed**
1/8   **teaspoon onion salt**
1/8   **teaspoon pepper**
1/2   **cup sliced celery**
2   **tablespoons chopped pimento**
        (optional)

Yield: 4 servings

Run hot water over peas in colander just until thawed; drain. Combine yogurt, mayonnaise, dillweed, onion salt and pepper in medium bowl; mix well. Add peas, celery and pimento; toss gently to mix. Chill for up to 24 hours.

Crunchy Sauerkraut Salad

1	16-ounce can sauerkraut
1	15-ounce can garbanzo beans
1	2-ounce jar chopped pimento
1	cup chopped onion
1	cup chopped celery
1/2	cup sugar
1/2	cup vinegar
1/2	cup vegetable oil

Yield: 8 servings

Drain sauerkraut, beans and pimento. Combine with onion and celery in large bowl; mix well. Combine sugar and vinegar in saucepan. Bring to a boil. Stir in oil; remove from heat. Pour over salad; mix well. Chill, covered, overnight.

Super Salad

6–8	cups torn romaine lettuce, spinach and leaf lettuce or other greens of choice
1	pint strawberries, sliced
1/2	red onion, thinly sliced
3/4	cup chopped walnuts
	Super Salad Dressing

Yield: 8 to 10 servings

Combine salad greens, strawberries, onion rings and walnuts in salad bowl; mix well. Chill until serving time. Add Super Salad Dressing just before serving; toss to coat well.

Try this; you are in for a great surprise.

Super Salad Dressing

1/2	cup mayonnaise
1/3	cup sugar
1/4	cup milk
2	tablespoons vinegar
1	tablespoon poppy seeds

Yield: 1 cup

Combine mayonnaise, sugar, milk, vinegar and poppy seeds in bowl; whisk until smooth. Chill for several hours.

Spinach Salad

1	**pound fresh spinach**
1	**medium red onion, thinly sliced**
6	**mushrooms, sliced**
1/4	**cup olive oil**
1/4	**cup orange juice**
2	**tablespoons soy sauce**
1/2	**teaspoon coarsely ground pepper**

Yield: 4 to 6 servings

Rinse and drain spinach, discarding stems; tear spinach into bite-sized pieces. Combine with onion rings and mushrooms in salad bowl. Chill until serving time. Combine olive oil, orange juice, soy sauce and pepper in jar with lid; shake to mix well. Chill until serving time. Add dressing at serving time; toss to coat well.

Add 1 cup chopped hard-cooked eggs and 1/4 cup crumbled crisp-fried bacon to serve as a main-dish salad.

Sweet Potato-Vinaigrette Salad

4	**cups chopped cooked sweet potatoes**
1	**cup pineapple tidbits**
1/2	**each green and red bell pepper, cut into short julienne strips**
	Ginger Vinaigrette

Yield: 5 to 6 servings

Combine sweet potatoes, pineapple and bell peppers in serving bowl. Add Ginger Vinaigrette; mix gently. Chill until serving time. Serve on bed of salad greens.

Ginger Vinaigrette

1/4	**cup vegetable oil**
1 1/2	**tablespoons cider vinegar**
1	**tablespoon honey or sugar**
2	**green onions, sliced**
1	**tablespoon minced gingerroot**
1/2	**teaspoon salt**

Yield: 3/4 cup

Combine vinegar, oil, honey, green onions, gingerroot and salt in bowl; mix well.

Curried Rice Salad

2	cups uncooked rice
4	cups chicken broth
1	medium piece of fresh gingerroot, grated
1	teaspoon curry powder
1/2	teaspoon turmeric
	Salt and pepper to taste
1/4	cup olive oil
	Juice of 2 lemons
1/2	cup golden raisins
1/2	cup raisins or currants
1	cup chopped green bell pepper
1 1/2	cups plain yogurt
1/2	cup almonds, toasted

Yield: 10 to 12 servings

Cook rice in mixture of chicken broth, ginger, curry powder, turmeric, salt and pepper in saucepan, using directions on rice package. Combine with olive oil and lemon juice in bowl; mix well. Marinate in refrigerator for several hours to overnight. Add raisins, green pepper and yogurt; mix well. Sprinkle with almonds; garnish with parsley.

This is a great dish for a buffet supper. Serve it with chicken, beef or lamb. The flavor improves if made a day in advance.

Marinated Vegetable Medley

	Salt to taste
	Flowerets of 1 small head cauliflower
2 1/2	cups thinly sliced carrots
2 1/2	cups thinly sliced yellow or pattypan squash
1	medium green bell pepper, cut into strips
1/2	cup thinly sliced green onions
2/3	cup vegetable oil
1/4	teaspoon grated lemon rind
1/3	cup fresh lemon juice
3/4	teaspoon prepared mustard
3/4	teaspoon each sugar, basil and garlic salt
1/4	teaspoon pepper

Yield: 6 to 8 servings

Bring 1 inch salted water to a boil in skillet over medium-high heat. Add cauliflower. Cook for 3 to 4 minutes or just until tender-crisp; remove to bowl with slotted spoon. Add carrots to water. Cook for 4 to 5 minutes or just until tender-crisp; remove to bowl. Add squash. Cook for 3 minutes; drain and add to bowl. Add green pepper and green onions. Combine oil, lemon rind, lemon juice, prepared mustard, sugar, basil, garlic salt and pepper in bowl; mix well. Add to vegetables; mix well. Marinate, covered, in refrigerator for up to 24 hours. Mix well before serving.

Zippy Beet Dressing

1	8-ounce can chopped or julienned beets
1/2	cup mayonnaise
1 1/2	teaspoons prepared horseradish
	Salt to taste

Yield: 1 1/2 cups

Drain beets, reserving liquid. Mash beets slightly with fork in bowl. Stir in mayonnaise, horseradish and salt. Add enough beet juice to make of desired consistency.

Serve this on lettuce wedges or salad greens.

White French Dressing

3/4	cup sugar
1	tablespoon salt
1	tablespoon dry mustard
1 1/2	teaspoons cornstarch
1 1/2	cups white wine vinegar
	Dash of white pepper
	Dash of cayenne pepper
3	cups vegetable oil

Yield: 1 quart

Combine sugar, salt, dry mustard, cornstarch, vinegar, white pepper and cayenne pepper in 1-quart saucepan; blend well. Bring to a boil over medium heat, stirring constantly. Simmer for 5 minutes, stirring frequently. Let stand until cool. Pour into mixer bowl. Add oil in a fine stream, beating constantly at medium speed. Store in covered container in refrigerator.

Mayonnaise

1	egg
1	tablespoon white wine vinegar or lemon juice
1	teaspoon dry mustard
1	cup vegetable oil

Yield: 1 cup

Combine egg, vinegar and dry mustard in blender container. Process for about 4 seconds or until blended. Add oil several drops at a time, processing constantly. Increase addition of oil to a fine steady stream as mixture thickens, processing constantly. Pour into bowl. Store, covered, in refrigerator.

Balsamic Vinaigrette

1	large clove of garlic, minced
1/2	cup extra-light olive oil
1/2	cup vegetable oil
3	tablespoons balsamic vinegar
1/2	teaspoon salt
1/4	teaspoon pepper

Yield: 1 1/2 cups

Combine garlic, olive oil, vegetable oil, vinegar, salt and pepper in jar with lid; shake to mix well. Store in refrigerator.

This is wonderful on greens or on potato salad made with tiny new potatoes.

Dijon Vinaigrette

2	tablespoons Dijon mustard
3/4	cup olive oil
1/4	cup wine vinegar
1/2	teaspoon salt
1/4	teaspoon pepper

Yield: 1 cup

Combine mustard, olive oil, vinegar, salt and pepper in bowl; mix well. Store in refrigerator.

Tarragon Salad Dressing

1/2	cup vegetable oil
1/4	cup white wine-tarragon vinegar
1 1/2	teaspoons sugar
1/2	teaspoon tarragon
	Hot pepper sauce to taste
1/4	teaspoon salt
1/8	teaspoon pepper

Yield: 3/4 cup

Combine oil, vinegar, sugar, tarragon, pepper sauce, salt and pepper in small bowl; whisk until smooth. Chill for 20 minutes or longer. Mix again just before serving.

Flavor improves if made at least 1 day ahead.

Mimbres Deer

Meat, Poultry & Fish

Turkey

It appears that, previous to Europeans' initial encounter with Native Americans, the only domesticated animals found in Mesoamerica and North America were the dog and the turkey. Both were eaten in Mexico, but the dog was considered an inferior food. Father Sahagún in his history of New Spain reported that "...turkey-meat was put on top, and the dog underneath to make it seem like more" when served at a feast. When the Spanish introduced cattle to the New World, the dog virtually disappeared from the dinner table. The turkey, however, gained wide acceptance in other parts of the world.

The Mexicans called the bird *uexolotl,* but the English called it "turkie-bird." It is probable that the turkey was first introduced to England in 1523-1524 by Turkish merchants who acquired the birds at a stop in Seville on their way to London. In Europe, the turkey is known as *coq d'inde, dinde,* or *dindon* in France, *galle d'india* in Italy, and *indianische henne* in Germany. And in India, the turkey is called *peru.*

The wild turkey is a gregarious and not too intelligent animal. Some researchers have speculated that Native peoples domesticated the turkey out of sheer frustration. The birds, once locating a food source like a grain storage bin, refused to leave even if threatened. Some scientists think that the turkey was confined and fed to prevent crop and storage destruction.

The turkey, or furkee, as they called it, enjoyed by the Pilgrims at Plymouth in 1621 was different from the pampered, plump bird we eat today. Leaner and "game-ier" than the supermarket variety, the turkey nevertheless was an important food for Native peoples and colonists alike. Benjamin Franklin argued that the turkey should become the national symbol of the new United States but was defeated by the argument that the bird was a scavenger and lacked intelligence and, therefore, would make a poor symbol of the new country.

Beef and Eggplant Stacks

1	medium eggplant
1/3	cup flour
1	teaspoon salt
	Pepper to taste
1/4	cup vegetable oil
1	pound ground beef
	Salt to taste
2	8-ounce cans tomato sauce
1	tablespoon grated Parmesan cheese
1/2–1	teaspoon oregano
1	cup shredded Cheddar cheese

Yield: 6 servings

Slice unpeeled eggplant crosswise into 1-inch slices. Coat with mixture of flour, 1 teaspoon salt and pepper. Brown lightly on both sides in heated oil in skillet; drain. Place in shallow baking dish. Shape ground beef into six 3/4 to 1-inch thick patties; season with salt and pepper to taste. Brown on both sides in skillet. Place patties on eggplant slices; spoon tomato sauce over top. Sprinkle with Parmesan cheese, oregano and Cheddar cheese. Bake at 350 degrees for 35 to 40 minutes or until done to taste.

Beer-Braised Beef

1	5-pound boneless beef chuck roast
	Salt and pepper to taste
2	tablespoons vegetable oil
3	large onions, cut into quarters
2	cloves of garlic, pressed
3	tablespoons flour
1	12-ounce can beer
	Turmeric to taste
1/8	teaspoon cinnamon
3	whole cloves
2	tablespoons tomato paste
1	bay leaf
1/4	teaspoon thyme
1	16-ounce can beef broth

Yield: 8 servings

Sprinkle roast with salt and pepper. Brown on all sides in hot oil in Dutch oven; remove roast from pan. Add onions and garlic to Dutch oven. Sauté until brown, stirring occasionally. Stir in flour. Cook until flour is brown, stirring constantly. Add beer, turmeric, cinnamon and cloves. Bring to a boil. Stir in tomato paste, bay leaf, thyme and beef broth. Add roast. Bring to a boil, basting roast with juices. Bake, covered, at 350 degrees for 2½ hours or until roast is tender; discard bay leaf and cloves. Remove roast to serving plate and slice. Serve with pan juices.

Serve with rice or noodles and a green salad.

Braised Brisket Carbonnade

1	3 to 4-pound beef brisket, trimmed
1	large onion, sliced
2	12-ounce cans beer
1/4	cup packed dark brown sugar
1	tablespoon Dijon mustard
1	tablespoon instant beef bouillon
	Coarsely ground pepper to taste
1/2	teaspoon dried thyme
1	bay leaf
3	cloves of garlic, pressed

Yield: 8 to 10 servings

Place beef in large Dutch oven; top with onion slices. Combine beer, brown sugar, mustard, beef bouillon, pepper, thyme, bay leaf and garlic in bowl; mix well. Pour over beef. Bake, covered, at 350 degrees for 3 hours or until tender. Remove beef to warm platter; slice thinly cross grain.

Discard bay leaf. Use pan juices to make gravy.

Meat Loaf

2	pounds ground beef
1	12-ounce can evaporated milk
1	envelope leek or French onion soup mix

Yield: 8 to 10 servings

Combine ground beef, evaporated milk and soup mix in bowl; mix well. Mixture will be soupy. Place in 5x9-inch loaf pan. Bake at 350 degrees for 1 1/2 hours.

This is delicious served hot or cold.

Agriculture on the Lower Colorado River ⌒

Before the dams on the Colorado River were built, the Native people along the lower part of the river in Arizona lived in an environment similar to that of the lower Nile in Egypt. The river ran full and wide, and large fish, weighing up to 60 pounds, were caught. When the river flooded in early summer, depositing rich silt, corn, beans, squash, melon and wheat were planted. The hot weather promoted rapid growth and a good harvest.

The tribes living in this area today are the Mohave, Chemehuevi, Quechan (Yuma) and the Cocopah.

Mock Cabbage Rolls

1¹/₂	pounds ground beef
2	onions, chopped
2	cloves of garlic, pressed
3	8-ounce cans tomato sauce
1	medium green bell pepper, chopped
1	stalk celery, sliced ¹/₄ inch thick
1	carrot, thinly sliced
¹/₄	teaspoon fennel seeds
¹/₂	teaspoon pepper
3	cups cooked white rice
1	medium head cabbage, shredded

Yield: 6 servings

Brown ground beef in skillet, stirring until crumbly; drain. Add onions and garlic. Sauté for several minutes. Stir in half of 1 can tomato sauce, green pepper, celery, carrot, fennel seeds, pepper and rice. Layer half the cabbage and remaining half can of tomato sauce in 1¹/₂-quart baking dish. Top with beef mixture, remaining cabbage and remaining tomato sauce. Bake, covered, at 350 degrees for 1 hour.

May sprinkle with Parmesan cheese at serving time.

Stuffed Peppers

6	large green bell peppers
	Salt to taste
1	pound lean ground beef
1	large onion, finely chopped
1	clove of garlic, pressed
1	teaspoon salt
¹/₄	teaspoon hot pepper sauce
1¹/₂	cups cooked rice
1	15-ounce can tomato sauce

Yield: 6 servings

Cut thin slice from stem end of each green pepper; cut peppers into halves lengthwise, discarding seeds and membrane. Cook with salt in boiling water to cover in saucepan for 5 minutes; drain. Invert peppers to drain well. Cook ground beef with onion and garlic in skillet, stirring until ground beef is crumbly and onion is tender; drain. Stir in 1 teaspoon salt, pepper sauce, rice and 1 cup tomato sauce. Spoon into peppers; arrange in 9x13-inch baking dish. Pour remaining tomato sauce over and around peppers. Bake, covered with foil, at 350 degrees for 45 minutes. Bake, uncovered, for 15 minutes longer.

Creole Beef Stew

3	tablespoons flour
1/2	teaspoon ground ginger
1	teaspoon salt
1/2	teaspoon celery salt
1/4	teaspoon garlic salt
1/4	teaspoon pepper
3	pounds chuck roast, cut into 2-inch cubes
2	tablespoons shortening or bacon drippings
1	16-ounce can tomatoes
3	medium onions, sliced
1/3	cup red wine vinegar
1/2	cup molasses
6–8	carrots, sliced diagonally 1 inch thick
1/2	cup raisins

Yield: 8 to 10 servings

Mix flour, ginger, salt, celery salt, garlic salt and pepper together. Toss with beef cubes, coating well. Brown beef in shortening in large heavy saucepan. Add tomatoes, onions, vinegar and molasses; mix well. Bring to a boil; reduce heat. Simmer, covered, for 2 hours. Add carrots and raisins. Simmer for 30 minutes or until carrots are tender.

Serve with rice, green salad and corn bread.

Sweet and Sour Beef

2	pounds lean beef, cubed
2	8-ounce cans tomato sauce
	Juice of 1 lemon
1/2	cup sugar
	Salt and pepper to taste

Yield: 8 servings

Sear beef cubes on all sides in skillet; remove to 2 1/2-quart baking dish. Combine tomato sauce, lemon juice, sugar, salt and pepper in bowl; mix well. Pour over beef. Bake, covered, at 325 degrees for 3 hours. Serve over hot cooked rice or noodles.

May make a day in advance and reheat to serve.

French Beef

1 1/2	pounds 2-inch beef stew meat
2	medium onions, sliced
2	tablespoons tapioca
2	beef bouillon cubes, crushed
1	8-ounce can mushrooms
1/2	cup water
1	cup dry red wine

Yield: 4 to 5 servings

Combine stew beef, onions, tapioca, bouillon, mushrooms, water and wine in bowl; mix well. Spoon into 3-quart baking dish. Bake, covered, at 350 degrees for 3 hours, stirring after 1 1/2 hours. Serve over rice or noodles.

Sweet and Spicy Short Ribs

3–4	pounds beef short ribs
1	cup catsup
1	tablespoon horseradish
1	cup water
1	tablespoon sugar
1	tablespoon vinegar
1	tablespoon Worcestershire sauce
1	tablespoon dry mustard
1	bay leaf
1	teaspoon salt
1/4	teaspoon pepper
2	medium onions, sliced

Yield: 4 servings

Combine short ribs, catsup, horseradish, water, sugar, vinegar, Worcestershire sauce, dry mustard, bay leaf, salt and pepper in large saucepan. Simmer, covered, for 2 hours or until beef is tender. Cool to room temperature. Chill for 2 hours to overnight. Skim fat from surface; discard bones and bay leaf. Spoon into 6-cup baking dish; top with onion slices. Bake, uncovered, in moderate oven for 30 minutes; baste with sauce. Bake, covered, for 30 minutes longer or until done to taste.

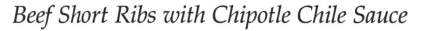

Beef Short Ribs with Chipotle Chile Sauce

4	pounds lean beef short ribs, cracked
1/2	cup flour
1/4	teaspoon onion powder
1/4	teaspoon garlic powder
1/2	teaspoon salt
1/2	cup olive oil
1	large onion, chopped
3	cloves of garlic, minced
3	canned chipotle chiles in adobo sauce
1/4	cup adobo sauce
2 1/2	cups beef broth
3	cups cooked rice

Yield: 4 to 5 servings

Trim fat from ribs. Mix 1/2 cup flour, onion powder, garlic powder and salt in bowl. Coat ribs with flour mixture, reserving remaining flour mixture. Brown ribs on all sides in heated olive oil in heavy 5-quart saucepan over medium-high heat; remove to platter. Drain all but 2 teaspoons oil from saucepan. Add onion and garlic. Sauté until tender. Stir in 1 tablespoon reserved flour mixture. Cook for 2 to 3 minutes, stirring constantly; push mixture to 1 side. Add chiles, mashing with back of spoon. Add adobo sauce; mix well. Cook for 2 minutes. Spread mixture evenly over bottom of saucepan. Place ribs on onion mixture. Add broth; reduce heat. Simmer, covered, for 1 to 1 1/2 hours or until meat is tender, basting occasionally. Skim fat from surface. Serve ribs over rice; spoon cooking juices over top.

May prepare dish in advance and reheat in microwave.

Eye of Round Garni

1	5 to 6-pound beef eye of round roast
1/3	cup soy sauce
1/3	cup wine
1/3	cup water
1/2	cup chopped onion
1/2	cup chopped celery
1/2	cup chopped green bell pepper
1	tablespoon flour
1	10-ounce can cream of mushroom soup

Yield: 8 to 10 servings

Combine roast with soy sauce, wine, water, onion, celery and green pepper in bowl. Marinate for 1 hour or longer. Shake flour in cooking bag; add beef and marinade. Place in 2-inch deep baking pan; pierce 6 holes in bag. Bake at 325 degrees for 1½ to 2 hours. Remove beef to serving plate, reserving cooking juices. Combine cooking juices with soup in saucepan. Cook until heated through, stirring to mix well. Serve with roast.

May cook roast wrapped in foil instead of using cooking bag if preferred.

Flank Steak with Mushroom and Pine Nut Stuffing

1	2-pound flank steak
1	large onion, chopped
1	clove of garlic, pressed
2	tablespoons olive oil
1/2	cup chopped mushrooms
1/4	cup coarsely chopped pine nuts
1/4	cup chopped parsley
1½	cups soft bread cubes
1/4	teaspoon oregano
1/4	teaspoon basil
1/2	teaspoon salt
	Freshly ground pepper to taste
1	egg, beaten
1	tablespoon vegetable oil
1/2	cup dry white wine

Yield: 6 servings

Pound steak with meat mallet; score lightly on both sides. Sauté onion and garlic in hot olive oil in skillet until brown. Add mushrooms. Sauté for 2 to 3 minutes. Add pine nuts, parsley, bread cubes, oregano, basil, salt, pepper and egg; mix well and remove from heat. Spread on steak. Roll up to enclose filling; secure with string at 2-inch intervals. Brown on all sides in vegetable oil in Dutch oven. Add wine. Bake, covered, at 350 degrees for 2 hours. Cut into 1-inch slices; serve with pan juices.

Mustard Steak

1/4	cup vegetable oil
1	Chateaubriand, 3 inches thick
32	ounces prepared mustard
1	large container salt

Yield: 8 servings

Rub oil over entire steak. Spread mustard 1/2 inch thick over top and sides of steak. Pour salt on mustard until salt stops being absorbed and remains white. Place coated side down directly on 1 to 2 layers very hot coals. Spread remaining side with mustard and coat with salt, wearing protective gloves. Build coals around steak until level with top, using tongs. Close top of grill, leaving vents open. Grill for 20 minutes, checking coals for even heat every 5 minutes. Lift steak and spread coals. Replace steak cooked side up on coals; build coals up around sides. Grill for 15 to 20 minutes longer or until done to taste. Slice into 1/8 to 1/4-inch slices to serve. It is important to use a steak 3 inches thick for this recipe. The mustard and salt will burn off, leaving a moist steak with a delicious flavor.

This recipe was contributed by Barbara Heard, wife of Bartlett B. Heard, Jr., grandson of Dwight B. and Maie Bartlett Heard. Mustard Steak was a great favorite at Heard family picnics.

Mexican Party Roast

1 **5 to 6-pound eye of round roast**
1/2 **cup vegetable oil**
1 **15-ounce can tomatoes**
2 **15-ounce cans tomato sauce**
1/2 **cup chopped onion**
3 **cloves of garlic, pressed**
1/2 **cup minced parsley**
1/2 **teaspoon cloves**
1/2 **teaspoon cinnamon**
  Salt to taste

Yield: 12 to 15 servings

Brown roast in oil in saucepan. Remove roast to large saucepan, reserving drippings. Add enough boiling water to cover roast. Simmer for 1 1/2 hours or until roast is tender. Add tomatoes, tomato sauce, onion, garlic, parsley, cloves, cinnamon and salt to reserved drippings in first saucepan; stir to deglaze saucepan. Simmer for 15 minutes. Remove roast to platter. Boil broth until reduced to 1 1/2 to 2 cups. Add tomato mixture and roast. Simmer for 30 minutes. Remove roast to platter. Chill roast and sauce until time to reheat. Slice roast into thin slices; arrange in overlapping layers in baking dish. Spoon sauce over top. Bake at 325 degrees for 30 minutes or until heated through. May reheat in microwave if preferred.

Spicy Orange Pot Roast

1 **4-pound bone-in blade-cut beef chuck roast**
2 **tablespoons fresh lemon juice**
6 **slices bacon, chopped**
1 **medium onion, chopped**
1 **clove of garlic, minced**
1 1/2 **cups orange juice**
1 **cup chopped peeled tomato**
1 **tablespoon sugar**
2 **teaspoons salt**
1 **teaspoon thyme**
1/2 **teaspoon nutmeg**
1/4 **teaspoon pepper**
1 **bay leaf**
2 **tablespoons cornstarch**
2 **tablespoons water**

Yield: 6 servings

Brush roast with lemon juice; let stand for 5 minutes. Sauté bacon with onion and garlic in electric skillet or heavy saucepan until bacon is crisp. Remove with slotted spoon. Brown roast on both sides in bacon drippings. Add bacon mixture, orange juice, tomato, sugar, salt, thyme, nutmeg, pepper and bay leaf. Simmer, covered, for 3 hours. Remove roast to warm platter. Pour cooking juices into 4-cup measure and skim fat; discard bay leaf. Combine with mixture of cornstarch and water in saucepan. Cook for 3 to 5 minutes or until thickened, stirring constantly. Serve with roast.

Moussaka

2	medium eggplant
1/2	cup olive oil
	Meat Sauce
	Custard Topping
	Grated Parmesan cheese

Yield: 10 to 12 servings

Cut stem ends from eggplant and slice 1/4 inch thick. Coat well with olive oil; arrange in single layer on baking sheet. Bake at 425 degrees for 30 minutes; reduce oven temperature to 350 degrees. Layer half the eggplant, Meat Sauce and remaining eggplant in 10x15-inch baking pan. Spread with Custard Topping; sprinkle with Parmesan cheese. Bake for 1 hour. Cut into squares to serve.

This recipe requires substantial preparation time but it is well worth the effort.

Meat Sauce

2	medium onions, chopped
1	tablespoon oil
1 1/2	pounds ground beef
2	teaspoons salt
2	6-ounce cans tomato paste
1/4	cup dry red wine
1/4	cup finely chopped parsley
1	cinnamon stick
2	cloves of garlic, pressed
3	tablespoons fine dry bread crumbs
1	cup grated Parmesan cheese

Sauté onions in oil in saucepan. Add ground beef. Cook until ground beef is brown and crumbly, stirring frequently. Add salt, tomato paste, wine, parsley, cinnamon stick and garlic. Simmer, covered, for 30 minutes; discard cinnamon stick. Simmer, uncovered, until thickened to desired consistency. Stir in bread crumbs and Parmesan cheese.

Custard Topping

1/2	cup flour
1/3	cup melted butter
1	quart milk
1	teaspoon salt
1/4	teaspoon nutmeg
1/2	cup grated Parmesan cheese
6	eggs, slightly beaten

Blend flour into melted butter in saucepan. Cook for 2 minutes, stirring constantly. Stir in milk gradually. Cook until thickened, stirring constantly. Add salt, nutmeg and Parmesan cheese. Stir a small amount of hot mixture into eggs; stir eggs into hot mixture.

Cheesy Hash and Spinach Pie

2	10-ounce packages frozen chopped spinach
2	eggs, beaten
1	10-ounce can cream of mushroom soup
1/2	cup flour
1	teaspoon prepared mustard
1	tablespoon prepared horseradish
1	15-ounce can corned beef hash
1	baked 9-inch deep-dish pie shell
1	cup shredded sharp Cheddar cheese
2	tablespoons chopped pimento

Yield: 6 servings

Cook spinach using package directions; drain well, pressing out excess moisture. Combine beaten eggs, soup, flour, mustard and horseradish in bowl; mix well. Stir in spinach. Spread corned beef hash in pie shell; spread spinach mixture over hash, mounding in center. Bake at 350 degrees for 45 minutes. Sprinkle with mixture of shredded cheese and pimento. Bake for 2 to 3 minutes longer. Let stand for 5 minutes before serving.

Swedish Ham Balls

1	pound ground ham
8	ounces lean ground pork
8	ounces lean ground beef
1	cup rolled oats
1	cup milk
2	eggs, slightly beaten
	Sauce for Ham Balls

Yield: 3 dozen

Combine ground ham, pork and beef with oats, milk and eggs in bowl; mix well. Shape into 1 1/2-inch balls with wet hands; place in 9x13-inch baking dish. Pour Sauce for Ham Balls over top. Bake at 325 degrees for 2 hours, turning every half hour.

May make in advance and chill until time to bake or reheat.

Sauce for Ham Balls

1	cup packed brown sugar
1	teaspoon dry mustard
1/2	cup vinegar
1/2	cup water

Mix brown sugar and dry mustard in bowl. Add vinegar and water; mix well.

Deviled Ham and Broccoli Casserole

1	10-ounce package frozen broccoli spears
6	eggs, hard-cooked
3	tablespoons mayonnaise-type salad dressing
1	tablespoon minced onion
1	teaspoon prepared mustard
1/2	teaspoon Worcestershire sauce
1	4.5-ounce can deviled ham
	Cream Sauce

Yield: 6 servings

Cook broccoli spears using package directions; drain well. Peel eggs; cut into halves. Remove yolks; reserve whites. Mash yolks in small bowl. Add salad dressing, onion, mustard, Worcestershire sauce and deviled ham; mix well. Spoon into reserved egg whites. Layer broccoli spears, stuffed eggs and Cream Sauce in baking dish. Bake at 325 degrees for 30 minutes.

Cream Sauce

2	tablespoons margarine
2	tablespoons flour
1	cup milk
1/2	teaspoon salt
1/2	cup shredded Cheddar cheese

Melt margarine in small saucepan. Blend in flour. Stir in milk. Cook until thickened, stirring constantly. Add salt and cheese. Heat until cheese melts, stirring constantly.

Ham and Wild Rice Casserole

1	6-ounce package long grain and wild rice mix
1	pound ham, cut into 1/2-inch cubes
1	cup sliced fresh mushrooms
1	10-ounce package frozen chopped broccoli or 10 ounces chopped fresh broccoli, partially cooked
1	cup chopped celery
1/2	cup finely chopped onion
1	cup shredded Cheddar cheese
1	10-ounce can cream of celery soup
1	cup mayonnaise
1	tablespoon Dijon mustard
1/2	teaspoon lemon pepper
1/2	cup grated Parmesan cheese

Yield: 10 to 12 servings

Cook rice using package directions; spread in greased 9x13-inch baking dish. Layer ham, mushrooms, broccoli, celery, onion and Cheddar cheese over rice. Combine soup, mayonnaise, mustard and lemon pepper in bowl; mix well. Spread over layers; sprinkle with Parmesan cheese. Bake at 350 degrees for 45 minutes.

Filipino-Style Pork Chops

4	loin pork chops
1/4	cup rice wine vinegar
	Salt and pepper to taste
1	egg, beaten
1	tablespoon water
2	tablespoons bread crumbs
1	clove of garlic, minced
1	teaspoon chopped parsley
2	tablespoons flour
2 1/2	tablespoons olive oil

Yield: 2 servings

Marinate pork chops in vinegar in shallow dish for 1 hour; drain and pat dry. Sprinkle with salt and pepper. Beat egg with water. Mix bread crumbs, garlic, parsley and salt and pepper to taste. Coat pork chops with flour. Dip into egg mixture; coat with bread crumb mixture. Brown on both sides in olive oil in skillet. Remove to baking dish. Bake, covered, at 325 degrees for 1 hour or until tender.

Stuffed Pork Chops in Wine Sauce

6	double loin pork chops
	Apple-Onion Stuffing
1	tablespoon butter
1/2	cup dry white wine
1–2	teaspoons cornstarch

Yield: 6 servings

Cut pockets in pork chops. Spoon Apple-Onion Stuffing into pockets in pork chops; secure openings with wooden picks. Brown on both sides in 1 tablespoon butter in Dutch oven. Add wine to depth of 1/4 inch. Bake, covered, at 350 degrees for 1 hour. Remove pork chops to warm platter. Bring cooking liquid to a boil. Stir in mixture of cornstarch and a small amount of water. Cook until thickened, stirring constantly. Adjust seasonings. Serve wine sauce with pork chops.

Apple-Onion Stuffing

1/2	cup chopped tart apple
1/2	cup chopped onion
1/4	cup chopped celery
3	tablespoons butter
1 1/2	cups bread cubes
1	teaspoon fennel seeds, crushed
1/4	cup chopped parsley
1/4	cup half and half

Sauté apple, onion and celery in 3 tablespoons butter in heavy skillet until tender. Add bread cubes, fennel seeds and parsley; mix well. Add half and half; mix gently.

Savory Baked Pork Chops

1	10-ounce can cream of celery soup
1	cup milk
1	cup uncooked instant rice
1/2	teaspoon salt
1/4	teaspoon sage
4–6	pork chops, 3/4 inch thick
2	tablespoons butter or margarine

Yield: 4 to 6 servings

Combine soup and milk in bowl; mix well. Add rice, salt and sage; mix well. Brown pork chops on both sides in butter in skillet. Remove to 5-cup baking dish; spoon rice mixture over and around chops. Bake, covered, at 350 degrees for 1 hour.

Pork Roast with Sauerkraut

1	5-pound pork roast
1	teaspoon salt
1/4	teaspoon onion powder
1/4	teaspoon garlic powder
1	tablespoon shortening
2	large onions, chopped
2	16-ounce cans sauerkraut
2	teaspoons caraway seeds

Yield: 5 to 6 servings

Sprinkle roast with salt, onion powder and garlic powder. Brown on all sides in shortening in heavy saucepan; remove to platter. Add onions to drippings in saucepan. Sauté until light brown. Add undrained sauerkraut and caraway seeds. Cook for 5 minutes. Make well in sauerkraut mixture; place roast and any accumulated meat juices into well. Simmer, covered, for 1 1/2 to 2 hours.

Choucroute Garni

8	ounces bacon, chopped
2	large onions, coarsely chopped
3	carrots, sliced
	Bouquet Garni
4–6	pounds fresh sauerkraut, rinsed, drained
2–4	cups fruity white wine
3–4	cups chicken broth
1	pound lean pork loin, cubed
8	ounces ham, cubed
1	pound smoked sausage, sliced
1	pound bratwurst, sliced
2	tart green apples, coarsely chopped

Yield: 10 servings

Cook bacon in large heavy saucepan over medium-low heat until drippings are rendered. Add onions and carrots. Cook for 8 to 10 minutes, stirring occasionally. Add Bouquet Garni, sauerkraut, wine and chicken broth. Bring to a boil; reduce heat. Simmer, covered, for 1 hour. Add pork, ham and sausages; mix well. Simmer, covered, for 1 hour. Add apples. Simmer for 20 minutes; discard Bouquet Garni. Serve with pumpernickel or rye bread.

May chill and reheat to serve.

Bouquet Garni

1/2	cup chopped parsley
2	bay leaves
10	black peppercorns
10	juniper berries
4	whole cloves

Tie parsley, bay leaves, peppercorns, juniper berries and cloves in cheesecloth bag or combine in large tea ball; set aside.

Veal Chops with Anchovy and Caper Sauce

6	veal loin chops, 3/4 inch thick
1/2	cup flour
1/4	cup vegetable oil
1/4	cup brandy
2	ounces prosciutto, minced
3	tablespoons butter
4	flat anchovy fillets
2	tablespoons capers, rinsed, drained
6	tablespoons half and half
3	tablespoons chopped fresh parsley

Yield: 6 servings

Coat veal chops with flour, shaking off excess. Place in hot oil in large heavy skillet. Cook for 8 to 10 minutes or until brown on both sides, turning once. Remove to warm platter. Keep warm, loosely covered, in 200-degree oven. Pour oil from skillet. Add brandy to skillet, stirring to deglaze. Bring to a boil. Boil until reduced by 1/2. Sauté prosciutto in butter in small skillet over medium heat for 1 minute. Add anchovies and capers, mashing to paste with fork. Stir brandy mixture into anchovy mixture. Blend in half and half. Cook until heated through. Spoon over chops; sprinkle with parsley.

This is good with green salad, hot crusty bread and a glass of dry white wine.

Veal Pearle

2 1/2	pounds veal scallops
	Salt to taste
1	tablespoon butter or margarine
1 1/2	cups hot water
1	beef bouillon cube
1	tablespoon chili sauce
1	tablespoon parsley flakes
1/4	cup sherry or white wine
2	tablespoons sweet vermouth
	Onion salt, nutmeg and pepper to taste

Yield: 6 servings

Sprinkle veal with salt to taste. Brown on both sides in butter in large skillet; remove to baking dish. Add hot water to skillet, stirring to deglaze. Add bouillon, chili sauce, parsley flakes, wines, salt, onion salt, nutmeg and pepper; mix well. Pour over veal. Bake, covered, at 350 degrees for 45 minutes or until bubbly; do not overbake.

Rolled Shoulder of Veal with Tomato and Mushroom Sauce

1	3¹/₂ to 4-pound rolled veal shoulder roast
2	cloves of garlic, pressed
2	teaspoons pepper
2	teaspoons paprika
3	medium onions, sliced
1	8-ounce can tomato sauce
1	4-ounce can sliced mushrooms

Yield: 6 to 8 servings

Rub roast with garlic, pepper and paprika. Wrap in foil or waxed paper. Chill overnight. Spread onions in roasting pan. Remove foil from roast; add to roasting pan. Top with tomato sauce and undrained mushrooms. Roast, tightly covered, at 350 degrees for 3 hours. Let stand for 15 minutes before slicing. Serve with cooking sauce.

Chicken and Artichoke Casserole

2	9-ounce packages frozen artichoke hearts
2	cloves of garlic
1	tablespoon olive oil
2²/₃	cups chopped cooked chicken
2	10-ounce cans cream of chicken soup
1	tablespoon fresh lemon juice
1	cup mayonnaise
1	teaspoon curry powder
1¹/₄	cups shredded sharp Cheddar cheese
1¹/₄	cups soft bread cubes
2	tablespoons melted butter

Yield: 8 servings

Cook artichoke hearts using package directions, adding garlic and olive oil; drain, discarding garlic. Layer artichokes and chicken in greased baking dish. Combine soup, lemon juice, mayonnaise and curry powder in bowl; mix well. Spoon over chicken; sprinkle with cheese. Toss bread cubes with melted butter in bowl; sprinkle over casserole. Bake at 350 degrees for 25 minutes.

Easy Baked Chicken

1	**3-pound chicken, cut up**
1/2	**envelope onion soup mix**
1/2	**cup Russian salad dressing**
1/2	**cup apricot jam**

Yield: 4 to 6 servings

Rinse chicken and pat dry; place in 8x8-inch baking dish. Combine soup mix, salad dressing and jam in bowl; mix well. Spoon over chicken. Bake at 350 degrees for 1½ hours or until tender.

Happy Legs

1½	**cups uncooked instant rice**
4	**chicken legs and thighs, skinned**
1	**8-ounce can pineapple tidbits**
1	**tablespoon Worcestershire sauce**
1/4	**cup fresh lemon Juice**

Yield: 4 servings

Sprinkle uncooked rice into 9x9-inch baking dish. Rinse chicken and pat dry; arrange over rice. Drain pineapple, reserving juice. Combine reserved juice with Worcestershire sauce and lemon juice in 2-cup measure. Add enough water to measure 1½ cups. Pour over chicken. Spoon pineapple over and around chicken. Bake, tightly covered with foil, at 350 degrees for 1½ hours.

To serve, place chicken in center of platter and spoon rice around chicken. Arrange cooked broccoli around edge of platter.

Oriental Chicken

2	broiler chickens, cut into quarters
2	tablespoons vegetable oil
1	clove of garlic, minced
1/2	cup light soy sauce
1 1/4	teaspoons finely chopped gingerroot
2	green onions, cut into 1-inch pieces
1	12-ounce can beer
1	tablespoon chopped cilantro
3	tablespoons cornstarch
3	tablespoons water
	Salt and pepper to taste

Yield: 6 servings

Rinse chicken and pat dry. Brown in oil in 5-quart Dutch oven. Add garlic, soy sauce, gingerroot, green onions, beer and cilantro; mix well. Bake, covered, at 350 degrees for 1 hour. Remove chicken to serving platter. Skim fat from surface of cooking liquid. Stir in mixture of cornstarch and water. Cook until thickened, stirring constantly. Season with salt and pepper. Spoon some of the sauce over chicken. Serve remaining sauce in bowl. Serve with hot cooked rice.

Omit salt if using regular soy sauce.

Oven-Barbecued Chicken

8	chicken breast halves, boned
1/2	teaspoon salt
1/8	teaspoon pepper
1/4	cup butter or margarine
1/4	cup fresh lemon juice
1/4	cup Worcestershire sauce
1/4	cup cider vinegar
1/4	cup catsup

Yield: 4 to 6 servings

Rinse chicken and pat dry; season with salt and pepper. Arrange skin side up in single layer in shallow baking pan. Broil 6 inches from heat source for 5 minutes or until light brown. Melt butter in small saucepan. Add lemon juice, Worcestershire sauce, vinegar and catsup. Bring to a boil. Cook for 1 minute, stirring constantly. Pour over chicken. Bake at 325 degrees for 1 hour, basting frequently.

Baked Chicken with Almonds

1/2	cup raisins
1/4	cup vodka
1/2	cup slivered almonds
1/2	cup butter or margarine
8	chicken breast halves, boned
1	teaspoon salt
1/2	teaspoon red pepper
1	10-ounce can cream of mushroom soup
1	10-ounce can Cheddar cheese soup
1	large onion, sliced

Yield: 6 to 8 servings

Soak raisins in vodka in small bowl. Sauté almonds in butter in skillet until light brown; remove almonds with slotted spoon. Rinse chicken and pat dry; sprinkle with salt and red pepper. Brown in drippings in skillet. Remove chicken to 9x13-inch baking dish. Spoon mixture of soups over chicken; top with onion slices and raisins. Bake, covered, at 375 degrees for 30 minutes. Add almonds. Bake, uncovered, for 20 minutes longer.

May make 1 day in advance and chill until baking time. Allow an additional 5 to 10 minutes for covered baking time.

Monterey Chicken

8	7 to 8-ounce whole chicken breasts, skinned, boned
1	7-ounce can whole green chiles, cut into strips
8	ounces Monterey Jack cheese, cut into 8 strips
1/2	cup fine dry bread crumbs
1/4	cup grated Parmesan cheese
1–3	teaspoons chili powder
1/2	teaspoon salt
1/4	teaspoon ground cumin
1/4	teaspoon freshly ground pepper
6	tablespoons melted butter

Yield: 8 servings

Rinse chicken and pat dry. Pound thin between sheets of waxed paper. Layer 1 strip of green chile and 1 strip of Monterey Jack cheese on each piece of chicken; roll chicken to enclose filling, tucking ends under. Combine bread crumbs, Parmesan cheese, chili powder, salt, cumin and pepper in shallow dish. Dip chicken rolls into melted butter; coat with bread crumb mixture. Arrange seam side down in baking dish; drizzle with remaining butter. Chill, covered, for 4 hours or longer. Bake in preheated 400-degree oven for 25 to 40 minutes or until chicken is cooked through. Garnish with sour cream and fresh lime slices.

Chicken with Lemon-Herb Sauce

6   chicken breast halves, boned
3   tablespoons flour
1/4   cup butter
1/2   cup vermouth
        Lemon-Herb Sauce

Yield: 6 servings

Rinse chicken and pat dry. Coat with flour. Brown in butter in skillet for 4 minutes on each side. Add vermouth. Cook over high heat for 5 minutes to reduce liquid. Simmer for 5 minutes longer. Serve with Lemon-Herb Sauce.

Lemon-Herb Sauce

6   tablespoons fresh lemon juice
1   teaspoon chopped garlic
1/2   teaspoon each dillweed and thyme
1   teaspoon each parsley, oregano, basil
            and pepper
1/2   teaspoon salt

Combine lemon juice, garlic, dillweed, thyme, parsley, oregano, basil, pepper and salt in saucepan. Simmer for 5 minutes.

Agave 〜

The agave plant, also known as mescal, and as the "century plant," was once one of the staple foods collected by the Western Apache. The plant matures in about 15 to 20 years and sends up a flowering stalk before it dies. Agave hearts are sweetest when collected just before the flower stalk emerges. The hearts were roasted in pits for one and one-half to two days and then pounded to a pulp, shaped into cakes and dried. Dried agave cakes may be eaten as is or mixed with water to make a gruel.

The practice of making mescal and tequila from the juice of the agave was not as prevalent in the Southwest as it currently is in Mexico.

Chicken Parisienne

4	chicken breasts
	Salt and pepper to taste
2	tablespoons olive oil
1	onion, cut into quarters
1	10-ounce can golden mushroom soup
2/3	cup sliced fresh mushrooms or
	1 3-ounce can mushrooms with liquid
1	cup sour cream
1/2	cup sherry
	Paprika, garlic powder, onion powder and freshly ground pepper to taste

Yield: 4 servings

Rinse chicken and pat dry; season with salt and pepper. Brown on both sides in olive oil in skillet. Remove chicken to plate. Add onion to drippings in skillet. Sauté for 3 minutes. Arrange chicken over onion. Combine soup, mushrooms, sour cream and sherry in bowl; mix well. Spoon over chicken. Sprinkle with salt and remaining seasonings to taste. Simmer for 15 minutes or until chicken is tender. Serve on rice or noodles.

May bake at 350 degrees for 1 hour if preferred.

Chicken Picante

1	2 1/2 to 3-pound broiler-fryer chicken, cut up
	Chicken broth or white wine
1/2	cup medium salsa
1/4	cup Dijon mustard
2	tablespoons fresh lime juice
1/2	teaspoon ground cumin

Yield: 4 servings

Rinse chicken and pat dry. Brown on all sides in skillet sprayed with nonfat cooking spray, adding a small amount of chicken broth if needed to prevent overbrowning. Combine salsa, mustard, lime juice and cumin in bowl; mix well. Spoon over chicken; reduce heat. Simmer, covered, for 20 minutes or until tender. Garnish with parsley or cilantro; serve with rice.

May substitute 4 to 6 chicken breast halves for cut-up chicken and reduce simmering time to 10 minutes or until tender.

Chicken Salad Bake

2	cups chopped cooked chicken
1	cup chopped celery
1/2	cup chopped onion
1	5-ounce can sliced water chestnuts, drained
1/2	cup shredded Cheddar cheese
1/2	cup mayonnaise
1	tablespoon fresh lemon juice
	Salt to taste
1/8	teaspoon pepper
1	cup canned shoestring potatoes

Yield: 4 servings

Combine chicken, celery, onion, water chestnuts, cheese, mayonnaise, lemon juice, salt and pepper in bowl; mix well. Spoon into 1 1/2-quart baking dish; sprinkle with potato sticks. Bake at 400 degrees for 20 to 25 minutes or until heated through.

May top with potato chips, chow mein noodles or onion rings instead of potato sticks if preferred. May add broccoli, mushrooms or other vegetables.

Mexican Chicken Wellington

1	cup chopped cooked chicken
1/2	cup 1/2-inch scallion pieces
1/2	cup shredded Monterey Jack cheese
1	2-ounce can sliced black olives, drained
1/2	cup taco sauce or jalapeño sauce
1	4-ounce can chopped green chiles, drained
1	4-ounce jar sliced pimentos, drained
1/4	teaspoon cumin
12	sheets phyllo dough
1/4	cup melted butter

Yield: 4 servings

Combine chicken, scallion pieces, cheese, olives, taco sauce, green chiles, pimentos and cumin in large bowl; mix well. Layer 6 sheets of phyllo dough on waxed paper, brushing each sheet sparingly with melted butter. Repeat process with remaining sheets to make a second stack. Spread chicken mixture crosswise over center 1/4 of each stack, leaving 1 1/2 inches uncovered on either side. Fold sides over filling; brush with butter. Roll phyllo from narrow side as for jelly rolls. Place rolls seam side down on buttered baking sheet; brush with butter. Bake at 375 degrees for 15 to 20 minutes or until golden brown. Cut each roll into halves. Serve immediately.

Szechuan Chicken with Peppers and Cashews

2	whole chicken breasts, skinned, boned
1/2–1	teaspoon crushed red pepper flakes
1/4	cup vegetable oil
1	green bell pepper, sliced into thin strips
1	red bell pepper, sliced into thin strips
1	yellow bell pepper, sliced into thin strips
	Ginger-Sherry Sauce
4	green onions, diagonally sliced
2 1/2	tablespoons cornstarch
1/4	cup water
1/2	cup unsalted cashews

Yield: 4 servings

Cut chicken into 3/4-inch pieces; rinse and pat dry. Stir-fry pepper flakes in hot oil in wok or skillet for 30 seconds. Add chicken. Stir-fry for 2 minutes; remove from wok. Stir-fry bell peppers in drippings in skillet for 1 minute. Return chicken to wok. Stir in Ginger-Sherry Sauce and green onions. Add mixture of cornstarch and 1/4 cup water. Cook until thickened, stirring constantly. Stir in cashews. Serve over steamed rice.

Ginger-Sherry Sauce

1/4	cup soy sauce
2	tablespoons dry sherry
4	teaspoons sugar
2 1/2	teaspoons vinegar
1	tablespoon grated gingerroot
1/3	cup water

Combine soy sauce, wine, sugar, vinegar, gingerroot and 1/3 cup water in bowl; mix well and set aside.

West African Chicken

12–14	meaty pieces of chicken, skinned
1	tablespoon salt
1	tablespoon ground ginger
1/4	cup vegetable oil
1	cup chopped onion
1	clove of garlic, pressed
1–2	tablespoons minced gingerroot
1/2	teaspoon red pepper flakes
1	4-ounce can chopped green chiles
2	16-ounce cans tomatoes, chopped
1	6-ounce can tomato paste
3/4	cup peanut butter
2	cups hot water

Yield: 6 to 8 servings

Rinse chicken and pat dry; sprinkle with salt and ground ginger. Brown on all sides in hot oil in large skillet; remove chicken. Sauté onion in drippings in skillet until tender. Add garlic, gingerroot, pepper flakes, chiles, tomatoes and tomato paste; mix well. Blend peanut butter into hot water in bowl. Add to skillet. Bring to a boil; reduce heat. Simmer for 5 minutes. Return chicken to skillet. Simmer, covered, for 35 minutes or until chicken is tender. Garnish with sliced scallions and pineapple cubes; serve with rice.

Turkey Bourguignon

1	12 to 16-ounce turkey leg, skinned
1	small yellow onion, thinly sliced
3	cloves of garlic
1	cup Burgundy or other dry red or white wine
1/2	teaspoon rosemary
1/2	teaspoon salt
1/2	teaspoon pepper
2	teaspoons flour
2	tablespoons water
4–6	fresh mushrooms, lightly sautéed
1/2	cup canned whole tiny onions
	Chopped parsley to taste

Yield: 2 servings

Combine turkey, onion and garlic in glass dish. Combine wine, rosemary, salt and pepper in bowl; mix well. Pour over turkey, turning to coat well. Marinate, covered, in refrigerator for up to 24 hours, turning turkey several times. Bake in preheated 325-degree oven for 2 hours, turning after 1 hour to cook evenly. Remove turkey to plate, reserving cooking juices; cool slightly. Shred turkey meat, discarding bones and tendons. Strain cooking juices into saucepan. Stir in mixture of flour and water. Cook until slightly thickened, stirring constantly. Add turkey, mushrooms, onions and parsley to taste. Cook until heated through. Serve with new potatoes or over rice or noodles.

Turkey Pilaf

1	12 to 14-ounce turkey leg, skinned
1	small onion, chopped
1	carrot, chopped
1	stalk celery, chopped
1/2	teaspoon thyme
1	bay leaf
1 3/4	cups chicken broth
1/2	cup uncooked long grain rice

Yield: 2 servings

Rinse turkey and pat dry; place in baking dish. Add onion, carrot, celery, thyme, bay leaf and chicken broth. Bake, tightly covered, at 325 degrees for 1 1/2 hours; discard bay leaf. Remove turkey and cool slightly. Shred turkey meat, discarding bones and tendons. Stir turkey and rice into juices remaining in baking dish. Bake for 40 to 45 minutes longer or until rice is tender and most of the liquid is absorbed.

Cheesy Turkey

3/4	cup macaroni, cooked
1 1/2	cups chopped cooked turkey
1	15-ounce can Italian tomatoes
1	large onion, chopped
2	cloves of garlic, minced
1/2	cup chopped green bell pepper
1/2	teaspoon marjoram
1	teaspoon oregano
1/2	teaspoon red pepper flakes
	Salt to taste
1/2	cup shredded mozzarella cheese
1/2	cup shredded Cheddar cheese
1/2	cup seasoned bread crumbs
1	tablespoon butter

Yield: 4 servings

Combine macaroni, turkey, tomatoes, onion, garlic, green pepper, marjoram, oregano, pepper flakes and salt in bowl; mix well. Mix mozzarella cheese and Cheddar cheese in bowl. Add half the cheese to turkey mixture; mix well. Spoon into 9x13-inch baking dish; sprinkle with remaining cheese. Top with bread crumbs; dot with butter. Bake at 350 degrees for 30 minutes or until brown and crusty.

This dish has lots of flavor and is a great way to use leftover turkey.

Golden Turkey Quiche

1	unbaked 9-inch deep-dish pie shell
1	cup chopped celery
1	small onion, chopped
1	tablespoon butter or margarine
1	cup chopped cooked turkey
2	tablespoons chopped pimento
3	eggs
1	cup milk
$1/4$	cup mayonnaise
2	tablespoons prepared mustard
1	teaspoon salt
1	cup shredded Cheddar or Monterey Jack cheese
	Paprika to taste

Yield: 4 to 6 servings

Bake pie shell at 375 degrees for 10 minutes. Sauté celery and onion in butter in skillet until tender. Stir in turkey and pimento. Beat eggs, milk, mayonnaise, mustard and salt in bowl until smooth. Stir in turkey mixture. Spoon into pie shell; sprinkle with cheese and paprika. Bake at 375 degrees for 35 to 40 minutes or until knife inserted near center comes out clean.

Crab Giovanni

1	cup chopped onion
8	ounces fresh mushrooms, sliced
2	cloves of garlic, minced or pressed
$1/2$	cup butter or margarine
8	ounces vermicelli, cooked
2–3	cups crab meat
$1/2$	cup sliced stuffed green olives
8	ounces sharp Cheddar cheese, shredded
$1/2$	cup sour cream
1	28-ounce can tomatoes, chopped
$1^1/2$	teaspoons salt
$1/2$	teaspoon basil

Yield: 8 to 10 servings

Sauté onion, mushrooms and garlic in butter in large skillet over low heat until tender. Add pasta, crab meat, olives, cheese, sour cream, tomatoes, salt and basil; mix well. Spoon into greased 3-quart baking dish. Bake at 350 degrees for 35 to 45 minutes or until bubbly. May prepare in advance and chill until baking time; allow 1 hour to bake.

For a spicier flavor, add a pinch of cayenne pepper and top with $1/2$ cup grated Parmesan cheese.

Crab Soufflé

1   7-ounce can crab meat, rinsed, drained
2   cups drained and flaked imitation crab meat
1¹/₂   cups thinly sliced water chestnuts
1   tablespoon fresh lemon juice
2   cups mayonnaise
6   slices white bread, crusts trimmed, cubed
2   cups half and half
2   hard-cooked eggs, chopped
1   small onion, grated
2   tablespoons chopped parsley
    Salt and pepper to taste
³/₄   cup crushed corn flakes

Yield: 12 to 16 servings

Combine crab meat, imitation crab meat, water chestnuts, lemon juice, mayonnaise, bread cubes, half and half, eggs, onion, parsley, salt and pepper in bowl; mix well. Spoon into greased 9x13-inch baking dish. Sprinkle with corn flakes. Bake at 350 degrees for 45 to 60 minutes or until light brown and bubbly.

May make 1 day ahead and chill, covered, until baking time. This is a wonderful luncheon dish served with a tossed green salad and rolls. It goes a long way because it is very rich.

Lobster Party Casserole

1   8-ounce package elbow macaroni
3   cups chopped cooked lobster meat
3   tablespoons fresh lemon juice
1   tablespoon grated onion
¹/₄   cup finely chopped green bell pepper
1   4-ounce can mushrooms, drained
2   tablespoons butter or margarine
2   tablespoons flour
¹/₄   teaspoon dry mustard
¹/₄   teaspoon seasoned salt
¹/₂   teaspoon salt
¹/₈   teaspoon pepper
2   cups milk
2   cups shredded American process cheese
¹/₄   cup sherry (optional)
¹/₄   cup crushed butter crackers
    Paprika

Yield: 4 to 6 servings

Cook macaroni using package directions; rinse and drain. Sprinkle lobster meat with lemon juice. Sauté onion, green pepper and mushrooms in butter in heated skillet until tender. Add flour, dry mustard, seasoned salt, salt and pepper. Stir in milk gradually. Cook until thickened, stirring constantly. Stir in 1¹/₂ cups cheese. Fold in macaroni, lobster and sherry. Spoon into 2-quart baking dish. Sprinkle with remaining ¹/₂ cup cheese, cracker crumbs and paprika. Bake at 350 degrees for 30 to 35 minutes or until bubbly.

May substitute imitation lobster, crab meat or shrimp or drained canned tuna, salmon or other cooked fish for lobster.

Crusty Baked Fish

1	pound fish fillets
3	tablespoons flour
1/2	teaspoon salt
1/8	teaspoon each celery salt and pepper
1	cup cracker crumbs
1/4	cup melted butter
1	cup milk
1	tablespoon chopped parsley
1/4	teaspoon paprika

Yield: 3 to 4 servings

Arrange fish in buttered shallow baking dish. Sprinkle with flour, salt, celery salt and pepper. Spread mixture of cracker crumbs and butter over top. Pour milk over fish; sprinkle with parsley and paprika. Bake at 375 degrees for 25 minutes or until top is brown and fish flakes easily. Serve on warmed platter.

Mediterranean Fish Stew

3	large onions, sliced
1	large green bell pepper, sliced into strips
1	16-ounce can tomatoes
1	large leek, sliced
2	carrots, sliced
2	tablespoons chili sauce
2	tablespoons anchovy paste
1	tablespoon fresh lemon juice
1	tablespoon salt
1	teaspoon thyme
1/2	teaspoon fennel seeds
1/4	teaspoon pepper
1	6-ounce can tomato paste
1/4	cup vegetable oil (optional)
2	pounds scallops
2	pounds halibut, skinned, boned

Yield: 6 to 8 servings

Combine onions, green pepper, tomatoes, leek, carrots, chili sauce, anchovy paste, lemon juice, salt, thyme, fennel seeds and pepper in large stockpot. Blend tomato paste and oil in small bowl. Add to stockpot; mix well. Bring to a boil; reduce heat. Simmer, covered, for 15 to 20 minutes. Cut large scallops into halves; cut fish into bite-sized pieces. Add to stew. Simmer, covered, for 15 minutes longer. Serve with hot French bread and chilled white wine.

Poached Salmon with Green Sauce

1	lemon
6	1-inch thick salmon steaks
1	onion, thinly sliced
12	sprigs of fresh dill
	Coarse salt and freshly ground pepper to taste
1½	cups fish broth or chicken broth
1½	cups dry white wine
6	thin lemon slices, seeded
6	tablespoons butter
	Green Sauce

Yield: 6 servings

Squeeze lemon juice over fish. Spread onion and dill in buttered baking pan large enough to hold fish in single layer. Arrange fish in prepared pan; sprinkle with salt and pepper. Pour broth and wine over fish. Top each steak with 1 lemon slice and 1 tablespoon butter. Cover tightly with foil. Bring to a boil on range top. Bake at 425 degrees for 10 minutes. Cool to room temperature. Chill until serving time. Serve with Green Sauce.

Green Sauce

3	tablespoons fresh lemon juice
1	tablespoon white wine vinegar
2	tablespoons Dijon mustard
1	cup vegetable oil
2	cups coarsely chopped chives
⅓	cup finely chopped fresh dill
½	cup drained capers

Yield: 2 cups

Combine lemon juice, vinegar, mustard, oil and chives in blender container; process until smooth. Combine with dill and capers in bowl; mix well. Chill until serving time.

May also serve as dip for vegetables or chips.

Sautéed Scallops Marguerita

1	pound sea scallops
2	medium cloves of garlic, minced
2	scallions, diagonally sliced
1	tablespoon chopped fresh cilantro
1/2	teaspoon red pepper flakes
	Juice of 1 lime
3	tablespoons Tequila
2	tablespoons olive oil

Yield: 4 servings

Remove tough connective tissue from sides of scallops; slice scallops 1/4 inch thick. Combine garlic, scallions, cilantro and red pepper flakes in small bowl. Mix lime juice and Tequila in small bowl. Sauté scallops in hot olive oil in large skillet over high heat for 1 minute; reduce heat. Add garlic mixture; mix well. Cook for 2 minutes longer. Add Tequila mixture. Bring to a boil. Serve immediately with tossed green salad and crusty French bread.

The ingredients in this recipe lend a Southwestern touch to sautéed scallops.

Shrimp Nanking

2	tablespoons sliced green onions
2	cups sliced mushrooms
2	tablespoons butter
1	pound shrimp, peeled, deveined
2	tablespoons soy sauce
2	tablespoons water
	Sugar to taste
1 1/2	tablespoons cornstarch
1	tablespoon water

Yield: 3 to 4 servings

Sauté green onions and mushrooms in butter in skillet over high heat for 2 minutes. Add shrimp, soy sauce, 2 tablespoons water and sugar. Simmer, covered, for 5 minutes or just until shrimp turn pink. Stir in mixture of cornstarch and 1 tablespoon water. Cook until thickened, stirring constantly. Serve over rice.

Santa Ana Bird

Eggs,
Cheese & Pasta

Beans

Over many centuries, the term "bean" has come to include a multitude of seeds of the legume family—and many of them belong to diverse genera. In the Americas, a single genus, *Phaseolus,* was cultivated before contact, Europeans initial encounter with Native Americans, and the most important of this group are the kidney, lima, pinto, wax and navy beans. Other beans were and are cultivated but have not made a major impact on world cuisines.

Beans have been grown in the Americas for more than 8,000 years, from Chile and Argentina to the St. Lawrence and upper Missouri River valleys. Beans are depicted in Peruvian textiles and ceramics and were collected as tribute by the Aztecs. As early as 1493, New World beans were introduced into Asia, Europe and East Africa. Old World varieties were brought by colonists to the Americas, and the explorers and settlers used the term "beans" and "pease" interchangeably, thus, confusing the botanical history.

New Englanders, preferring sweet dishes, were not attracted to spicy ones. They delighted in beans slow-simmered in maple sugar, which evolved into Boston baked beans. From the Narraganset peoples, the colonists learned to cook whole corn kernels and lima beans together. The Native peoples called this dish *succotash,* meaning "cooked whole grains." In Virginia and North Carolina, Native Americans made a traditional stew of squirrel, corn, tomatoes and beans which the settlers adopted. Substituting beef or chicken for squirrel, it is now known as "Brunswick Stew."

Beans are a primary source of protein in Mesoamerica. Hours of cooking, however, was the only method of preparing beans. Refried beans were possible only after European contact when animal fat became available to fry food.

Since beans were known and used by both the Old and New Worlds previous to European contact, both populations were quick to recognize that new varieties would be useful and could be used in similar ways. Beans from the Americas were grown widely in Europe by the 16th century, but the precise details of their introductions and dispersals are lacking. Since beans were instantly recognizable, they were readily added to the cuisines of the world.

Swiss Cheese Scramble

2	cups trimmed soft bread cubes
1³/₄	cups milk
8	eggs, slightly beaten
³/₄	teaspoon salt
¹/₈	teaspoon pepper
2	tablespoons butter or margarine
¹/₄	teaspoon seasoned salt
8	ounces Swiss cheese, sliced
2	tablespoons melted butter or margarine
¹/₂	cup fine dry bread crumbs
8	slices crisp-fried bacon, crumbled

Yield: 8 servings

Combine 2 cups bread cubes with milk in bowl; mix well. Let stand for 5 minutes. Drain, reserving milk. Combine reserved milk, eggs, salt and pepper in bowl; mix well. Scramble egg mixture in 2 tablespoons butter in skillet until soft, stirring frequently. Stir in bread cubes. Spoon into 9x9-inch shallow baking dish or 9-inch round baking dish. Sprinkle with seasoned salt. Arrange cheese slices over mixture. Sprinkle with mixture of 2 tablespoons melted butter and ¹/₂ cup bread crumbs. Top with crumbled bacon. Bake at 400 degrees for 10 to 15 minutes or until cheese melts.

Great brunch dish!

Three Cheese Pizza

1	10-ounce can refrigerated pizza dough
1¹/₂	cups ricotta cheese
1	cup shredded mozzarella cheese
2	tablespoons finely chopped onion
¹/₂	teaspoon Italian seasoning
¹/₄	cup pesto sauce
1	large tomato, thinly sliced
¹/₂	cup shredded Parmesan cheese

Yield: 4 to 6 servings

Press pizza dough into 12-inch pizza pan or 9x12-inch baking pan. Spread with ricotta cheese. Sprinkle with mozzarella cheese. Sprinkle onion and seasoning over cheese layer. Dot with pesto sauce. Arrange tomato slices over top. Sprinkle with Parmesan cheese. Bake at 400 degrees for 15 to 20 minutes or until lightly browned.

Spinach and Mushroom Frittata

1	clove of garlic, pressed
	White of 5 scallions, sliced
2	shallots, minced
8	ounces fresh mushrooms, sliced
3	tablespoons butter
3	10-ounce packages frozen chopped spinach, thawed
1	tablespoon butter
6	eggs
3	tablespoons whipping cream
1	tablespoon minced parsley
1/2	teaspoon dried thyme
1	teaspoon dried basil
1/2	teaspoon salt
1/2	teaspoon pepper
1/2	cup grated Parmesan cheese
1	tablespoon olive oil

Yield: 6 servings

Sauté garlic, scallions, shallots and mushrooms in 3 tablespoons butter in skillet over medium heat for 3 minutes. Remove to colander with slotted spoon. Squeeze spinach dry. Add 1 tablespoon butter to skillet. Heat until melted. Add spinach. Sauté until liquid has evaporated. Combine with sautéed mushroom mixture. Beat eggs in large bowl until frothy. Add cream, herbs, salt, pepper and half the Parmesan cheese; beat until well blended. Drain sautéed vegetables well; stir into egg mixture. Pour olive oil into 2-quart casserole or quiche pan; rotate casserole to coat bottom and side with olive oil. Pour in egg mixture. Bake at 375 degrees for 20 to 25 minutes. or until set. Sprinkle with remaining Parmesan cheese. Place under preheated broiler for 1 minute. Serve immediately.

Frittata is good served as an appetizer, side dish or luncheon dish.

Holiday Brunch Eggs

1/2	cup butter, softened
8	slices soft white bread, trimmed
2	cups shredded Cheddar cheese
1/2	teaspoon garlic powder
1/2	teaspoon nutmeg
2	chicken bouillon cubes
1/2	cup hot water
1/2	cup white wine or dry sherry
4	eggs, beaten

Yield: 6 servings

Butter 3-quart casserole generously. Spread remaining butter on bread slices. Layer bread and cheese in prepared casserole, sprinkling each layer with garlic powder and nutmeg. Dissolve bouillon cubes in hot water; cool slightly. Whisk dissolved bouillon and wine into eggs in bowl. Pour over bread and cheese layers. Refrigerate, covered, overnight. Bake, uncovered, at 325 degrees for 1 hour or until puffed and golden brown.

Cheesy Black Bean and Brown Rice Casserole

1 1/2	cups uncooked brown rice
3	cloves of garlic, pressed
1	large onion, finely chopped
1/2	cup chopped green bell pepper
2	tablespoons vegetable oil
2	cups cooked black beans
8	ounces ricotta cheese
1/4	cup skim milk
3 1/2	cups shredded Cheddar cheese
	Pepper or hot pepper sauce to taste

Yield: 6 servings

Cook brown rice using package directions. Sauté garlic, onion and green pepper in oil in skillet until tender but not brown. Combine with beans in bowl. Add cooked rice; mix gently. Combine ricotta cheese and skim milk in bowl; mix well. Stir in 3 cups Cheddar cheese. Alternate layers of rice mixture and cheese mixture in greased 2-quart casserole, ending with rice mixture. Sprinkle with pepper. Bake at 350 degrees for 30 minutes. Sprinkle with remaining 1/2 cup Cheddar cheese. Let stand until Cheddar cheese melts.

Cheese and Egg Tortilla Roll

6	eggs, beaten
2	tablespoons water
4	teaspoons butter
1	cup shredded Cheddar cheese
6	8-inch flour tortillas

Yield: 6 servings

Beat eggs with water. Melt enough butter in hot 8-inch skillet over medium heat to coat bottom of skillet. Add ¼ cup egg mixture. Cook until partially set. Sprinkle with about 2½ tablespoons cheese. Cover with tortilla; press gently. Cook until tortilla is warm to touch indicating that egg mixture is cooked through. Invert onto large sheet of foil; roll as for jelly roll. Keep warm. Repeat with remaining ingredients. Serve with favorite salsa.

Burden Baskets ⌒

Burden baskets were made by many native American cultures, each having its own distinctive style. They were made in different sizes to carry berries, meat and large loads of firewood. The Apache burden basket still is being made in many sizes and can be found in Southwestern shops. Conical in shape, it includes an attached leather tumpline which is rested on the forehead for carrying, freeing both hands for work. Burden basketmakers cut "tin" cans, discarded by the United States military personnel, into small cones and attached them to leather strings hanging from the basket. Much gathering was done in groups, and the jingle of these metal cones was called "women's music."

Antipasto Salad

2	small fresh broccoli spears
8	ounces spiral or shell macaroni
5	ounces Italian hard salami, sliced
1	small red onion, thinly sliced
1	cup whole pitted black olives
1	cup thinly sliced celery
1	cup cherry tomato halves
1/4	cup sliced green bell pepper
1/4	cup sliced red bell pepper
1/4	cup sliced yellow bell pepper
8	ounces mozzarella cheese, cubed
	Italian Salad Dressing
8	ounces fresh mushrooms, sliced

Yield: 6 servings

Blanch broccoli spears for 3 to 4 minutes or until a brilliant green color; rinse with cold water to halt cooking. Drain well and cut into bite-sized pieces. Cook macaroni *al dente* using package directions; rinse with cold water and drain well. Combine broccoli, macaroni, salami, onion, olives, celery, tomatoes, bell peppers, cheese and Italian Salad Dressing in large bowl; toss to mix. Add mushrooms just before serving; toss to mix.

Salad may be held for up to 3 hours before serving.

Italian Salad Dressing

1/4	cup capers, drained
1	clove of garlic, pressed
1	shallot, minced
1/2	teaspoon pepper
1	small dried de árbol chile, sliced
1/2	teaspoon crushed fennel seed
1	tablespoon dry white wine
2	tablespoons fresh lemon juice
1	envelope Italian salad dressing mix
1/2	cup olive oil

Yield: 3/4 cup

Combine capers, garlic, shallot, pepper, de árbol chile, fennel seed, white wine, lemon juice and salad dressing mix in small bowl; mix well. Add olive oil in fine stream, whisking constantly until salad dressing appears creamy as olive oil emulsifies.

Athenian Tortellini Salad

2	9-ounce packages refrigerated cheese tortellini
1	green bell pepper, cut into thin strips
1	red bell pepper, cut into thin strips
1	small red onion, thinly sliced
1/4	cup sliced black or Greek olives Minty Salad Dressing
1/2	cup crumbled feta cheese

Yield: 8 to 10 servings

Cook tortellini using package directions; drain well. Combine with bell peppers, onion and olives in large bowl. Add Minty Salad Dressing; toss gently to mix. Chill, covered, overnight. Add feta cheese just before serving; toss to mix.

Minty Salad Dressing

1/2	cup white vinegar
1/2	cup olive oil
3	tablespoons fresh lemon juice
2	tablespoons dry sherry
1 1/2	teaspoons seasoned salt
1	teaspoon garlic powder
1/4	teaspoon crushed red pepper
1	teaspoon black pepper
3	tablespoons chopped fresh mint or 1 tablespoon dried mint

Yield: 1 1/2 cups

Combine vinegar, olive oil, lemon juice and sherry in jar. Add seasoned salt, garlic powder, red pepper, black pepper and mint. Cover jar; shake until well mixed.

Artichoke-Pasta Salad

8	ounces corkscrew-shaped pasta
2	6-ounce jars marinated artichoke hearts
1/4	cup grated Parmesan cheese
1/2	cup bread crumbs
1	tablespoon red wine vinegar
1/3	cup chopped celery
1/3	cup chopped green bell pepper
1	medium tomato, chopped
1/4	cup chopped red onion

Yield: 4 servings

Cook pasta *al dente* using package directions; rinse with cold water and drain well. Combine with undrained artichoke hearts, cheese, bread crumbs, vinegar, celery, green pepper, tomato and onion in large bowl; toss gently to mix. Chill until serving time.

Chicken and Pasta Salad with Curried Tarragon Dressing

8	ounces rotelle pasta
3	cups 1-inch cubes cooked chicken
1 1/2	cups cooked broccoli flowerets
3/4	cup chopped red bell pepper
1	tablespoon vegetable oil
1 1/2	teaspoons curry powder
2/3	cup mayonnaise
1	teaspoon salt
1/4	teaspoon pepper
1	teaspoon crushed tarragon leaves

Yield: 6 servings

Cook pasta *al dente* using package directions; rinse with cold water and drain well. Combine pasta, chicken, broccoli and red bell pepper in large bowl. Heat oil in small skillet. Add curry powder. Cook for 30 seconds or until fragrant, stirring constantly. Combine curry mixture with mayonnaise, salt, pepper and tarragon in small bowl; blend well. Add to chicken mixture; mix gently. Chill until serving time.

Cold Tortellini Salad

8	ounces tortellini
1	cup chopped green bell pepper
1	cup chopped red onion
1	cup chopped zucchini
2	cups chopped tomatoes
	Spicy Vinaigrette
1	cup shredded Cheddar cheese

Yield: 8 to 10 servings

Cook tortellini al dente using package directions; rinse with cold water and drain well. Combine with green pepper, onion, zucchini and tomatoes in large bowl. Add Spicy Vinaigrette to tortellini and vegetables; toss to mix. Chill for 4 hours or longer. Sprinkle with cheese just before serving.

Spicy Vinaigrette

1	cup olive oil
3/4	cup wine vinegar
1/2	teaspoon pepper
1/2	teaspoon cumin
1	teaspoon chili powder
1	teaspoon dry mustard
1	teaspoon paprika
2	cloves of garlic, minced

Yield: 2 cups

Combine olive oil, vinegar, pepper, cumin, chili powder, dry mustard, paprika and garlic in jar; cover tightly and shake until well mixed.

Rainbow Pasta Salad

8	ounces corkscrew-shaped rainbow pasta
1	small cucumber
1	cup sliced fresh mushrooms
1	large tomato, chopped
1/2	cup chopped green bell pepper
1/2	cup sliced pitted black olives
1/2	cup sliced stuffed green olives
1/4	cup minced onion
1/2	cup chopped celery
	Paprika Vinaigrette

Yield: 6 to 8 servings

Cook pasta *al dente* using package directions; rinse with cold water and drain well. Cut cucumber lengthwise into quarters; slice. Combine pasta, cucumber, mushrooms, tomato, green pepper, olives, onion and celery in large bowl. Pour Paprika Vinaigrette over pasta mixture; toss gently to mix. Chill until serving time.

Paprika Vinaigrette

6	tablespoons olive oil
2	tablespoons red wine vinegar
1	teaspoon seasoned salt
1/4	teaspoon freshly ground pepper
1/4	teaspoon paprika

Yield: 1/2 cup

Combine olive oil, vinegar, seasoned salt, pepper and paprika in small bowl; mix well.

Swiss Cheese and Olive Pasta Salad

12	ounces small shell or elbow macaroni
6	ounces Swiss cheese, cubed
1	bunch green onions, chopped
1¹/₄	cups sliced stuffed green olives
	Mustard Vinaigrette Salad Dressing

Yield: 8 to 10 servings

Cook macaroni *al dente* using package directions; rinse with cold water and drain well. Combine with cheese, green onions and green olives in large bowl. Add Mustard Vinaigrette Salad Dressing; toss to mix. Chill until serving time.

Mustard Vinaigrette Salad Dressing

¹/₂	cup olive oil
1	tablespoon fresh lemon juice or vinegar
1	teaspoon Dijon mustard
¹/₂	teaspoon salt
¹/₂	teaspoon pepper

Yield: ¹/₂ cup

Combine olive oil, lemon juice, mustard, salt and pepper in small bowl; beat with wire whisk until well blended.

Creamy Fettucini Primavera

8	ounces fettucini
1	cup broccoli flowerets
1	cup julienned carrots
¹/₂	cup chopped red bell pepper
1³/₄	cups low-fat milk
8	ounces light cream cheese, cubed
¹/₂	cup chopped green onions
¹/₄	teaspoon garlic powder
1	cup julienned cooked turkey
¹/₂	cup grated Parmesan cheese

Yield: 6 servings

Prepare fettucini using package directions. Add broccoli, carrots and red pepper 5 minutes before cooking process ends; drain. Combine milk, cream cheese, green onions and garlic powder in saucepan; mix well. Cook over low heat until smooth, stirring constantly. Stir in turkey and Parmesan cheese. Toss fettucini and vegetables with turkey sauce in bowl. Serve immediately.

Herbed Shrimp Pasta

1	pound shrimp
8	ounces snow peas
8	ounces fusilli
2	cups chopped plum tomatoes
1/4	cup chopped fresh tarragon, dill or parsley
2	teaspoons finely grated orange zest
1/4	cup olive oil
	Salt and freshly ground pepper to taste
1/4	cup fresh orange juice

Yield: 6 servings

Clean and cook shrimp; set aside to cool. Blanch snow peas until bright green in color; rinse with cold water to stop cooking process and drain well. Cook pasta *al dente* using package directions; rinse with cold water and drain well. Combine shrimp, snow peas, pasta, tomatoes, tarragon, orange zest, olive oil, salt and pepper in large bowl; toss to mix. Add orange juice just before serving; adjust seasonings. Serve immediately.

Creamy Cheese Pasta Sauce

1	8-ounce package cream cheese, cubed
3/4	cup milk
1/2	cup grated Parmesan cheese
	Nutmeg and pepper to taste

Yield: 1 1/2 cups

Combine cream cheese, milk and Parmesan cheese in 1-quart microwave safe bowl. Microwave on Medium for 6 to 8 minutes or until sauce is smooth, stirring every 2 minutes. Stir in nutmeg and pepper. Toss with desired amount of hot cooked pasta.

May prepare in 1-quart saucepan over medium heat, stirring constantly; do not boil.

Tomato-Herb Sauce for Pasta

1	medium onion, finely chopped
1	large clove of garlic, minced
2	tablespoons extra-light olive oil
1	14½-ounce can tomatoes
1	8-ounce can tomato sauce
½	teaspoon sugar
4½	teaspoons oregano
½	teaspoon basil
½	teaspoon rosemary
¼	teaspoon salt
⅛	teaspoon pepper

Yield: enough for 1 pound pasta

Sauté onion and garlic in olive oil in saucepan until tender. Add tomatoes, tomato sauce, sugar and seasonings. Simmer, uncovered, for 45 to 60 minutes or until of desired consistency, stirring occasionally. Serve over hot cooked pasta.

Sauce may be stored in refrigerator for up to 1 week or frozen for up to 3 months.

Chicken Fettucini

4	chicken breast halves
1	8-ounce bottle of light Dijon Vinaigrette salad dressing
1	tablespoon vegetable oil
1	tablespoon margarine
	Garlic powder and pepper to taste
¼	cup grated Parmesan cheese
½	cup Italian-style dry bread crumbs
½	cup dry sherry
4	servings hot cooked fettucini

Yield: 4 servings

Rinse chicken; pat dry. Marinate chicken in salad dressing for 1 hour. Heat oil and margarine in large skillet. Drain chicken, reserving marinade. Arrange chicken in prepared skillet. Sprinkle with garlic powder, pepper, Parmesan cheese and bread crumbs. Cook until brown on both sides and tender, turning once. Remove chicken; keep warm. Add reserved marinade diluted with an equal part water to skillet. Stir in sherry. Cook until thickened, stirring constantly. May add additional bread crumbs to thicken if desired. Serve chicken and sauce over hot fettucini.

Serve a green salad and garlic bread with this quick and easy dish.

Fettucini with Pine Nuts

1/2	cup pine nuts
1	tablespoon unsalted butter
1	pound uncooked fettucini
11	tablespoons unsalted butter
1/2	cup grated Parmesan cheese
	Freshly ground pepper to taste

Yield: 4 servings

Sauté pine nuts in 1 tablespoon butter in skillet until golden brown. Cook fettucini *al dente* using package directions; rinse with hot water and drain well. Add remaining 11 tablespoons butter to hot fettucini in large bowl; toss until butter melts and coats fettucini. Add pine nuts, Parmesan cheese and pepper; toss until well mixed. Serve immediately.

Pasta with Smoked Salmon and Caviar

1 1/2	pounds thin spaghetti or other favorite pasta
11	tablespoons butter
2	cups half and half cream
1/4	pound smoked salmon, thinly sliced
1/4	teaspoon salt
	White pepper to taste
1	4-ounce jar golden caviar

Yield: 6 servings

Cook spaghetti *al dente* using package directions; rinse with hot water, drain and return to saucepan. Add 3 tablespoons butter; toss until butter melts and coats spaghetti. Melt remaining 8 tablespoons butter in large skillet. Stir in half and half cream. Bring to a boil, stirring occasionally. Cook over medium heat for 5 to 6 minutes or until reduced to desired consistency. Cut salmon into small pieces; add to sauce. Add white pepper and spaghetti to sauce; toss until coated. Heat to serving temperature if necessary. Serve immediately. Garnish each serving with a spoonful of caviar.

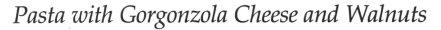

Pasta with Gorgonzola Cheese and Walnuts

1¹/₂   **pounds fusilli, penne or ziti**
        Gorgonzola Cheese Sauce
1   **cup coarsely chopped walnuts**
¹/₂   **cup freshly grated Romano or**
        Parmesan cheese

Yield: 6 servings

Cook pasta *al dente* using package directions; rinse with hot water, drain and return to saucepan. Add hot Gorgonzola Cheese Sauce. Heat over low heat, stirring gently until pasta is coated. Stir in walnuts. Turn pasta onto serving dish. Sprinkle with Romano or Parmesan cheese. Serve immediately.

Good with tossed salad and garlic bread.

Gorgonzola Cheese Sauce

5   **shallots or green onions, finely**
        chopped
2   **tablespoons butter**
5   **teaspoons chopped fresh thyme or**
        1¹/₂ teaspoons dried thyme
2   **cups half and half cream**
8   **ounces gorgonzola, cambozola or**
        other bleu cheese, crumbled
        Freshly ground pepper to taste

Yield: 2¹/₂ cups

Sauté shallots in butter in medium skillet over medium heat for 5 minutes or until translucent. Stir in thyme, half and half cream and gorgonzola cheese. Heat until cheese melts and sauce is slightly thickened, stirring constantly. Season with pepper. Sauce may be stored in covered container in refrigerator overnight and reheated over low heat.

Spaghetti Supper

1	pound coarsely ground beef
1/4	cup flour
1/2	teaspoon salt
1/8	teaspoon pepper
1	1.4-ounce envelope onion soup mix
2	cloves of garlic, pressed
2 1/2	cups water
1	tablespoon flour
1	cup sour cream
7	ounces uncooked spaghetti
1	cup buttered bread crumbs

Yield: 6 servings

Brown ground beef in skillet, stirring until crumbly; drain. Mix 1/4 cup flour, salt, pepper, and soup mix in saucepan. Add garlic and water. Cook until thickened, stirring constantly. Blend 1 tablespoon flour into sour cream. Stir sour cream mixture and ground beef into sauce. Cook spaghetti *al dente* using package directions; rinse with hot water and drain well. Place in greased 2 1/2-quart casserole. Ladle sauce over spaghetti; top with bread crumbs. Bake at 350 degrees for 30 minutes.

Spinach-Cheese Kugel

12	ounces noodles
1	10-ounce package frozen chopped spinach
3	eggs, beaten
2	cups sour cream
1	1.4-ounce envelope onion soup mix
1	cup shredded Cheddar cheese

Yield: 8 servings

Cook noodles using package directions; rinse and drain well. Cook spinach using package directions; drain well. Combine noodles with eggs in large bowl. Combine sour cream, soup mix, 3/4 cup cheese and spinach in small bowl; mix well. Add to noodle mixture; mix well. Pour into greased 9x13-inch baking pan. Top with remaining 1/4 cup cheese. Bake at 350 degrees for 1 hour. Let stand for 10 minutes. Cut into squares.

Eggplant-Stuffed Shells

8	ounces jumbo macaroni shells or tubes
1	large clove of garlic, thinly sliced
1/4	cup vegetable oil
1	1-pound eggplant, peeled, chopped
1/2	cup finely chopped onion
1/2	cup water
1	32-ounce jar spaghetti sauce
1	cup low-fat cottage cheese
4	egg whites
1/2	cup Italian-style bread crumbs
1	teaspoon oregano
1/8	teaspoon pepper
8	ounces mozzarella cheese, sliced

Yield: 8 servings

Cook macaroni shells *al dente* using package directions; rinse with water, drain and set aside. Sauté garlic in oil in skillet until brown; discard garlic. Add eggplant and onion to garlic oil. Sauté for 5 minutes. Add 1/2 cup water. Simmer, covered, for 10 minutes or until tender, stirring occasionally. Cool. Pour half the spaghetti sauce into 9x13-inch baking pan. Combine cottage cheese, egg whites, bread crumbs, oregano and pepper in bowl; mix well. Add eggplant mixture; mix well. Spoon into macaroni shells; arrange in prepared baking pan. Pour remaining spaghetti sauce over shells. Top with mozzarella cheese. Bake, covered, at 375 degrees for 20 minutes. Bake, uncovered, for 10 minutes longer.

May be prepared and refrigerated until ready to bake. Add an additional 10 minutes to covered baking time if chilled.

O'odham Man-in-the-Maze

Southwest

Chiles

Five hundred years ago, the peoples of the Old World had not tasted, seen, or heard of a chile pepper. There was not even a word for chile before 1492. The first explorers wrote of "bushes like rosebushes which make a fruit as long as cinnamon, full of small grains as biting as pepper." The Spanish went on to state that the Carib peoples of the Caribbean Islands ate the fruit as they ate apples. Called "aji" by the Native peoples, the spice was labeled by Columbus as "pimiento," or pepper, a spice from the Far East which he was seeking.

It now appears that chile peppers originated in South America, somewhere south of the wet forests of the Amazon and the semi-arid cerrado of Brazil. From there, wild capsicums, or chiles, spread by human and animal migrations throughout Mesoamerica and the Amazon. At the time of European contact, the chile pepper was the most common spice used by the Native Americans. When the Spanish invaded Mexico in 1519, they came to identify the spice by its Nahuatl name, "chilli." The Spanish subsequently called it "chile" and the English converted it to "chili."*

Both the Spanish and the Portuguese were responsible for introducing chiles to cuisines around the world, beginning as early as 1493. By 1548, chile peppers had been introduced into Africa, India, Indonesia, China, Japan, England and Hungary (where they are known as paprika). Ironically, except for the American Southwest and the area that is now Florida, chiles remained unknown north of Mexico until recently. Because of Spanish and Portuguese trade monopolies, the chile pepper traveled from the Americas to the Old World and back again to Europe via the Orient, all before the Pilgrims set foot on Plymouth Rock in 1620. During its travels, the chile pepper was completely incorporated into the cuisines of the people of Asia, Africa, the Middle East, and the Far East, and new botanical strains were developed that are unknown in the Americas. It is estimated that, in the early 1600s, the peoples of lowland South America utilized 40 varieties of peppers. In Mexico today, there are believed to be 92 varieties in use.

*In this cookbook "chile" refers to the pepper, "chiles" is the plural, and "chili powder" refers to a mixture of seasonings that includes chiles.

Jalapeño Appetizer

1	4-ounce can jalapeño peppers, drained
1	7-ounce can tuna
2	sweet pickles, finely chopped
1/4	cup mayonnaise

Yield: 8 to 10 servings

Remove stem ends of peppers and cut lengthwise into halves, discarding seeds; rinse well. Mix tuna, pickles and mayonnaise in bowl. Spoon into peppers; arrange on serving plate. Serve with crackers or corn chips.

Marinated Pimento-Stuffed Olives

1	21-ounce jar pimento-stuffed green olives
6–8	dried japonés chiles, crushed
5	cloves of garlic, chopped
1/4	teaspoon crushed thyme
1/8	teaspoon crushed oregano
1/8	teaspoon crushed basil
1/2	cup virgin olive oil
1	cup white wine or dry sherry

Yield: about 2 cups

Drain olives, reserving liquid; return olives to jar. Combine chiles, garlic, thyme, oregano, basil, olive oil and wine in small bowl. Pour over olives; fill jar with reserved liquid, covering olives completely. Store, tightly covered, at room temperature for 2 to 3 weeks, shaking jar occasionally. Drain to serve.

Bell Peppers Stuffed with Ricotta

2	each medium yellow, red and green bell peppers
3	cups whole milk ricotta cheese
2	eggs
1/3	cup freshly grated Parmesan cheese
3	cloves of garlic, pressed
1/4	teaspoon dried rosemary, crushed
1/4	teaspoon dried basil, crushed
	Salt and pepper to taste
	Garlic and Basil Dressing

Yield: 6 servings

Place bell peppers on rack in broiler pan. Broil until blistered and blackened on all sides. Place in paper bag; let stand for 20 minutes. Peel peppers and rinse under running water. Cut off 1-inch slice from stem ends of peppers; discard seeds. Pat peppers dry with paper towels. Arrange cut side up in greased 9x13-inch baking dish. Combine ricotta cheese, eggs, Parmesan cheese, garlic, rosemary and basil in medium bowl; mix well. Season with salt and pepper. Spoon into peppers. Bake at 325 degrees for 35 minutes or until tops are set and crusty. Chill, covered, for 4 to 5 hours. Cut stuffed peppers crosswise into 1/2-inch slices; overlap slices on serving plate. Top with Garlic and Basil Dressing.

May prepare this dish the day before; slice peppers and dress at serving time.

Garlic and Basil Dressing

3	cloves of garlic
3	tablespoons red wine vinegar
1	tablespoon Dijon mustard
1	tablespoon tomato paste
1/2	cup virgin olive oil
1/4	cup coarsely chopped fresh basil
	Salt and pepper to taste

Yield: 1 cup

Crush garlic to paste in bowl. Add vinegar, mustard and tomato paste; whisk until smooth. Add olive oil gradually, whisking constantly. Stir in basil, salt and pepper.

Mexican Cheese Squares

8	ounces Cheddar cheese, shredded
8	ounces Monterey Jack cheese, shredded
3	eggs
1/2	cup green taco sauce

Yield: 36 squares

Combine cheeses in bowl; mix well. Beat eggs with taco sauce in bowl. Layer half the cheese mixture, egg mixture and remaining cheese mixture in greased 9x9-inch baking pan. Bake at 350 degrees for 30 minutes. Cool to room temperature. Cut into 1 1/2-inch squares. The flavor of these squares improves if chilled overnight.

Cheesecake Appetizer

1	cup fine dry bread crumbs
1 1/2	pounds cream cheese, softened
1	cup shredded Cheddar cheese
1/2	cup cream
3	eggs
1	tablespoon chili powder
	Salt to taste
1	cup minced ham
1/4–1/2	cup minced seeded jalapeño peppers

Yield: 24 to 30 servings

Butter side of 9-inch springform pan. Press bread crumbs over bottom and part of the way up side of pan. Combine cream cheese, Cheddar cheese and cream in large mixer bowl; mix well. Beat in eggs 1 at a time. Add chili powder and salt; mix well. Stir in ham and peppers. Spoon into prepared pan. Bake in preheated 325-degree oven for 1 1/4 hours or until set. Cool to room temperature. Chill until serving time. Place on serving plate. Run sharp knife around edge of pan; remove side. Garnish with parsley and small jalapeño peppers. Serve with crackers.

Oaxacan Peanuts

10–12	small dried japonés chiles, coarsely crushed
2	tablespoons olive oil
4	cloves of garlic, minced
2	pounds salted dry-roasted peanuts
1	teaspoon chili powder
1	teaspoon kosher salt

Yield: 2 pounds

Sauté peppers in olive oil in heavy cast-iron skillet over medium heat. Add garlic. Cook for 1 minute, stirring constantly. Add peanuts. Cook for 5 minutes or until light brown, stirring constantly. Sprinkle with chili powder; mix well. Remove from heat. Sprinkle with salt; mix well. Cool to room temperature. Store in airtight container.

These are also good in salad. You may substitute pecan halves for peanuts.

Tex-Mex Dip

2	9-ounce cans jalapeño bean dip
3	avocados
1/2	cup mayonnaise
1	tablespoon fresh lemon juice
2	cups sour cream
3/4	cup shredded Cheddar cheese
2	scallions, chopped

Yield: 12 servings

Spread bean dip in serving dish. Mash avocados with mayonnaise and lemon juice in bowl, mixing well. Spread over bean dip. Layer sour cream, shredded cheese and scallions over top. Serve with nacho chips.

Japonés ～

Japonés are Japanese hot chiles that are actually dried serrano chiles and are very hot.

Jalapeño Carrots

2	bunches baby carrots, peeled
1	medium onion, thinly sliced
1	cup olive oil
1	cup white vinegar
1	teaspoon sugar
4–5	canned jalapeño peppers, seeds removed

Yield: 20 servings

Steam carrots in saucepan for 6 to 8 minutes or until tender-crisp. Pour mixture of onion, olive oil, vinegar, sugar and jalapeño peppers over carrots in bowl. Chill, covered, overnight.

Guacamole Dip

2	ripe avocados, peeled, seeds removed
1	medium tomato, chopped
1	teaspoon salt
1	medium onion, chopped
1	jalapeño pepper or
	1 7-ounce can
	chopped green chiles
1/2	teaspoon garlic salt
2	teaspoons lemon juice
	Salt and pepper to taste

Yield: 8 servings

Combine avocados, tomato, salt, onion, jalapeño pepper, garlic salt, lemon juice, salt and pepper in blender container. Process at medium speed until blended. Spoon into serving bowl. Serve with corn chips.

Jalapeño Chiles ⌐

The jalapeño chile is named after the town of Jalapa in the Mexican state of Vera Cruz. It is a fairly small dark green chile, approximately 2 to 3 inches long and 1½ inches in diameter, with a green vegetable flavor. Jalapeños can be added to almost any food. It is probably one of the best known of the hot chiles.

Tequila Cocktail

1½   ounces white Tequila
1   tablespoon fresh lime juice
         Salt to taste
         Lemon-lime soda

Yield: 1 serving

Combine Tequila and lime juice in an old-fashioned glass. Add pinch of salt and ice. Fill glass with lemon-lime soda.

Serve with appetizers such as stuffed jalapeño peppers or a plate of sliced jicama, cucumber and orange, sprinkled with chili powder.

Berry Sangria

½   cup sugar
1   750-milliliter bottle of Beaujolais, chilled
2   cups cranberry-raspberry juice cocktail
½   cup sugar
1   pint strawberries
1   pint raspberries
2   tablespoons sugar
2   oranges, thinly sliced

Yield: 6 cups

Dissolve ½ cup sugar in wine and cranberry-raspberry juice in large pitcher. Chill in refrigerator. Combine ½ cup sugar with half the strawberries and raspberries in blender container; process until smooth. Add to wine mixture. Chill until serving time. Slice remaining strawberries; mix with 2 tablespoons sugar in bowl. Chill, covered. Add sliced strawberries, remaining raspberries and orange slices to sangria at serving time. Serve from pitcher.

Indian Fry Bread

¹/₂	cup shortening or lard
3	cups self-rising flour or mixture of 3 cups all-purpose flour, 1¹/₂ tablespoons baking powder and 1¹/₂ teaspoons salt
1	cup (about) warm water
	Oil for frying

Yield: 18 servings

Cut shortening into flour in bowl until crumbly. Add warm water gradually, mixing to form soft dough. Knead lightly until dough is no longer sticky. Shape into 2¹/₂ to 3-inch balls. Let rest, covered with plastic wrap, for 30 minutes. Shape each ball into flat circle with oiled hands, thinning first around edges and patting between heels of hands. Poke a small hole in the center of each circle to prevent puffing and to yield crisper bread. Fry in 2 inches oil heated to 375 degrees in skillet until golden brown on both sides, turning once; drain on paper towels. Serve hot with toppings of honey, confectioners' sugar or refried beans sprinkled with salt.

Native Americans serve fry bread as a base for tacos. It is by far the most popular food item at the Heard Museum Guild Indian Fair and Market, which is held annually on the first Saturday and Sunday of March. The Indian women shaping the bread at the Fair display a high degree of skill and grace as they "slap" the dough back and forth between their hands until it is just right.

Mexican Corn Bread

1	cup cornmeal
1/2	cup flour
1	teaspoon baking soda
1/2	teaspoon salt
1/3	cup melted shortening
1/2	cup milk
2	eggs, beaten
1	cup whole kernel corn
1	7-ounce can chopped green chiles
1	cup shredded Cheddar cheese

Yield: 9 servings

Mix cornmeal, flour, baking soda and salt in bowl. Add shortening, milk, eggs and corn; mix well. Spread half the batter in greased 8x8-inch baking pan. Layer chiles and half the cheese over batter. Spread with remaining batter and top with remaining cheese. Bake at 350 degrees for 1 hour or until knife inserted in center comes out clean.

Cowboy Bread

4	cups all-purpose flour
1	cup blue corn flour
3	tablespoons baking powder
1	teaspoon salt
1 2/3	cups (about) warm water

Yield: 8 servings

Mix all-purpose flour, corn flour, baking powder and salt in bowl. Add enough warm water to form soft dough, mixing lightly. Knead lightly in bowl until dough is no longer sticky. Let rest, covered, for 1 hour. Shape into 8 balls; press and roll into thin circles. Cook on lightly greased griddle until brown on both sides, turning once. Serve warm. May reheat to serve.

Blue Corn ⌁

Blue corn has been grown by the Hopi for hundreds of years. It is now being grown commercially using strains of the ancient varieties. Blue corn chips, blue corn tortillas and blue corn mixes are gaining popularity in food stores.

Soft Flour Tortillas

2	cups flour
1½	teaspoons baking powder
1	teaspoon salt
¼	cup shortening
½	cup lukewarm water

Yield: 1 dozen

Mix flour, baking powder and salt in large bowl. Cut in shortening until mixture resembles coarse crumbs. Stir in ½ cup water all at once with fork. Knead in bowl, adding additional water 1 teaspoon at a time until mixture forms soft dough. Knead on floured surface for 5 to 6 minutes or until smooth. Let rest for 10 minutes. Divide into 12 portions. Roll each portion into 9-inch circle, turning frequently and adding flour as needed to prevent sticking. Cook tortillas on heated ungreased griddle until dry and brown in spots, turning once. Wrap stacked tortillas in kitchen towel to keep warm.

Apache Ash Bread

2	cups flour
1	tablespoon baking powder
½	teaspoon salt
¾–1	cup water

Yield: 2 (7-inch) loaves

Mix flour, baking powder and salt in bowl. Add enough water to form soft dough. Knead lightly until dough is somewhat elastic. Shape into 2 balls. Let rest, covered, for 20 to 30 minutes. Brown 1 at a time on bottom on hot griddle; remove to baking sheet. Bake at 375 degrees for 10 to 12 minutes; do not overbake. Serve warm or cooled.

The loaves originally were placed in the ashes and coals of the camp fire to bake and the ashes then tapped off with a stick. The Western Apaches today serve tortillas and fry bread primarily, but Apache Ash Bread and Apache Acorn Stew (page 187) are still made for traditional ceremonies.

Acapulco Shellfish Chowder

2½	quarts bottled clam broth or chicken broth
½	cup white wine
1	bay leaf
3	cloves of garlic, minced
⅛	teaspoon ground saffron
3–4	large fresh jalapeño peppers, seeded, minced
3	large tomatoes, chopped
18–20	small steamer clams, scrubbed
2	pounds skinned fish fillets such as halibut, lingcod, rockfish or monkfish
8	ounces sea scallops
	Club soda
8	ounces medium shrimp, peeled, deveined
	Salt and pepper to taste
¼	cup chopped fresh cilantro

Yield: 10 to 12 servings

Combine clam broth, wine, bay leaf, garlic, saffron and jalapeño peppers in heavy 8-quart saucepan. Bring to a boil; reduce heat. Simmer, covered, for 25 minutes. Add tomatoes. Bring to a boil. Add clams. Simmer, covered, for 5 minutes. Cut fish into ½-inch pieces. Rinse scallops with club soda and cut into halves. Add fish, scallops and shrimp to chowder. Simmer for 4 to 5 minutes or until clams open and other shellfish is cooked through; discard bay leaf. Season with salt and pepper. Top servings with cilantro; garnish with lime wedges.

Piki Bread ⁓

Piki bread is an Indian bread of Hopi origin. Hopi women prepare piki bread at the Heard Museum Guild Indian Fair and Market each year.

Piki batter is thin and consists of finely ground blue corn flour, water and plant ashes. The ash is usually made from the four-winged saltbush or sagebrush. The alkaline in the ash helps preserve the desirable blue color and adds flavor to the product and minerals to the diet.

The piki stone, approximately 18 inches wide, 24 inches long and several inches thick, is heated and then greased lightly with crushed watermelon seeds which are burned black. A cloth is used to grease the stone between bakings. The expertise necessary to put a thin film of batter on the hot stone, without burning the hand, is developed through years of practice. It takes 3 to 4 swipes of the hand to leave on the stone an even film of batter, which cooks instantly. It is peeled off and placed on top of the next sheet being baked to absorb steam and become pliable. It then is folded sideways into thirds and rolled up, front to back, into 8 to 10-inch rolls.

Albondigas Soup

1	14-ounce can peeled tomatoes
3	47-ounce cans chicken broth
1	10-ounce can beef broth
3	cups water
1	large onion, minced
2	cloves of garlic, minced
2	tablespoons minced fresh cilantro
2	green onions, minced
1	large dried whole ancho, pasilla or chipotle chile, seeded, crushed
1/2	teaspoon crushed oregano
1/2	teaspoon salt
	Meatballs
1/4	cup uncooked rice

Yield: 6 to 8 servings

Crush tomatoes. Reserve 3 tablespoons drained crushed tomatoes for meatballs. Combine remaining tomatoes and juice with chicken broth, beef broth, water, onion, garlic, cilantro, green onions, chile, oregano and salt in heavy 5-quart saucepan. Bring to a boil. Add Meatballs. Simmer for 5 minutes. Add rice. Simmer, covered, for 20 minutes or until rice is tender and meatballs are cooked through. Garnish servings with additional cilantro. Serve with lime wedges.

Meatballs

3	tablespoons reserved drained crushed tomatoes
1 1/2	pounds ground sirloin or round steak
1 1/2	tablespoons uncooked rice
1/2	medium onion, finely chopped
2	tablespoons minced fresh cilantro
1/4	teaspoon oregano
1/2	teaspoon salt
1/4	teaspoon pepper

Combine reserved tomatoes with ground sirloin, rice, onion, cilantro, oregano, salt and pepper in bowl; mix well. Shape into 1-inch meatballs.

Oaxacan Black Bean and Oxtail Soup

1½	pounds beef oxtails
1	tablespoon olive oil or vegetable oil
2	large onions, chopped
4	cloves of garlic, crushed
5	quarts beef broth
½	cup dry sherry
1½	teaspoons ground cumin
1	teaspoon cayenne pepper
¼	teaspoon ground allspice
4	cups dried black beans
	Salt and pepper to taste
4	corn or flour tortillas
½–¾	cup vegetable oil for frying
¾	cup thinly sliced green onions
1	large tomato, chopped
1	cup shredded Monterey Jack cheese

Yield: 12 to 16 servings

Brown oxtails in olive oil in heavy 10-quart saucepan, turning often; remove oxtails to platter. Add onions and garlic to drippings in saucepan. Sauté for 5 to 6 minutes or until tender. Return oxtails to saucepan with broth, wine, cumin, cayenne pepper and allspice. Simmer, covered, for 1 hour. Sort and rinse beans. Add to soup. Bring to a boil; reduce heat. Simmer, covered, for 1½ to 2 hours or until beans are tender. Remove oxtails to platter; remove meat from bones and discard bones. Process soup ½ at a time in blender or food processor. Combine with meat in saucepan. Season with salt and pepper. Simmer until heated through. Cut tortillas into ¼-inch strips. Fry ¼ at a time in hot oil in 10-inch skillet over medium-high heat until crisp and golden brown; drain. Season lightly with salt. Sprinkle servings of soup with tortilla strips, green onions, tomato and cheese.

Indian Corn Soup

1	pound dried navy beans
3	14-ounce cans chicken broth
3	4-ounce cans chopped green chiles
1	large onion, chopped
1/2	bunch fresh cilantro, chopped
3	16-ounce cans white hominy
1	tablespoon cumin
1	tablespoon ground oregano
1/2	teaspoon ground red pepper
3	large cloves of garlic, pressed
1/2	teaspoon black pepper
2	tablespoons butter or margarine
3	slices bacon, chopped
4	cups chopped cooked chicken breasts
1	cup shredded Cheddar cheese
1/4	cup flour

Yield: 10 to 12 servings

Sort and rinse beans. Bring to a boil in water to cover in heavy 6-quart saucepan. Let stand overnight. Drain 1/3 of the water from saucepan. Add chicken broth, chiles, onion, cilantro, hominy, cumin, oregano, red pepper, garlic, black pepper, butter, bacon and chicken; mix well. Simmer for 3 to 4 hours or until beans are tender. Add cheese, stirring until melted. Mix flour with enough water to blend well in small bowl. Stir into soup. Cook for 10 minutes or until thickened, stirring constantly. Serve with corn tortillas or corn chips.

Ted Charveze, Isleta, was a creator of fine gem jewelry. Sandy, his widow, has kindly shared this delicious recipe for one of his favorite dishes.

Dried Corn ⌒

Parched, or roasted, corn on the cob is husked and strung up to dry completely. When it is to be used for a winter meal, the corn is plunged into boiling water or added to a vegetable dish or stew so that it regains its soft texture and sweet flavor.

Chicken and Ham Hock Posole

6	chicken thighs
2	large meaty smoked ham hocks
2	large onions, coarsely chopped
3	cloves of garlic, pressed
1	teaspoon oregano
1/2	teaspoon cumin
2	tablespoons New Mexico red chili powder
	Salt to taste
3	14-ounce cans chicken broth
4	cups (about) water
1–2	dried red chile pods, broken into halves
1	30-ounce can hominy, drained
1/2	cup chopped cilantro
1/2	cup thinly sliced green onions
3	tablespoons chile caribe
2	large avocados, chopped

Yield: 6 to 8 servings

Rinse chicken and pat dry. Combine with ham hocks, onions, garlic, oregano, cumin, chili powder and salt in heavy 8-quart saucepan. Add chicken broth and enough water to cover ingredients by 3 inches. Bring to a boil over high heat; reduce heat. Stir in red chiles. Simmer, covered, for 1 1/2 to 2 hours or until chicken is fork tender. Remove chicken and ham hocks; let stand until cool. Cut meat from bones, discarding bones. Add meat to soup with hominy. Cook for 20 to 35 minutes or until heated through. Serve with cilantro, green onions, chile caribe and avocados for topping.

The ham hocks give this dish a wonderful smoky flavor.

Mock Posole

2	cloves of garlic, minced or pressed
2	large onions, chopped
1	tablespoon oregano
2	tablespoons vegetable oil
1	2 1/2 to 3-pound chicken or 2 whole chicken breasts, cooked, chopped
2	4-ounce cans chopped green chiles
1	11 to 16-ounce can corn
1	2-ounce can sliced black olives, drained
6	cups homemade or canned chicken broth

Yield: 6 servings

Sauté garlic, onions and oregano in oil in saucepan. Add chicken, green chiles, undrained corn, olives and chicken broth; mix well. Simmer for 10 minutes or until done to taste.

Chicken and Rice Soup with Chipotle Chiles

1	whole chicken breast
6	cups canned chicken broth
1	7-ounce can chipotle in adobo sauce
1	medium onion, minced
1	teaspoon minced garlic
1/2	cup uncooked long grain white rice
2	carrots, peeled, thinly sliced
	Juice of 1 lime
1/2	teaspoon salt
1	avocado, chopped
1/4	cup minced cilantro

Yield: 4 to 6 servings

Rinse chicken and pat dry. Combine with chicken broth in heavy 5-quart saucepan. Drain chipotle, reserving 2 tablespoons sauce. Add chipotle, reserved sauce, onion and garlic to saucepan. Bring to a boil over high heat; reduce heat. Simmer for 20 to 25 minutes or until chicken is cooked through. Remove chicken to platter; let stand until cool. Stir rice and carrots into soup. Simmer, covered, for 20 minutes or until rice is tender. Chop chicken into bite-sized pieces, discarding skin and bones. Return chicken to soup. Season with lime juice and salt. Top servings with avocado and cilantro.

Gourd Containers

Gourds were carried as small containers long before pottery reached North America. The strong rind of the gourd made it suitable for canteens, containers, dippers and rattles. Each gourd variety has a different shape. A practical water canteen was made from the crookneck gourd, which was allowed to dry on the vine. A round opening was cut into the top of the dried gourd and it was boiled for about 30 minutes. The seeds and fibrous pulp were then scraped out of the inside. A "cork," carved to fit out of cottonwood root or other wood, was inserted in the top and a shoulder strap, of agave fiber, was knotted into a sling around the bulb. This lightweight container was filled with water and carried over the shoulder.

Mexican Bean Soup

2	cups dried pinto beans
4	slices bacon, chopped
1	large onion, finely chopped
2	cloves of garlic, pressed
3	jalapeño peppers, seeded, minced
2	teaspoons hot chili powder
1	14-ounce can tomatoes, chopped
6	cups chicken broth
6	corn tortillas
	Oil for frying
1/2	cup cubed sharp Cheddar cheese
1/2	cup sour cream
1/2	cup chopped green chiles
1/4	cup minced cilantro

Yield: 6 servings

Sort and rinse beans. Soak in water to cover in bowl overnight; drain and rinse. Place in slow cooker. Fry bacon in skillet until crisp; remove bacon. Drain all but 3 tablespoons drippings from skillet. Add onion, garlic and peppers to drippings in skillet. Sauté for 2 minutes. Stir in chili powder. Cook for 30 seconds, stirring constantly. Add undrained tomatoes. Cook for 3 minutes. Add to slow cooker with chicken broth and bacon and enough water to cover by 3 inches. Cook on High for 6 hours. Cut tortillas into 1/4-inch strips. Fry in oil until golden brown; drain. Place tortilla strips and cheese cubes in soup bowls. Ladle soup into bowls; top with sour cream, green chiles and cilantro.

May cook in heavy 5-quart saucepan on stove top for 2 to 2 1/2 hours if preferred.

Tepary Beans ⁓

Tepary beans are well adapted to the harsh environmental conditions of the Southwest. Teparies have long been popular with the O'odham people. Smaller than kidney beans, they can be white or brown in color. Crops are ready in early summer and the beans are preserved by drying. Tepary beans have a distinctive flavor and can be used in any recipe calling for pinto beans. Teparies, an excellent source of protein, are high in carbohydrate and calcium and contain potassium, iron and phosphorus.

Shrimp Jicama Salad with Piquant Tequila Dressing

3	heads butter lettuce, torn
1½	pounds peeled salad shrimp, cooked
1	medium jicama, cut into julienne strips
2	large avocados, sliced
	Tequila Dressing
2	large tomato wedges

Yield: 6 servings

Place lettuce in salad bowl. Top with shrimp, jicama and avocados. Add Tequila Dressing; toss lightly. Top with tomato wedges.

Tequila Dressing

½	cup mayonnaise
2½	tablespoons fresh lemon juice
1	tablespoon white wine Worcestershire sauce
½	teaspoon dillweed
½	teaspoon cayenne pepper
¼	teaspoon dry mustard
	Juice of ½ lime
½	teaspoon grated lemon zest
¾	teaspoon grated lime zest
1	cup sour cream
½	teaspoon Tequila

Yield: 2 cups

Combine mayonnaise, lemon juice, Worcestershire sauce, dillweed, cayenne pepper, dry mustard, lime juice, lemon zest and lime zest in bowl; whisk until well mixed. Stir in sour cream and Tequila. Chill for 3 hours.

Virginia L. Yates, Heard Museum Guild member, submitted this prize-winning recipe, which was created especially for the Zest of the Southwest Recipe Contest sponsored by The Arizona Republic newpaper, Phoenix, Arizona in October, 1987. Used with permission.

Taco Salad

1	pound ground beef
	Salt and pepper to taste
1	6-ounce can pitted ripe olives, sliced
1	head lettuce, shredded
1	16-ounce can red kidney beans, drained, rinsed
3	medium tomatoes, chopped
1	4-ounce can chopped green chiles
	Taco Salad Dressing
3/4	cup shredded Cheddar cheese
3/4	cup coarsely crushed corn chips

Yield: 6 to 8 servings

Brown ground beef with salt and pepper in skillet, stirring until crumbly; drain. Combine ground beef, olives, lettuce, kidney beans, tomatoes and chiles in bowl; mix well. Chill, covered, in refrigerator. Toss salad ingredients with chilled Taco Salad Dressing in serving bowl. Top with cheese and corn chips just before serving.

Taco Salad Dressing

3/4	cup sour cream
3	tablespoons Italian salad dressing
1/4	teaspoon pepper
1	teaspoon chili powder
3/4	teaspoon salt
2	avocados, peeled, chopped

Yield: 1 cup

Combine sour cream, Italian salad dressing, pepper, chili powder, salt and avocados in bowl; mix well. Chill in refrigerator.

Makes a nice addition to a buffet.

Ensalada Esmeralda

1	pound zucchini, cut into thick slices
	Salt to taste
	Italian dressing
3	ounces cream cheese, chopped
2	tablespoons chopped onion
1	avocado, peeled, chopped
2	green chiles, peeled, cut into strips
	Pepper to taste
	Romaine lettuce

Yield: 4 to 6 servings

Cook zucchini in boiling salted water in saucepan for 5 minutes or until tender-crisp; drain. Combine zucchini and Italian dressing in bowl; mix well. Marinate in refrigerator for 3 hours or longer. Combine cream cheese, onion, avocado and chiles in bowl; mix well. Season with salt and pepper. Stir in zucchini. Chill for 30 minutes. Serve on bed of romaine lettuce.

Cactus Salad with Feta Cheese and Cilantro Dressing

1	head romaine lettuce, torn
1	head red leaf lettuce, torn
1	15-ounce jar Nopalitas cactus
1	large red onion, sliced into rings
2	large tomatoes, cut into wedges
4	ounces feta cheese, crumbled
3/4	cup pitted black olives
1/2	cup pecan halves
	Cilantro Dressing

Yield: 8 servings

Chill lettuce for 2 hours or longer. Drain, rinse and chop cactus; chill in refrigerator. Arrange lettuce on shallow platter. Top with cactus, onion rings, tomatoes, cheese, olives and pecans. Drizzle with Cilantro Dressing; toss to mix well.

Nopalitas taste much like tart green beans.

Cilantro Dressing

1/2	cup olive oil
1/4	cup fresh lime juice
1	clove of garlic, pressed
1/4	cup chopped fresh cilantro
1/2	teaspoon hot pepper sauce

Yield: 1 cup

Combine olive oil, lime juice, garlic, cilantro and pepper sauce in bowl; mix well.

Spinach and Cactus Salad

1	pound spinach
1	bunch watercress
1	15-ounce jar Nopalitas cactus
1	medium red onion, sliced into rings
1	bunch radishes, sliced
8	ounces Monterey Jack cheese, cubed
12	cherry tomatoes, cut into halves
2	large avocados, sliced
	Balsamic Dressing

Yield: 6 to 8 servings

Tear spinach and watercress into bite-sized pieces, discarding stems. Wrap in paper towels and chill in plastic bag for 2 hours or longer. Rinse, drain and chop cactus. Combine spinach, watercress, cactus, onion, radishes, cheese, tomatoes and avocados in large salad bowl. Add Balsamic Dressing; toss to mix well.

Balsamic Dressing

4	large New Mexico red chiles
1/4	cup olive oil
1/4	cup balsamic vinegar
	Juice of 1/2 lime
1	clove of garlic, pressed
1	teaspoon Dijon mustard
	Salt and pepper to taste

Yield: 1 cup

Cut chiles crosswise into thin strips, discarding seeds and stems. Fry in hot olive oil in large skillet over low heat, stirring constantly. Remove and discard chiles, reserving oil. Combine reserved oil with vinegar, lime juice, garlic, mustard, salt and pepper in bowl; mix well.

New Mexico Red Chiles ～

New Mexico red chiles are similar in appearance to the Anaheim chiles but hotter in flavor. New Mexico chili powder is pure ground New Mexico red chiles.

Black Bean and Rice Salad

1	16-ounce can black beans, drained, rinsed
3	cups cooked rice
1	medium red bell pepper, chopped
1	medium green bell pepper, chopped
4	green onions, chopped
1/4	cup minced fresh cilantro
1/3	cup olive oil
1/4	cup fresh lime juice
	Salt and freshly ground pepper to taste
	Lettuce leaves
2	avocados, sliced
1	papaya, peeled, seeded, sliced
	Sections of 2 oranges

Yield: 6 servings

Combine beans, rice, bell peppers, green onions and cilantro in large bowl; mix well. Whisk olive oil and lime juice together in small bowl. Pour over bean and rice mixture; mix well. Season with salt and pepper. Chill, covered, for several hours to overnight. Spoon into serving bowl lined with lettuce. Top with avocados, papaya and orange sections.

This is good served with Red Chili Barbecued Chicken (page 184).

Chile and Beef for Sandwiches

1	6-pound pot roast
1	large onion, sliced
1/2	cup strong coffee
1	28-ounce can tomatoes, drained
1	7-ounce can roasted green chiles, rinsed, seeded, cut into strips
	Salt and pepper to taste

Yield: 8 to 10 servings

Brown roast on all sides in nonstick saucepan. Add onion and coffee. Simmer until roast is tender. Remove roast from saucepan, reserving cooking liquid. Cool roast and reserved liquid. Shred roast, discarding fat. Return to saucepan with tomatoes, chiles, salt and pepper. Simmer for 3 to 4 hours or until done to taste, adding liquid if needed. Serve hot on rolls or with pita bread.

Christmas Eve Salad

1	fresh pineapple or 1 20-ounce can pineapple chunks
4	large oranges
1	medium head iceberg lettuce, shredded
3	medium beets, cooked, peeled, thinly sliced or 1 16-ounce can sliced beets, drained
2	large red apples, thinly sliced
4	bananas, sliced
1	medium jicama, peeled, julienned
1/2	cup salted peanuts
	Seeds of 2 pomegranates
1/4	cup vegetable oil
2	tablespoons red wine vinegar
1/2	cup plain yogurt or sour cream
	Salt to taste

Yield: 10 to 12 servings

Peel and cube pineapple or drain canned pineapple over bowl to catch juice. Peel and thinly slice oranges over bowl to catch juice; reserve fruit juices. Line large shallow bowl with lettuce. Arrange pineapple, oranges, beets, apples, bananas and jicama in decorative pattern over lettuce. Sprinkle with peanuts and pomegranate seeds. Combine reserved juices with oil, vinegar, yogurt and salt in bowl; mix well. Drizzle over salad.

This salad does not hold well and should be served as soon as it is assembled, since the juices from the fruit will continue to flow.

Mexican Quiche

10	eggs
1/2	cup flour
1	teaspoon baking powder
2	cups small curd cottage cheese
4–5	drops of hot pepper sauce
1/2	teaspoon salt
1/2	cup melted butter
1	7-ounce can sliced green chiles
1	pound sharp Cheddar cheese, shredded

Yield: 24 servings

Beat eggs in bowl. Add flour, baking powder, cottage cheese, pepper sauce, salt, butter, green chiles and cheese; mix well. Spoon into 10x15-inch baking pan. Bake at 400 degrees for 10 minutes; reduce oven temperature to 300 degrees. Bake for 40 minutes or until brown on top. Cool slightly. Cut into squares.

This makes a good appetizer. It may be frozen and reheated.

Fajitas

¹/₄	cup soy sauce
¹/₄	cup vegetable oil
¹/₄	cup fresh lime juice
1	pound beef skirt, flank steak or round steak
6	chicken breast fillets
1	green or red bell pepper, sliced
1	onion, cut into wedges
1	tomato, chopped
1	jalapeño pepper, chopped (optional)
10	large flour tortillas

Yield: 10 servings

Combine soy sauce, oil and lime juice in bowl; mix well. Combine steak and marinade in plastic food storage bag; mix well. Marinate for 8 to 12 hours in refrigerator. Rinse chicken and pat dry. Add to marinade. Marinate in refrigerator for 1 to 3 hours. Drain, reserving marinade. Grill chicken and beef over hot coals for 5 minutes on each side or broil until cooked through. Cut cross grain into thin slices. Cook bell pepper, onion, tomato and jalapeño pepper in a small amount of the reserved marinade in skillet until tender-crisp. Add chicken and beef; toss to mix well. Cook tortillas in ungreased medium-hot skillet until heated and softened, turning several times. Serve fajita filling on sizzling platter with hot tortillas. Serve with sour cream and avocado or guacamole.

May stir-fry marinated meat with vegetables instead of grilling if preferred. May stack 5 tortillas at a time between 2 slightly dampened towels and microwave on High for 45 seconds.

Chalupas

16	ounces dried pinto beans
1	3-pound pork loin roast
2	cloves of garlic, chopped
2	tablespoons cumin
1	4-ounce can chopped green chiles
2	tablespoons red chili powder
1	teaspoon oregano leaves
1	tablespoon salt
4–5	drops of hot pepper sauce

Yield: 12 servings

Sort and rinse beans. Combine beans with roast, garlic, cumin, green chiles, chili powder, oregano, salt and pepper sauce in heavy 5-quart saucepan. Add water to cover. Simmer, covered, for 6 hours or until beans and roast are tender, adding water if needed. Remove roast and cube or shred roast, discarding skin and bones. Return meat to saucepan. Simmer, uncovered, for 1 hour or until of desired consistency. May serve in bowls with warm tortillas. May serve over corn chips or crisp tortillas with toppings of shredded lettuce, chopped onion, chopped tomatoes, chopped avocados, shredded longhorn or Monterey Jack cheese and hot sauce. May prepare in advance and reheat.

This recipe is prepared by Lucy Toledo and her family for the Feast Day at Jemez Pueblo.

Pima Storeroom ⌒

The Pima and Tohono O'odham have been known for their hospitality. Visitors are presented with food when they arrive and given more to take along when they leave.

George Webb, born in 1893, recalls his early memories of growing up in his book, **A Pima Remembers**. He describes an early Pima storeroom. " . . .there would be three or four large size storage baskets. There would be smaller baskets and ollas full of mesquite bean cakes, balls of cactus fruit, cactus seeds, dried meat in sacks, cheese and salt. In one corner, stacked in straw, would be muskmelons, watermelons and pumpkins. Hanging from the ceiling would be bundles of fox-tail weed, split willow branches and devil's claw for basket making. In those days the Pima always had plenty."

Chicken Fajitas

6	chicken breast fillets
1	teaspoon seasoned salt
1/4	teaspoon garlic powder
1/4	teaspoon onion powder
2	tablespoons olive oil
1/2	green bell pepper, cut into strips
1	each red and yellow bell pepper, cut into strips
1	large onion, sliced into rings
2	large tomatoes, sliced
5	tablespoons minced cilantro
12	soft flour tortillas, warmed
2	limes, quartered
1/2	cup salsa

Yield: 6 servings

Cut chicken into strips; rinse and pat dry. Stir-fry chicken with seasoned salt, garlic powder and onion powder in 1 tablespoon olive oil in large skillet just until chicken is cooked through; do not overcook. Remove chicken from skillet. Add remaining 1 tablespoon oil, bell peppers and onion to skillet. Stir-fry for 2 to 3 minutes or until tender-crisp. Add tomatoes, cilantro and chicken. Cook until heated through. Spoon into warm tortillas; squeeze limes over filling. Roll tortillas to enclose filling. Serve with salsa, sour cream, guacamole and black olives.

Chicken Mole

6	chicken breast fillets
	Chicken broth or white wine
1	cup tomato sauce
1/2	cup medium picante sauce
5	teaspoons baking cocoa
1	teaspoon ground cumin
2	cloves of garlic, minced
1/2	teaspoon paprika
1 1/2	teaspoons Worcestershire sauce
1/4	cup red wine or grape juice
	Ground cloves, nutmeg and allspice to taste

Yield: 6 servings

Rinse chicken and pat dry. Pound 1/2 inch thick. Brown lightly on both sides in skillet sprayed with nonstick cooking spray, adding a small amount of chicken broth or white wine if needed to prevent overbrowning. Combine tomato sauce, picante sauce, baking cocoa, cumin, garlic, paprika, Worcestershire sauce, red wine, cloves, nutmeg and allspice in bowl; mix well. Pour over chicken. Bring to a boil; reduce heat. Simmer, covered, for 10 minutes.

This sauce is also good to marinate game hens; bake in sauce at 375 degrees for 45 to 50 minutes, basting frequently.

Carlos' Chicken Mole

1	2¹/₂-pound chicken or 6 chicken breast halves
¹/₄	cup chopped cilantro
6	cloves of garlic, minced
1	yellow onion, chopped
¹/₄	teaspoon pepper
3	cups water
2	ounces unsweetened baking chocolate
2	8-ounce cans tomato sauce
1	tablespoon honey
2	tablespoons (rounded) peanut butter
2	tablespoons (heaping) sesame tahini
1	teaspoon cumin
1	teaspoon chili powder
¹/₄	teaspoon cinnamon
	Salt or lime juice to taste
¹/₂	cup masa harina

Yield: 4 servings

Rinse chicken and pat dry. Combine with cilantro, garlic, onion, pepper and water in pressure cooker. Cook using manufacturer's directions. Drain, reserving broth. Cool chicken and chop into bite-sized pieces, discarding skin and bones. Combine ¹/₃ cup reserved chicken broth with chocolate in 8-quart saucepan. Cook until chocolate melts, stirring to mix well. Add tomato sauce, honey, peanut butter, tahini, cumin, chili powder and cinnamon. Simmer for 20 minutes. Add 1 cup reserved chicken broth; mix well. Add chicken and salt. Blend ²/₃ cup reserved chicken broth with masa harina in bowl. Stir into chicken mixture. Cook until thickened, stirring constantly. Serve with warm corn tortillas, refried black beans, green salad and pickled jalapeño peppers.

R. Carlos Nakai, a Ute-Navajo, is a renowned composer and international performer of music for the flute. He displays just as much creativity in the kitchen.

Green Chile Frittata

1/2	cup flour
1	teaspoon baking powder
10	eggs, slightly beaten
1/2	cup melted butter or margarine, cooled
2	cups small curd cottage cheese
16	ounces Monterey Jack cheese, shredded
3	4-ounce cans diced green chiles
	Salt to taste

Yield: 18 servings

Combine flour and baking powder in bowl; mix well. Stir in eggs and butter. Add cottage cheese, Monterey Jack cheese, chiies and salt. Spoon into 9x13-inch baking dish. Bake at 350 degrees for 35 to 45 minutes or until set. Cut into squares. Serve hot.

May be served as a luncheon entree.

Baked Chiles Rellenos

6	egg whites
6	egg yolks, slightly beaten
1	tablespoon flour
1/4	teaspoon salt
1	4-ounce can chopped green chiles, drained
4	ounces Monterey Jack cheese, shredded
4	ounces Cheddar cheese, shredded
	Sour cream
	Salsa

Yield: 8 servings

Beat egg whites in mixer bowl until soft peaks form. Combine egg yolks, flour and salt; mix well. Fold in beaten egg whites. Spoon half the mixture into greased 8x12-inch baking dish. Sprinkle with chiles and cheeses. Top with remaining egg mixture. Bake at 325 degrees for 25 minutes. Top with sour cream and salsa.

Homemade Chorizo

1/4	cup New Mexico hot red chili powder
3	tablespoons salt
2	tablespoons hot paprika
1	tablespoon minced garlic
2	tablespoons dried red chile flakes
1 1/2	teaspoons dried oregano, crumbled
1/2	teaspoon ground cumin
1/4	cup water or Tequila
3	tablespoons red wine vinegar
5	pounds boneless pork shoulder, ground medium coarse

Yield: 5 pounds

Combine chili powder, salt, paprika, garlic, chile flakes, oregano, cumin, water and vinegar in large bowl. Add pork, kneading to mix well. Marinate, covered, in refrigerator overnight. Shape into patties 2 1/2 to 3 inches in diameter. Stack 6 to 8 patties together with waxed paper between layers; wrap in plastic wrap and heavy-duty foil. Freeze until needed.

This sausage is great for breakfast, cooked with scrambled eggs and served in warmed soft tortillas, or crumbled and fried and added to beans for tostados.

Blue Corn Enchiladas

12	blue corn tortillas
1/4	cup vegetable oil
3	cups Basic Red Chile Sauce (page 198)
1/2	cup shredded Monterey Jack cheese
1/2	cup shredded Cheddar cheese
1	medium onion, minced
4	fried eggs

Yield: 4 servings

Soften each tortilla in oil in skillet for 3 seconds; drain. Spoon thin layer of Basic Red Chile Sauce on each of 4 ovenproof plates. Layer tortillas, remaining chile sauce, cheeses and onion 1/3 at a time on each prepared plate. Bake at 300 degrees for 10 minutes or until cheese melts. Top each with 1 egg. Garnish with shredded lettuce. Serve immediately.

May substitute Dried Red Chile Sauce (page 199).

Green Chile and Chicken Enchiladas

2	cups drained canned tomatoes with 1/3 cup juice
1	clove of garlic, minced
	Pinch of sugar
10	drops of hot pepper sauce
1/2	teaspoon salt
2	tablespoons vegetable oil
2	7-ounce cans green chiles, rinsed, seeded, cut into strips
1	cup chopped onion
1/2	teaspoon salt
2	tablespoons vegetable oil
12	corn tortillas
2	cups shredded cooked chicken
1	cup sour cream
	Milk
1 1/2	cups shredded longhorn cheese

Yield: 6 to 8 servings

Process tomatoes with 1/3 cup juice, garlic, sugar, pepper sauce and 1/2 teaspoon salt in blender until smooth. Cook mixture in 2 tablespoons oil in skillet for 10 minutes; remove to bowl. Add chiles, onion, 1/2 teaspoon salt and 2 tablespoons oil to skillet. Cook for 10 minutes. Wrap tortillas in microwave-safe wrap. Microwave on Medium just until softened. Arrange 6 tortillas in overlapping layer in round 10-inch baking dish. Layer chicken, half the green chile mixture, half the tomato mixture, half the mixture of sour cream and a small amount of milk and half the cheese over tortillas. Arrange remaining tortillas over layers. Repeat layers with remaining ingredients. Bake at 350 degrees for 25 minutes. Serve immediately. Serve with refried beans and tossed salad.

Chiles Rellenos Casserole

8	whole New Mexico green chiles, roasted, peeled
8	ounces jalapeño Monterey Jack cheese, cut into strips
3/4	cup shredded Cheddar cheese
1	small onion, minced
2	cloves of garlic, pressed
1	tablespoon olive oil
3	eggs
1/4	cup flour
3/4	cup milk
1/4	teaspoon salt

Yield: 6 to 8 servings

Cut slit down side of each chile; remove seeds carefully. Place 1 strip Monterey Jack cheese in each chile; arrange in 9x13-inch baking dish sprayed with nonstick cooking spray. Sprinkle with Cheddar cheese. Sauté onion and garlic in olive oil in skillet until tender. Beat eggs with flour in bowl. Add milk, salt and onion mixture. Pour over chiles. Bake at 350 degrees for 35 minutes or until knife inserted in center comes out clean and casserole is light brown. Cool for several minutes before serving.

Green Corn Tamales

1	package dried corn husks
2	cups shortening
5	pounds masa
3	tablespoons baking powder
2	teaspoons salt
1	cup cream-style corn
3	cups chopped green chiles
1	cup shredded Monterey Jack cheese
1	cup shredded longhorn cheese

Yield: 2 dozen

Soak corn husks in very hot water in sink for 1 hour. Clean off silk and debris; drain and pat dry. Cream shortening in mixer bowl until light and smooth. Add masa, baking powder, salt and corn; mix well. Place corn husks 1 at a time on work surface. Spread enough masa mixture onto husk to cover upper half of husk. Spoon 2 teaspoons of chiles down center of masa; sprinkle with 2 teaspoons of combined cheeses. Fold in 1 side of husk; roll tightly to enclose filling. Fold pointed end of husk toward center. Repeat with remaining husks. Arrange tamales open end up in large kettle or steamer. Add desired amount of water. Bring to a boil; reduce heat. Steam, covered, for 1 hour or until masa is firm and pulls easily from husk.

May prepare tamales in advance and freeze until needed. Reheat, wrapped in plastic wrap, in microwave.

Anaheim or California Chiles ⌐

Anaheim chiles, the most widely available chile in the Southwest, are a smooth, bright shiny green, about 7 inches long and 1½ inches wide. They are mild to hot in flavor and their large size makes them ideal for stuffing. Anaheims are also available canned or frozen, and in this form probably are the most common chile used in the United States.

Chilaquiles

12	stale corn tortillas, cut into wedges
	Oil for frying
	Salt to taste
1	large onion, chopped
1	clove of garlic, minced
3¹/₄	cups Basic Red Chile Sauce (page 198)
	Chicken broth or water
³/₄	cup shredded Monterey Jack cheese
³/₄	cup shredded Cheddar cheese

Yield: 4 to 6 servings

Fry tortillas in ¹/₄ inch oil in heavy skillet until firm but not crisp; drain, reserving 1 tablespoon oil in skillet. Sprinkle tortillas lightly with salt. Sauté onion and garlic in reserved oil in skillet until tender. Add Basic Red Chile Sauce. Simmer for 10 minutes, thinning with chicken broth if needed for desired consistency. Alternate layers of sauce, tortilla wedges and cheeses in 8x8-inch baking dish sprayed with nonstick cooking spray until all ingredients are used. Bake at 350 degrees for 35 to 40 minutes or until bubbly.

This is a good brunch dish topped with sunny side-up eggs.

Chipotle Chile ⌒

Chipotle, the dried, smoked jalapeño chile, is a dull tan to coffee brown in color. It is dried over a mesquite fire which gives it a sweet and smoky flavor. About ¹/₅ of Mexico's jalapeño crop is processed as chipotle.

Canned chipotles in adobo sauce are chipotles that have been stewed in a lightly seasoned liquid. They are very popular in southwestern cooking, providing a delicious flavor.

Red Chili Barbecued Chicken

1	cup olive oil
4	cloves of garlic, pressed
1¹/₂	tablespoons chili powder
1	tablespoon fresh lime juice
1¹/₂	teaspoons cumin
1	teaspoon coriander
¹/₄	teaspoon cayenne pepper
2	teaspoons hot pepper sauce
1	teaspoon salt
¹/₂	teaspoon freshly ground black pepper
2	2¹/₂ to 3-pound whole chickens
	Salt and black pepper to taste

Yield: 4 servings

Combine olive oil, garlic, chili powder, lime juice, cumin, coriander, cayenne pepper, pepper sauce, 1 teaspoon salt and ¹/₂ teaspoon black pepper in medium bowl; mix well. Rinse chickens inside and out and pat dry. Separate skin carefully from breast and back of chickens. Spoon 2 to 3 tablespoons marinade under skin; massage gently to spread evenly. Place in large dish; pour remaining marinade over chickens. Marinate, covered, in refrigerator for 4 hours to overnight. Drain, reserving marinade. Season chickens with salt and black pepper to taste. Place on rotisserie on grill over drip pan; baste with reserved marinade. Grill, covered, until chickens begin to brown, brushing with marinade every 10 minutes. Grill over low coals for 1 hour longer, basting occasionally. May cut up chicken and cook directly on grill if rotisserie is not available.

Add water-soaked mesquite or hickory chips to coals to give a great smoky flavor.

Using Fresh Chiles ⌒

Select fresh chiles that are dry, firm and heavy for their size. The skin should be shiny, smooth and unblemished. Wash and dry the chiles, wrap them in paper towels and store in the crisper section of the refrigerator. They should keep for two or three weeks. Do not store chiles in plastic bags as moisture will accumulate and hasten spoiling.

Pork Chops Marinated in Red Chile Sauce

1¹/₄	quarts Basic Red Chile Sauce (page 198)
1	tablespoon red wine vinegar
¹/₂	onion, coarsely chopped
3	cloves of garlic, pressed
1–2	tablespoons dried red chile flakes
1	teaspoon sugar
¹/₂	teaspoon cumin
1	teaspoon crushed oregano
1¹/₄	teaspoons salt
	Water
12	pork chops, ¹/₄ to ¹/₂ inch thick
2	onions
¹/₂	cup water

Yield: 6 servings

Combine Basic Red Chile Sauce, vinegar, chopped onion, garlic, chile flakes, sugar, cumin, oregano and salt in blender container; process until smooth, adding a small amount of water 1 tablespoon at a time until mixture is of desired consistency. Coat both sides of pork chops with sauce. Cut 2 onions into 12 slices. Arrange pork chops and onion slices in overlapping layer in 9x13-inch baking dish. Top with remaining sauce. Chill, covered with foil, overnight to 24 hours. Add ¹/₂ cup water. Bake, covered with foil, in preheated 325-degree oven for 1¹/₂ hours or until tender.

May marinate and bake peeled and quartered potatoes with chops.

Chile de Árbol ~

Chiles de árbol are literally "chiles of the tree." These bright, red chiles are very small and very hot. They have a tannic, smoky and grassy flavor and produce a searing acidic heat on the tip of the tongue. Chiles de árbol are primarily used in powdered form in sauces, soups and stews.

Festive Pork Chops

6–10	pork chops
	Water
1	medium onion, chopped
1	red bell pepper, chopped
1	green bell pepper, chopped
1/2	bunch cilantro, chopped
1	bunch green onions, chopped
1	8-ounce can tomato sauce
1	cup water

Yield: 6 to 10 servings

Place pork chops in large skillet. Add 1/2 inch water. Simmer, covered, just until tender. Cook, uncovered, until light brown on both sides. Add onion, bell peppers, cilantro and green onions. Cook until vegetables are tender-crisp, stirring occasionally. Add tomato sauce and 1 cup water. Cook until sauce is of desired consistency, stirring occasionally. Serve with Cowboy Bread (page 160) and green salad.

Mary Lomahaftewa, who is a Choctaw, shares this dish with us from the cooking class she taught at The Heard Museum. It is a favorite with her son and husband, who is a Hopi. Her son requested it, with Cowboy Bread, for his high school graduation party.

Apache Acorn Stew

2–3	**pounds cubed stew beef**
2	**quarts water**
	Salt to taste
2	**cups flour**
1/2	**teaspoon salt**
3/4	**cup (about) water**
1	**cup ground acorn meal**
1	**cup cold water**

Yield: 6 to 8 servings

Combine beef with 2 quarts water in saucepan. Bring to a boil; reduce heat. Simmer, covered, for 1½ to 2 hours or until beef is very tender. Season with salt to taste. Mix flour, ½ teaspoon salt and enough of ¾ cup water to form a soft dough. Knead until slightly elastic. Divide dough into 2 balls; let rest, covered, for 30 minutes. Roll or pat dough on floured surface; cut into ¾x4-inch strips. Drop into boiling stew. Cook, uncovered, for 10 to 12 minutes or until cooked through, stirring occasionally. Mix acorn meal with 1 cup cold water in bowl. Stir into simmering stew. Cook for 10 to 15 minutes longer or until thickened to desired consistency. Serve with Apache Ash Bread (page 161).

Acorns ⌒

The Western Apaches harvest acorns in the areas of Payson, Mt. Graham and Ash Creek in Arizona. The right to harvest acorns in these areas was given in perpetuity to the Western Apaches in a treaty with the United States government. Picking the acorns is a tradition that has been preserved and handed down to each generation. Acorns also are available in some reservation trading posts and Mexican food stores under the name of "bellotas." The flavor of the acorns differs from area to area and tree to tree. The desert acorns, from the Emory oaks, have little tannin and require only shelling and grinding.

Jalapeño Grits Casserole

1/2	cup quick-cooking grits
1	teaspoon salt
1 1/2	cups boiling water
6	ounces jalapeño cheese, shredded
8	ounces Cheddar cheese, shredded
4	eggs, beaten
1/4	teaspoon garlic powder
1/4	teaspoon dry mustard

Yield: 6 to 8 servings

Cook grits with salt in water in saucepan over medium heat for 6 minutes, stirring occasionally. Add jalapeño cheese and 1 1/4 cups Cheddar cheese; stir until cheeses melt. Beat eggs with garlic powder and dry mustard in bowl. Stir a small amount of hot grits mixture into egg mixture; stir eggs into hot grits. Spoon into baking dish. Bake at 350 degrees for 20 to 30 minutes or until set. Top with remaining 3/4 cup Cheddar cheese; let stand until cheese melts.

Serve at breakfast or at other meals as an alternative to rice or potatoes.

Arizona Beans

2	pounds dried pinto, Anasazi or other beans
2	large onions, chopped
4	cloves of garlic, minced
1/2	teaspoon pepper
1/2	teaspoon cumin seeds
1	4-ounce can taco sauce
1	4-ounce can chopped green chiles
1	29-ounce can tomatoes with jalapeño peppers
1	teaspoon New Mexico hot chili powder (optional)

Yield: 8 servings

Sort and rinse beans. Soak beans in water to cover in bowl overnight or bring to a boil in saucepan and let stand for 1 hour; drain. Combine with enough water to cover by 2 inches in saucepan. Cook over medium heat for 1 hour, adding water as needed. Add onions, garlic, pepper, cumin seeds, taco sauce, chiles, tomatoes and chili powder; mix well. Cook for 1 hour longer or until beans are tender. May cook in slow cooker for 6 to 8 hours if preferred.

Sauté chopped beef or ground turkey with chopped onion and add to beans for a main dish.

Arizona Tepary Beans

2–3	cups dried tepary beans
4–6	slices bacon or 4 ounces chopped salt pork
1	medium onion, chopped
2	tablespoons red chili powder or crushed dried chiles to taste

Yield: 8 to 10 servings

Soak beans in water to cover in bowl overnight or bring to a boil in saucepan and let stand for 1 hour; drain. Combine beans with bacon, onion and chili powder in slow cooker; add water to cover. Cook on Low for 10 to 12 hours or on High for 4 to 6 hours.

Sand Parching of Beans ⌒

Juanita Tiger Kavena, in her book **Hopi Cookery**, says that "The reservation has very sandy soil, so sand of the right quality for parching corn and beans is readily available. Furthermore, it doesn't cling like the moist sands of coastal areas but readily falls away from the toasted foods."

Mrs. Kavena explains that "the Hopi parch white tepary beans in hot clean sand until light brown. They are then sprinkled with salt water (1 tablespoon of salt dissolved in 1 cup water) and dried in the oven. These are used as a snack."

Native American Green Chile Balls

2   pounds pork
2   pounds beef
2   sweet onions, finely chopped
2   tablespoons (about) vegetable oil
3   4-ounce cans chopped green chiles
1/2 cup sugar
1/2 cup raisins
2   eggs, separated
1/2 cup flour
2/3 cup shortening

Yield: 3¹/₂ dozen

Cook pork and beef in water to cover in saucepan until tender; drain. Grind pork and beef. Sauté onions in oil in skillet. Combine with pork, beef, chiles, sugar and raisins in bowl; mix well. Shape into small oval balls with floured hands. Beat egg yolks in bowl. Beat egg whites in mixer bowl until very stiff peaks form. Fold in egg yolks. Spread in shallow dish. Coat balls with egg mixture. Lift out with spoon and place in heated shortening in saucepan. Fry until golden brown, turning gently to brown evenly; drain on paper towels.

This dish is served as dessert for weddings and feast days.

Early Food Containers ⌐

Basketmaking is an ancient technique. The nomadic lifestyle of early hunters and gatherers required that possessions be few and practical. Baskets were a logical choice as they were light in weight, easy to transport, and unbreakable. Twining was the earliest known basketry technique. Most utilitarian basketry was made by plain or diagonal twining. This technique produces a very strong basket. Twined baskets were used as parching trays, water jars, and burden or firewood collecting baskets, to gather seeds, to cook and serve food, and for storage.

Basketry jars were used to transport and store water. These baskets were waterproofed by covering the interior and exterior with heated pitch from the piñon tree. Cooking in baskets was accomplished by heating a number of rocks in the campfire and then placing several in a basket with the food and water. As the rocks started to cool, they were exchanged for the hotter ones. This exchange continued until the food was cooked.

The introduction of pottery and, subsequently, metal containers decreased the need for utilitarian basketry, but basket weaving by many Native Americans for commercial sale has become an important source of income.

Orange Flan

2	quarts half and half or light cream, scalded
2	teaspoons vanilla extract
8	eggs
4	egg yolks
1/2	cup orange juice
1/4	cup sugar
1	tablespoon grated orange zest
2	cups sugar
1	cup water

Yield: 12 servings

Cook half and half in saucepan until reduced to about 6 cups; remove from heat. Stir in vanilla. Beat eggs, egg yolks, orange juice, 1/4 cup sugar and orange zest in bowl. Add hot half and half very gradually to egg mixture, stirring constantly; set aside. Stir 2 cups sugar into water in skillet. Cook until syrup is golden brown. Spoon into 12 custard cups, rotating cups to coat evenly. Let stand for several minutes. Spoon custard mixture into prepared cups; place in large pan with boiling water to reach halfway up sides of cups. Bake at 325 degrees for 25 minutes or until knife inserted in center comes out clean. Chill for 8 to 12 hours. Invert onto serving dishes.

Pineapple and Lime Flan

2/3	cup sugar
6	eggs
1	14-ounce can sweetened condensed milk
3/4	cup milk
	Grated zest of 1 lime
1/3	cup fresh lime juice
1	20-ounce can juice-pack crushed pineapple

Yield: 8 to 10 servings

Sprinkle sugar in heavy skillet; do not stir. Cook over low heat until sugar melts and begins to form light brown syrup; stir to mix well. Pour immediately into shallow 8-cup mold, rotating mold to coat evenly; set aside. Beat eggs slightly in large bowl. Add condensed milk, milk, lime zest and lime juice. Stir in undrained pineapple. Spoon into cooled mold. Place in shallow pan; add hot water to depth of 1/2 inch. Bake in preheated 350-degree oven for 1 hour or until small knife inserted into center comes out clean. Cool to room temperature. Chill overnight. Run knife around edge of mold to loosen. Place rimmed plate over mold; invert quickly onto plate.

Pumpkin Flan

1	cup milk
1	cup whipping cream
1/2	cup packed light brown sugar
1/2	cup canned solid-pack pumpkin
3	eggs, slightly beaten
2	egg yolks, slightly beaten
1	teaspoon vanilla extract
1/4	teaspoon cinnamon
1/4	teaspoon grated nutmeg
	Pinch each of allspice, cloves and salt
2	teaspoons sugar
1/2	teaspoon cinnamon

Yield: 8 servings

Fit buttered circle of waxed paper into each of 8 buttered 1/2-cup ramekins. Combine milk, cream and brown sugar in saucepan. Bring to a boil; remove from heat. Whisk pumpkin, eggs, egg yolks, vanilla, 1/4 teaspoon cinnamon, nutmeg, allspice, cloves and salt in bowl. Whisk in cream mixture. Spoon into prepared ramekins. Place in large baking pan; add boiling water to reach halfway up sides of ramekins. Bake at 350 degrees for 30 to 40 minutes or until knife inserted in center comes out clean. Cool to room temperature. Chill for 8 hours. Run knife around edges of ramekins; invert onto plate, discarding waxed paper. Sprinkle with mixture of sugar and 1/2 teaspoon cinnamon.

Empañadas

2   **cups flour**
2   **teaspoons baking powder**
1   **teaspoon salt**
1/2   **cup shortening**
1/3   **cup (about) ice water**
1   **21-ounce can apple pie filling**
       Oil for frying

Yield: 12 servings

Sift flour, baking powder and salt into bowl. Cut in shortening as for pastry. Add enough ice water to form dough. Divide into 12 portions. Roll each portion into 3 to 4-inch circle on floured surface. Spoon pie filling onto half of each circle. Fold dough over to enclose filling, moistening edge with water and pressing to seal. Fry in 425-degree oil in skillet until golden brown. Drain on paper towels. May bake at 400 degrees for 15 to 20 minutes if preferred.

May use other fillings such as crushed pineapple with grated coconut, mashed sweet potatoes with pineapple and almonds, fruit preserves, cherry pie filling or pumpkin pie filling.

Empañaditas ⌒

Empañaditas, a popular holiday food in the Southwest, are a smaller version of empañadas. The pastry dough is filled with a mixture of dried fruits, pork, and piñon nuts, a southwestern style of mincemeat, and fried in oil or shortening.

Sopaipillas

1³/₄	cups flour
2	teaspoons baking powder
1	teaspoon salt
2	tablespoons shortening
²/₃	cup cold water
	Oil for frying

Yield: 20 servings

Sift flour, baking powder and salt into bowl. Cut in shortening until crumbly. Add enough cold water gradually to form dough. Knead gently on lightly floured surface until smooth. Let rest, covered, for 5 minutes. Roll into 12x15-inch rectangle ¹/₁₆ to ¹/₈ inch thick. Cut into 3x3 or 2x3-inch pieces. Drop a few pieces at a time into preheated 400-degree oil in saucepan. Fry for 2 to 3 minutes on each side or until puffed, turning several times to brown evenly.

Serve sopaipillas with soup or guacamole or as dessert with butter, cinnamon and sugar, or honey.

Sopaipillas ⌒

Sopaipillas, feathery-light pillows of fried dough, are one of the favorite breads of the Southwest. They puff up like a soufflé when dropped into hot oil. Sopaipillas, developed by New Mexico settlers, were based on the Indian fry bread common to the Pueblo and Navajo. Sopaipillas, served with honey, can be eaten as an accompaniment to a meal, or as a main dish stuffed with meat or other fillings.

Mexican Wedding Cakes

1	cup butter, softened
2	cups sifted flour
1/2	cup sugar
1	teaspoon vanilla extract
1	cup finely chopped pecans
1/2	cup confectioners' sugar

Yield: 36 servings

Combine butter, flour and sugar in bowl, stirring until blended. Add vanilla and pecans; mix well. Chill for 30 minutes. Shape into small balls. Place on baking sheet; flatten slightly. Bake at 350 degrees for 10 to 12 minutes or until light brown; roll in confectioners' sugar. Place on wire rack to cool completely. Roll in confectioners' sugar.

Poppy Seed Cookies

1	cup shortening
1/2	cup sugar
2	egg yolks
3	cups flour
1/2	teaspoon baking powder
	Salt to taste
1/2	cup poppy seeds

Yield: 48 servings

Cream shortening and sugar in mixer bowl until light and fluffy. Add egg yolks, flour, baking powder and salt, beating until smooth. May add more flour to thicken. Stir in poppy seeds. Shape into small balls; twist to elongate ends. Place on cookie sheet. Bake at 350 degrees for 10 to 12 minutes or until light brown. Remove to wire rack to cool completely.

Cochiti Pueblo Indian Bread Pudding

1	cup sugar
2¹/₃	cups water
1	teaspoon ground cinnamon
¹/₄	teaspoon ground cloves
8	slices Indian bread, lightly buttered, toasted
1	cup seedless raisins
1¹/₂	cups shredded sharp Cheddar cheese

Yield: 6 servings

Sprinkle sugar in heavy skillet. Cook over medium heat for 4 minutes or until sugar is light brown, stirring frequently with wooden spoon. Add water gradually. Cook until sugar dissolves, stirring frequently. Stir in cinnamon and cloves; reduce heat to low. Simmer while preparing pudding ingredients. Break toasted bread into 1-inch pieces. Layer toast pieces, raisins and cheese ¹/₄ at a time in lightly buttered 2-quart baking dish. Pour hot syrup over layers; toss gently to mix. Bake at 350 degrees for 20 minutes or until cheese melts and liquid is absorbed. Serve hot or warm. May substitute white bread for Indian bread.

This dessert is a favorite at Pueblo Fiestas all along the Rio Grande in New Mexico.

Sonoran Seasoning

2	tablespoons New Mexico chili powder
2	teaspoons ground cumin
1	tablespoon garlic powder
1	tablespoon onion powder
2	teaspoons paprika
6	tablespoons salt
1¹/₂	teaspoons smoked hickory salt
2¹/₂	teaspoons black pepper
1	teaspoon cayenne pepper

Yield: ¹/₂ cup

Spread chili powder in small baking pan. Bake in preheated 250-degree oven for 5 to 6 minutes or just until chili powder begins to toast. Combine with cumin, garlic powder, onion powder, paprika, salt, hickory salt, black pepper and cayenne pepper in bowl; mix well. Cool completely. Store in covered jar.

This seasoning is excellent on grilled meat, poultry, seafood and vegetables.

Fresh Green Chile Salsa

1	clove of garlic
1	fresh jalapeño pepper, seeded, minced
1	small onion, minced
4	large fresh green chiles, roasted, peeled, minced
1	large fresh tomato, coarsely chopped
3	canned tomatoes, chopped, with 1/2 cup juice
3	tablespoons minced fresh cilantro
1	tablespoon olive oil
1/2	teaspoon salt
	Pepper to taste

Yield: 2 1/2 cups

Mash garlic to paste in bowl. Add jalapeño pepper, onion, chiles, fresh tomato, tomatoes with juice, cilantro, olive oil, salt and pepper; mix well. Chill, covered, for 2 to 4 hours to blend flavors.

This salsa is good on tacos, steak and burritos or on fried or scrambled eggs, or as a dip with chips.

Pico de Gallo Salsa

6–8	dried large chiles de árbol, crushed
2/3	cup chopped canned tomatoes with 1/4 cup juice
2	medium tomatoes, finely chopped
1	medium onion, minced
1/2	cup finely chopped cucumber
3	tablespoons minced fresh cilantro
2	tablespoons cider vinegar
2	tablespoons olive oil
1/2	teaspoon salt

Yield: 3 cups

Combine chiles, tomatoes with juice, fresh tomatoes, onion, cucumber and cilantro in bowl. Add vinegar, olive oil and salt; mix well. Chill, covered, for 4 hours.

The árbol is a small hot red chile with a smoky flavor. This salsa is good for fajitas and tacos or served with chips.

Basic Green Chile Sauce

2	cloves of garlic, minced
1	large onion, minced
6	tablespoons olive oil
6	tablespoons flour
2	cups chopped peeled roasted fresh green chiles or 1 16-ounce can chopped green chiles
3	large fresh tomatoes, chopped, or 1 cup chopped canned tomatoes
1/2	teaspoon oregano, crushed
1/4	teaspoon cumin
1/2	teaspoon salt
2 1/2	cups water or chicken broth

Yield: 3 cups

Sauté garlic and onion in hot olive oil in 3-quart saucepan until golden brown. Stir in flour. Cook until light brown, stirring constantly. Add chiles, tomatoes, oregano, cumin and salt; mix well. Whisk in water. Cook over low heat for 15 minutes or until reduced by 1/2.

Use this sauce on enchiladas, burritos and eggs or in green chile stew.

Basic Red Chile Sauce

5	tablespoons minced onion
2	cloves of garlic, minced
1/4,	cup (or more) vegetable oil
1/4	cup flour
2/3	cup New Mexico chili powder
3 1/2	cups (or more) water
1/4	teaspoon oregano, crushed
1 1/4	teaspoons cumin
1	teaspoon salt

Yield: 4 cups

Sauté onion and garlic in hot oil in 2-quart saucepan until golden brown. Stir in flour. Cook for 4 minutes or until light brown, stirring frequently. Stir in chili powder. Cook for 3 minutes or until chili powder begins to turn dark brown, stirring constantly and adding 1 additional tablespoon oil if mixture becomes too dry. Whisk in water, oregano, cumin and salt. Bring to a boil, stirring constantly; reduce heat. Cook for 5 to 6 minutes or until thickened, stirring constantly. May add a small amount of additional water if needed for desired consistency.

This basic sauce is used for enchiladas, tamales, red chile stew, red chile burritos and on eggs.

Dried Red Chile Sauce

24	dried red chiles
2	cloves of garlic, pressed
1	large onion, minced
3	tablespoons shortening
3	tablespoons flour
1	teaspoon salt
1/4	teaspoon cumin
	Oregano to taste

Yield: 4 cups

Wash chiles, discarding seeds. Cook in water to cover in saucepan for 10 to 15 minutes; drain, reserving cooking water. Process chiles in blender or food processor until smooth, adding a small amount of reserved cooking water if needed for smooth consistency. Press mixture through sieve into bowl. Sauté garlic and onion in shortening in 2-quart saucepan until tender. Stir in flour. Cook until golden brown, stirring constantly. Add chile purée and 2 cups reserved cooking water. Cook until sauce is thick enough to coat spoon, adding additional reserved cooking water if needed for desired consistency. Stir in salt, cumin and oregano. Cook for 10 minutes longer.

This sauce is the basis for the red chile sauce used for enchiladas, tamales and red chile stew.

Taco Sauce

1 1/2	cups tomato sauce
1	7-ounce can jalapeño salsa
1	small onion, chopped
2	cloves of garlic, minced
1/4–1/2	teaspoon oregano
1/2	teaspoon salt
2	teaspoons vinegar
6	tepín chiles, crushed

Yield: 3 cups

Combine tomato sauce, salsa, onion, garlic, oregano, salt, vinegar and chiles in blender container; process until smooth. Chill, covered, for 2 to 4 hours to blend flavors.

Serve this sauce on tacos, cheese crisps and chips.

Roasted Fresh Green Chiles

Fresh green chiles

Yield: variable

Rinse fresh green chiles and pat dry. Place on grill or rack in broiler pan. Grill or broil until skin is blistered on all sides, turning frequently; do not burn. Place chiles in double-thickness paper bag; close bag. Allow to steam in bag for 10 to 15 minutes. Remove skins from chiles, beginning at stem end and pulling down. Remove stems and some of the seeds, which are the hottest part of a chile. May freeze for use when needed.

Early Pottery ⌐

As the hunters and gatherers became more dependent on agriculture, pottery was introduced. Pottery offered an important new means of storage that was dry and safe from rodents and insects. Porous, unglazed Pueblo pottery was ideal for storing food. Moisture in the food could escape through the vessel wall, preventing spoilage.

Pottery styles became more diversified. Pottery was used extensively as utilitarian vessels until metal containers replaced pottery.

Ceramic vessels are being made today by many Pueblo peoples for ceremonial use and for commercial sale.

Hopi Clouds

Vegetables
& Side Dishes

Potatoes

The indigenous peoples of the Andes have been cultivating the potato for at least 4,000 years. The Spanish took the potato back to Europe to replace many grains, such as wheat, rye and oats, that were difficult to grow. By 1573, large quantities of potatoes were used in Spain. From Spain, the potato was introduced into Italy and was so common a food by 1601 that it was eaten even by the poor. Sir Francis Drake is thought to have introduced the potato to England and Ireland sometime after 1586.

Some Europeans were reluctant to accept the potato. It was the first vegetable they had encountered that was grown from tubers rather than seeds. Nevertheless, the potato gained in importance in countries where food was in short supply, because potato farming utilizes land and manpower to a better advantage than growing wheat.

The favorite snack food, potato chips, was created at the Moon Lake Lodge in Saratoga Springs, New York, in 1853. Native American chef George Crum made the first chips in frustration when an irate customer sent back his French fries twice, stating that they were too thick and not sufficiently crisp. The chips, initially called Saratoga Chips, were so successful that Crum opened his own restaurant.

Sweet Potatoes

Columbus encountered new foods when he reached the homeland of the Arawak and Carib peoples in 1492. One of the foods that most fascinated the Spanish was "a cooked root that had the flavor of chestnuts." Frequently confused with yams, a more strongly colored, sweet tuber native to Africa, the sweet potato is a true potato. The Caribbean sweet potato quickly became a favorite of the Spanish explorers, and Columbus took the sweet potato back to the court of Queen Isabella. Columbus called the tuber by the Arawak name, *batata,* which was later changed to the English "potato."

Because the sweet potato is harder to preserve than the white potato, it never gained the popularity in Europe that it enjoys in Africa and Asia. The Chinese, for example, make the sweet potato into a thin noodle that rivals wheat noodles in popularity.

Asparagus Supreme

1	pound fresh asparagus
	Salt and pepper to taste
2	tablespoons chopped onion
2	tablespoons chopped celery
2	tablespoons grated Parmesan cheese
1/4	cup dry bread crumbs
1/4	cup melted butter or margarine
1/4	cup toasted slivered almonds

Yield: 3 to 4 servings

Break off tough ends of asparagus; place spears in shallow baking dish. Season with salt and pepper; sprinkle with onion, celery, Parmesan cheese and bread crumbs. Drizzle with butter. Bake, covered, at 375 degrees for 45 minutes. Sprinkle with almonds to serve.

Microwave Broccoli and Cauliflower Medley

1/4	cup sliced almonds
1	tablespoon butter
1	cup chopped broccoli
1	cup chopped cauliflower
1	teaspoon soy sauce

Yield: 3 servings

Sauté almonds in butter in skillet until light brown. Combine with broccoli, cauliflower and soy sauce in glass dish; mix well. Microwave on High for 4 minutes.

Cholla Buds ⌐

Cholla buds, collected in the spring, are a popular food with many Native Americans. The buds are covered with spines, which must be removed before cooking. The Hopi clean the spines from the buds by putting the buds in a yucca-sifter basket with several pieces of sandstone. They are rolled and shaken, back and forth until the spines are removed. The spineless buds are then steamed or boiled and served as a vegetable. The flavor is a blend of asparagus and artichokes. Cholla buds are low in calories and a 4-ounce serving provides more calcium than an 8-ounce glass of milk.

Broccoli and Cheese

2	10-ounce packages frozen chopped broccoli, thawed, drained
1/3	cup chopped onion
1/2	teaspoon salt
1/3	cup butter
1/2	cup grated Parmesan cheese

Yield: 6 servings

Sauté broccoli and onion with salt in butter in saucepan until tender. Add Parmesan cheese; toss lightly.

Broccoli and Walnut Casserole

3	pounds fresh broccoli or
	3 10-ounce packages frozen broccoli
1/4	cup flour
1 1/2	tablespoons instant chicken bouillon
1/2	cup melted butter
2	cups milk
6	tablespoons butter
2/3	cup hot water
2	cups stuffing mix
2/3	cup chopped walnuts

Yield: 10 servings

Cook broccoli just until tender using package directions; drain. Arrange in buttered 9x13-inch baking dish. Stir flour and bouillon into 1/2 cup melted butter in saucepan. Add milk. Cook until thickened, stirring constantly. Spoon over broccoli. Melt 6 tablespoons butter in hot water in bowl. Stir in stuffing mix. Add walnuts; mix well. Spread over casserole. Bake at 350 degrees for 30 minutes.

Brussels Sprouts with Caramelized Onions

1	**large onion, thinly sliced**
1	**tablespoon olive oil**
1/4	**teaspoon salt**
	Freshly ground pepper to taste
1/2	**cup water**
3/4	**cup dry white wine**
12	**ounces fresh Brussels sprouts**

Yield: 4 servings

Combine onion, olive oil, salt, pepper and water in saucepan. Bring to a boil over high heat; reduce heat to medium. Cook, loosely covered, for 50 to 60 minutes or until caramelized, stirring occasionally. Stir in wine. Bring to a boil. Cook for 8 to 10 minutes or until most of the wine has evaporated. Steam Brussels sprouts in saucepan for 5 to 6 minutes or until tender; drain. Combine with onion in serving dish; toss lightly.

Dilly Green Beans

1	**16-ounce can cut green beans**
1/2	**cup sour cream**
1	**teaspoon fresh lemon juice**
1/8	**teaspoon white pepper**
1	**teaspoon dillweed**

Yield: 4 servings

Heat undrained green beans in saucepan until bubbly. Combine sour cream, lemon juice, pepper and dillweed in small saucepan. Cook until heated through. Drain green beans; place in serving dish. Spoon dill sauce over top.

Green Beans Provençale

1	pound fresh green beans
	Salt to taste
1	clove of garlic, pressed
1	tablespoon olive oil
4	Roma tomatoes, sliced
¹⁄₄	cup tomato juice
1	bay leaf
	Freshly ground pepper to taste

Yield: 6 servings

Trim beans and cut into 2-inch pieces. Combine with salt and boiling water to cover in saucepan. Cook until tender-crisp; drain. Sauté garlic in olive oil in skillet until golden brown. Add tomatoes, tomato juice, salt and bay leaf. Cook for 2 minutes. Add green beans and pepper. Cook for 2 to 3 minutes or until heated through; discard bay leaf.

Sweet and Sour Green Beans

1	16-ounce can whole green beans
¹⁄₄	cup vinegar
¹⁄₄	cup sugar
1	tablespoon vegetable oil

Yield: 4 servings

Drain beans, reserving ¹⁄₄ cup liquid. Combine reserved liquid with vinegar, sugar and oil in saucepan. Bring to a boil; remove from heat. Add beans; let stand for several hours. Serve cold or reheat at serving time.

Devil's Claw (Martynia) ⌇

Devil's claw is cultivated in the Southwest for use as food and as a fiber for basketry. It is a low-lying plant that produces a small green fruit hooked on one end. The young and tender pod, only 1 to 2 inches long, may be steamed and eaten as an okra-like vegetable. The whole green pods may also be pickled. As the pod matures and dries, the hook splits in two and the pod opens, releasing the seeds. The seeds may be dried, cracked, and eaten like sunflower seeds or ground to make mush. The long dark hooks of the mature fruit provide the fiber used to create the black design found in baskets made by Native Americans.

Sautéed Cabbage with Bacon

4	slices bacon, coarsely chopped
1	onion, coarsely chopped
1/2	medium head cabbage, coarsely chopped
1	clove of garlic, pressed
1	7-ounce can chopped tomatoes
	Salt and pepper to taste

Yield: 4 to 6 servings

Fry bacon in skillet until crisp; remove bacon with slotted spoon and drain all but 3 tablespoons drippings from skillet. Sauté onion, cabbage and garlic in reserved drippings until tender. Add undrained tomatoes, salt and pepper; mix well. Simmer for 7 to 8 minutes or until heated through.

Sautéed Red Cabbage

1	medium onion
2	tablespoons butter
1	pound red cabbage, cut into 1/2-inch pieces
1	large unpeeled Granny Smith apple, cut into 1/2-inch pieces
	Salt and pepper to taste
1/8	teaspoon ground cloves
1	tablespoon fresh lemon juice

Yield: 4 to 6 servings

Sauté onion in butter in skillet over medium heat for 3 minutes or until tender. Add cabbage and apple; mix well. Sprinkle with salt, pepper and cloves. Simmer, covered, for 15 minutes or until cabbage is tender, stirring occasionally. Drizzle with lemon juice.

Carrot and Zucchini Casserole

3	large carrots, cut into 2-inch strips
	Salt to taste
3/4	cup boiling water
3	small zucchini, cut into 1/4-inch slices
12	cherry tomatoes, cut in half
2	tablespoons cornstarch
1 1/2	cups milk
2	tablespoons butter or margarine
1	teaspoon salt
	Cayenne pepper to taste
1	cup shredded sharp Cheddar cheese
1/2	cup slivered almonds

Yield: 5 to 6 servings

Cook carrots with salt to taste in boiling water in saucepan for 5 minutes or until tender-crisp; drain. Place carrots, zucchini and tomatoes in 8x13-inch baking dish. Combine cornstarch, milk, butter, 1 teaspoon salt and cayenne pepper in saucepan; mix well. Cook over medium heat until thickened, stirring constantly. Add half the cheese, stirring until melted. Spoon over vegetables; sprinkle with remaining cheese and almonds. Bake at 375 degrees for 30 minutes or until zucchini is tender-crisp.

This casserole is especially colorful for the holidays.

Glazed Curried Carrots

1 1/4	pounds carrots, julienned
1 1/2	tablespoons honey
1	tablespoon fresh lemon juice
1 1/2	teaspoons Dijon mustard
1/2	teaspoon curry powder
1	tablespoon vegetable oil
1 1/2	teaspoons butter
1	tablespoon brown sugar
1/3	cup golden raisins

Yield: 6 servings

Steam carrots in covered pan for 8 to 10 minutes or until tender; remove cover and set aside. Combine honey, lemon juice, mustard and curry powder in small bowl; mix well. Drain carrots. Sauté in mixture of oil and butter in large skillet over medium heat for 3 minutes. Sprinkle with brown sugar and raisins. Cook for 2 minutes, stirring constantly. Add honey mixture. Cook for 3 minutes or until carrots are glazed, stirring constantly. Serve immediately.

Steamed Collards and Red Bell Peppers

1½	pounds collard greens
1	large clove of garlic, thinly sliced
1	teaspoon salt
½	teaspoon pepper
3	tablespoons olive oil
1	small red bell pepper, thinly sliced into strips
1	medium lemon, cut into 8 wedges

Yield: 4 servings

Wash greens, discarding stems. Slice crosswise into ¾-inch strips. Cook, covered, with garlic, salt and pepper in hot oil in large skillet for 10 minutes or until tender. Add bell pepper. Steam, covered, for 5 minutes or until pepper is tender. Remove pepper with slotted spoon. Spoon greens into serving bowl; arrange pepper over greens. Serve immediately with lemon wedges.

Eggplant Casserole

1	eggplant, peeled and sliced
	Salt to taste
2	onions, thinly sliced
8–12	ounces fresh mushrooms, sliced
¼	teaspoon oregano
	Garlic powder to taste
2	cups tomato juice
⅓	cup grated Parmesan cheese

Yield: 4 to 6 servings

Sprinkle eggplant with salt in bowl; weight with plate. Let stand for 30 to 45 minutes. Rinse eggplant and pat dry. Alternate layers of eggplant, onions and mushrooms in 1 to 1½-quart baking dish until all ingredients are used, sprinkling layers with oregano and garlic powder. Pour tomato juice over layers; sprinkle with Parmesan cheese. Bake, covered, at 325 degrees for 30 to 35 minutes. Bake, uncovered, for 15 minutes longer.

This dish is excellent with grilled meat. Just add a salad and rolls to complete the menu.

Eggplant Gratin

1	large unpeeled eggplant, cut into 1/2-inch cubes
1	clove of garlic, pressed
2	large onions, finely chopped
2	tablespoons olive oil
1/3	cup minced fresh parsley
	Salt and pepper to taste
1/2	cup grated Parmesan cheese
1/4	cup dry bread crumbs
3	tablespoons minced fresh parsley
1	tablespoon olive oil

Yield: 2 servings

Steam eggplant for 10 to 12 minutes or until tender; drain well in colander. Sauté garlic and onions in 2 tablespoons hot olive oil in skillet until golden brown. Add eggplant, 1/3 cup parsley, salt and pepper; mix well. Spread evenly in shallow baking dish. Mix Parmesan cheese, bread crumbs and 3 tablespoons parsley in bowl; sprinkle over casserole. Drizzle with 1 tablespoon olive oil. Bake at 400 degrees for 20 to 25 minutes or until bubbly.

This can also be served as a main dish with a green salad and crusty rolls.

Fennel Braised with Vermouth

2	large fennel bulbs with tops
1	small onion, finely chopped
1	clove of garlic, pressed
2	tablespoons olive oil
3/4	cup dry vermouth
1/3	cup half and half
	Salt and pepper to taste
1/2	cup freshly grated Parmesan cheese

Yield: 4 servings

Cut fennel bulbs into 1/2-inch slices. Chop 2 tablespoons leafy tops. Sauté onion and garlic in olive oil in large deep skillet until tender. Add sliced fennel bulbs; mix to coat well. Cook for 3 to 4 minutes, stirring constantly. Add vermouth. Cook for 7 to 8 minutes or until fennel is tender-crisp. Add chopped fennel tops, half and half, salt and pepper. Cook for 5 minutes or until sauce is slightly thickened. Sprinkle with Parmesan cheese; serve immediately.

This is good with pork and veal.

Baked Onion Casserole

1	**10-ounce can cream of mushroom soup**
1/2	**cup milk**
6	**large onions, thinly sliced**
1/2	**teaspoon salt**
	Pepper to taste
1	**cup shredded Swiss cheese**

Yield: 4 to 6 servings

Combine soup and milk in bowl; mix well. Spread 1/4 cup of the mixture in buttered 8 or 9-inch baking dish. Layer half the onions, salt, pepper and cheese in prepared dish. Top with remaining onions, salt, pepper, soup mixture and cheese. Bake at 350 degrees for 45 minutes or until golden brown and bubbly.

This dish is great with beef tenderloin.

Baked Stuffed Onions

6	**medium Vidalia or other sweet onions**
1	**clove of garlic, pressed**
1/2	**teaspoon vegetable oil**
1	**bunch spinach, coarsely chopped**
1/2	**teaspoon salt**
1/4	**cup golden raisins, plumped**
1/2	**cup plain yogurt**
1/4	**cup toasted pine nuts**
1	**tablespoon grated orange zest**
1/8	**teaspoon nutmeg**
3	**tablespoons fresh bread crumbs**

Yield: 6 servings

Trim thin slice from root ends of onions to level. Cut 1/2-inch slice from tops of onions and reserve. Hollow out onions with melon baller, leaving 1/2-inch shells; reserve centers. Place onion shells on rack in steamer over 1 inch boiling water. Steam, covered, for 10 to 15 minutes or until onions appear tender when pierced with point of knife; invert to drain. Chop reserved onion slices and centers. Sauté chopped onion and garlic in oil in skillet over medium heat until brown. Add spinach. Cook until spinach is wilted. Add salt. Cook until moisture has evaporated, stirring occasionally. Cool in bowl. Add raisins, yogurt, pine nuts, orange zest and nutmeg; mix well. Spoon spinach mixture into drained onion shells; spread any remaining stuffing mixture in baking dish. Place onions in prepared dish; sprinkle with bread crumbs. Bake at 350 degrees for 20 to 25 minutes. Broil just until golden brown. Serve with additional stuffing mixture.

Potato and Escarole Gratin with Rosemary

3	large unpeeled baking potatoes, thinly sliced
1	large onion, thinly sliced
1/4	teaspoon salt
1	tablespoon olive oil
1	small to medium head escarole, coarsely chopped
	Freshly ground pepper to taste
1	tablespoon olive oil
2	cloves of garlic, pressed
1	teaspoon rosemary, crushed
1/4	teaspoon salt
1/4	cup half and half

Yield: 4 to 6 servings

Combine potatoes with cool water to cover in bowl; set aside. Sauté onion with 1/4 teaspoon salt in 1 tablespoon olive oil in deep heavy skillet for 8 to 10 minutes or until tender. Add escarole and pepper. Cook for 2 to 3 minutes or until escarole is wilted, stirring constantly; remove from heat. Drain potatoes and pat dry. Combine with 1 tablespoon olive oil, garlic, rosemary and 1/4 teaspoon salt in bowl; mix well. Layer half the potatoes, escarole mixture and remaining potatoes in 8x8-inch baking dish. Bake, covered, at 450 degrees for 30 minutes. Pour half and half evenly over layers. Bake, uncovered, for 30 minutes longer or until potatoes are light brown and tender. *May substitute spinach for escarole.*

Baked Sliced Potatoes

4	large unpeeled baking potatoes
1/4	cup melted butter or margarine
1/4	cup vegetable oil
2	cloves of garlic, minced or pressed
1/2–1	teaspoon salt
1/2	teaspoon dried thyme leaves

Yield: 4 servings

Cut potatoes into 1/4-inch slices; arrange in overlapping layer in buttered 9x13-inch baking dish. Brush with mixture of butter and oil; drizzle remaining oil mixture over top. Sprinkle with garlic, salt and thyme. Bake at 400 degrees for 25 to 30 minutes or until potatoes are tender and edges are brown. Serve immediately.

Make-Ahead Mashed Potatoes

6	medium potatoes, peeled, cut into quarters
	Salt to taste
1/2	cup sour cream
1	3-ounce package cream cheese, chopped
1	teaspoon onion salt
1/4	teaspoon pepper
2	tablespoons butter or margarine
1/4–1/2	cup milk

Yield: 6 servings

Cook potatoes, covered, in salted boiling water to cover in saucepan for 20 to 25 minutes or until tender or microwave in 1/2 cup water in glass dish on High for 15 to 20 minutes; drain. Mash potatoes by hand or with mixer at low speed until smooth. Add sour cream, cream cheese, onion salt, pepper and 1 tablespoon butter. Add milk, beating until mixture is smooth and fluffy. Spoon into greased 1 1/2-quart baking dish; dot with remaining 1 tablespoon butter. Let stand until baking time or chill, covered with foil, for up to 24 hours. Bake at 350 degrees for 45 minutes or until heated through or microwave, covered, on High for 8 to 10 minutes, stirring once. May double recipe and bake in 3-quart dish for 1 hour or microwave doubled recipe in 2 dishes.

Bavarian Sauerkraut

1	7-ounce package long grain and wild rice mix
1	medium green bell pepper, chopped
1	medium onion, chopped
3	tablespoons margarine
2	cups drained sauerkraut
2	tablespoons honey
1	tablespoon caraway seeds
1/2	teaspoon seasoned salt
	Pepper to taste

Yield: 6 to 8 servings

Cook rice mix using package directions. Sauté green pepper and onion in margarine in saucepan until tender. Stir in sauerkraut, honey, caraway seeds and seasoned salt. Add rice and pepper; toss to mix well. Cook until heated through.

This is excellent with grilled meats that do not have a gravy.

Spinach Squares

2	10-ounce packages frozen chopped spinach
6	eggs
16	ounces cottage cheese
	Garlic salt, salt and pepper to taste
1¹/₂	cups shredded Cheddar cheese

Yield: 8 to 10 servings

Cook spinach using package directions; drain. Beat eggs in mixer bowl until light. Add cottage cheese, spinach, garlic salt, salt, pepper and 1 cup cheese; mix well. Spoon into greased 9x9-inch baking dish; sprinkle with remaining ¹/₂ cup cheese. Bake at 350 degrees for 45 minutes or until set. Cut into squares to serve.

Spinach Torte

2	10-ounce packages frozen chopped spinach
1	10-ounce can cream of mushroom soup
¹/₄	cup milk
2	eggs, beaten
2	tablespoons grated Parmesan cheese
	Salt and pepper to taste
	Butter

Yield: 8 servings

Cook spinach using package directions; drain. Combine soup and milk in bowl. Add eggs, Parmesan cheese, salt and pepper; mix well. Fold in spinach. Spoon into greased 2-quart baking dish; dot with butter. Bake at 350 degrees for 30 minutes or until set.

Wild Plants ⌒

There is a revival of interest in the use of wild plants commonly used by Native people of the Southwest. Shirley Blatchford, who grew up in Cochiti Pueblo, New Mexico, tells how her grandmother gathered wild plants: "In March, mushrooms were gathered. Later in the spring, the wild spinach which grew along the canal banks was picked. She would venture out further to gather large amounts of young beeweed and cook it in a large pot. People in Cochiti would come and barter for a bowl of it, offering coffee, fabric, or food staples in return. Wild Celery was a popular green. It needs to be picked before the yellow flowers form. The celery root also may be eaten. Clusters of small red sumac berries (rhus glabra) were gathered in late summer and fall. They were used to make 'Indian Kool-Aid'."

Squash and Green Chiles

2	pounds squash, chopped
1/2	cup chopped onion
	Salt to taste
1	4-ounce can chopped green chiles
2	eggs
3/4	cup half and half
1/2	cup buttered bread crumbs
1/2	cup shredded Cheddar cheese

Yield: 6 servings

Cook squash and onion in salted boiling water in saucepan just until tender; drain. Add chiles; mash to mix well. Beat eggs with half and half in bowl. Add to squash; mix well. Stir in half the bread crumbs and cheese. Spoon into buttered baking dish; top with remaining bread crumbs and cheese. Bake at 325 degrees for 25 to 30 minutes or until set.

You may use summer squash, yellow crookneck squash or zucchini in this dish.

Baked Summer Squash

2–2 1/2	pounds yellow squash
1/2	cup sour cream
1/4	cup melted butter
2	green onions with tops, minced
	Salt and pepper to taste
	Buttered fresh bread crumbs
1/4	cup grated Parmesan cheese (optional)

Yield: 6 servings

Slice squash 1/4 inch thick. Cook in a small amount of water in saucepan for 5 to 10 minutes or just until tender; drain. Mash lightly and drain again. Add sour cream, butter, green onions, salt and pepper; mix well. Spoon into buttered 1-quart baking dish. Top with bread crumbs and Parmesan cheese. Chill until baking time. Bake in preheated 350-degree oven for 25 minutes or until bubbly.

Squash Casserole

1	pound winter squash, sliced
2	onions, sliced
	Salt to taste
1/4	cup butter or margarine
1	egg
1/4	cup milk
1	teaspoon sugar
	Pepper to taste
1	cup shredded Cheddar cheese
1	cup bread crumbs

Yield: 4 servings

Cook squash and onions in salted boiling water in saucepan until tender-crisp; drain. Beat until smooth. Add butter, egg, milk, sugar, salt, pepper and 2/3 cup cheese; mix well. Spoon into buttered baking dish; top with remaining 1/3 cup cheese and bread crumbs. Bake at 350 degrees for 30 to 35 minutes or until light brown.

Indian Squash

2	zucchini, chopped
2	summer squash, chopped
2	yellow squash, chopped
1	yellow onion, chopped
	Kernels of 1 ear fresh corn
1	tablespoon bacon drippings
	Salt and pepper to taste

Yield: 4 servings

Combine squash, onion and corn in heavy saucepan. Stir in bacon drippings, salt and pepper; mix well. Cook over high heat for several minutes or until squash is tender and onion is slightly brown around edges, stirring occasionally.

May substitute 1 drained 15-ounce can whole kernel corn for fresh corn, adding about halfway through cooking time. May use any soft-skinned squash in this recipe.

Spaghetti Squash

1   **small spaghetti squash**
1   **small onion, chopped**
1   **teaspoon basil**
2   **tablespoons olive oil**
2   **tomatoes, chopped**
       Salt and pepper to taste

Yield: 4 servings

Pierce squash in several places with fork; place on baking sheet. Bake at 350 degrees for 1 hour or until fork-tender. Sauté onion and basil in olive oil in medium skillet for 5 minutes. Add tomatoes. Cook for 10 minutes, stirring frequently. Season with salt and pepper. Simmer while preparing squash. Cut squash into halves lengthwise, discarding seeds. Remove strands to skillet with fork; mix gently. Cook just until heated through, tossing gently. Garnish servings with grated Parmesan cheese.

Gold and Green Zucchini Casserole

2   **pounds zucchini**
       Salt to taste
1/2   **cup water**
2   **eggs, beaten**
1/2   **teaspoon salt**
1/8   **teaspoon pepper**
1   **teaspoon grated onion**
1   **12-ounce can whole kernel corn, drained**
8   **ounces mild Cheddar cheese, shredded**

Yield: 5 to 6 servings

Slice zucchini 1/4 inch thick. Cook with salt to taste in water in saucepan for 10 minutes or until tender; drain. Mash well. Combine eggs, 1/2 teaspoon salt, pepper and onion in bowl; mix well. Stir in zucchini, corn and half the cheese. Spoon into greased 2-quart baking dish; top with remaining cheese. Bake at 350 degrees for 30 to 40 minutes or until set.

This is a wonderful vegetarian dish to take to potluck dinners.

Skillet Zucchini

6	medium zucchini
1	bunch green onions, chopped
1/2	cup chopped parsley
1	clove of garlic, minced
3	tablespoons olive oil
	Salt and pepper to taste
3	tablespoons water

Yield: 6 to 8 servings

Slice zucchini 1/2 inch thick. Combine with green onions, parsley and garlic in bowl. Sauté vegetable mixture in heated olive oil in skillet until light brown. Add salt, pepper and water. Simmer, covered, just until zucchini is tender-crisp.

Zucchini Pancakes

1/3	cup flour
1/2	teaspoon baking powder
1/8	teaspoon freshly grated pepper
1/4	cup freshly grated Parmesan cheese
1	medium onion, finely chopped
2	eggs, slightly beaten
2	cups shredded unpeeled zucchini

Yield: 12 to 14 servings

Mix flour, baking powder, pepper and Parmesan cheese in bowl. Add onion, eggs and zucchini; mix well. Drop by tablespoonfuls onto heated nonstick griddle. Cook until brown on both sides. Serve warm.

May freeze on plastic wrap and store in plastic bag; reheat in 325-degree oven.

Broiled Tomatoes

4	medium tomatoes
	Dijon mustard
	Salt, black pepper and cayenne pepper to taste
1/2	cup seasoned dry bread crumbs
1/2	cup grated Parmesan cheese
6	tablespoons melted butter

Yield: 8 servings

Cut tomatoes into halves. Spread cut sides of tomatoes with mustard; sprinkle with salt, black pepper and cayenne pepper. Toss bread crumbs and Parmesan cheese with butter in small bowl. Sprinkle on tomatoes; place on baking sheet. Broil 12 inches from heat source until tomatoes are tender and topping is brown.

Tomatoes Stuffed with Zucchini

6	medium tomatoes
	Salt and pepper to taste
6	medium unpeeled zucchini, thinly sliced
1 1/2	teaspoons dried basil leaves
1/4	cup olive oil
2	cloves of garlic, pressed
2	tablespoons finely chopped fresh parsley
2	tablespoons butter
1	tablespoon finely chopped fresh parsley

Yield: 6 servings

Cut tops from tomatoes and scoop out pulp. Sprinkle with salt and pepper; invert to drain. Stir-fry zucchini and basil in olive oil in large skillet over medium-high heat for 4 to 5 minutes. Remove to drain on paper towel; sprinkle with salt and pepper. Sauté garlic and 2 tablespoons parsley in butter in same skillet for 2 minutes. Return zucchini to skillet; mix well. Spoon into tomato shells; sprinkle with 1 tablespoon parsley. Place in greased baking dish. Bake at 375 degrees for 15 minutes.

This dish goes well with baked chicken.

Italian Ratatouille

1	large white onion, chopped
2	cloves of garlic, minced
2	tablespoons olive oil
1	14-ounce can chopped peeled tomatoes
1	each red and yellow bell pepper, cut into 1½-inch squares
1	medium unpeeled eggplant, cut into 1½-inch squares
	Salt and pepper to taste

Yield: 8 servings

Sauté onion and garlic in olive oil in large heavy skillet for 10 minutes or until tender. Add tomatoes, peppers and eggplant; season generously with salt and pepper. Cook for 30 to 40 minutes or until most of the liquid has evaporated, stirring occasionally. Spoon onto serving platter. May drizzle with extra-virgin olive oil and garnish with minced fresh parsley.

This dish may be made in advance, cooled and chilled, covered, for up to 2 days. Serve cold or reheat gently to serve.

Dilled Vegetables

1	6-ounce jar marinated artichoke hearts
3	tomatoes, cut into quarters
2	6-ounce zucchini, thinly sliced
2	6-ounce yellow squash, thinly sliced
2	teaspoons fresh lemon juice
1	teaspoon dillweed
¼	teaspoon sugar
½	teaspoon salt

Yield: 4 to 6 servings

Combine undrained artichoke hearts, tomatoes, zucchini, yellow squash, lemon juice, dillweed, sugar and salt in saucepan. Cook for 5 minutes or until squash is tender, stirring occasionally.

Julienne Vegetable Sauté

1	green bell pepper
1	red bell pepper
2	large carrots
2	large zucchini
1	medium onion, chopped
2	cloves of garlic, pressed
1/3	cup vegetable oil
2	teaspoons dried basil
1/2	teaspoon salt

Yield: 6 to 8 servings

Cut peppers, carrots and zucchini into 1/4x2-inch julienne strips. Sauté peppers, carrots, onion and garlic in oil in heated large skillet for 5 minutes. Add zucchini. Sauté for 2 minutes longer. Stir in basil and salt; serve immediately.

Mixed Vegetable Gratin

2	very large unpeeled baking potatoes, thinly sliced
3	medium zucchini, sliced 1/8 inch thick
10	Italian plum tomatoes, sliced 1/4 inch thick
1	cup shredded Gruyère cheese
1	teaspoon *fines herbes*
	Salt and pepper to taste
2	cloves of garlic, pressed
1/2	cup extra-virgin olive oil
10	fresh basil leaves, shredded

Yield: 6 to 8 servings

Layer potatoes, zucchini, tomatoes, cheese, *fines herbes*, salt and pepper 1/2 at a time in shallow oval 9x12-inch baking dish. Sauté garlic in olive oil in small saucepan for 5 to 6 minutes. Drizzle oil over vegetables. Bake at 425 degrees for 45 to 50 minutes or until vegetables are tender. Sprinkle with basil.

This dish is very good with lamb or veal.

Barley and Mushroom Pilaf

1	cup uncooked barley
2	tablespoons butter or margarine
1	large onion, chopped
8	ounces mushrooms, sliced
2	tablespoons butter or margarine
2½	cups chicken broth
1	cup toasted almonds (optional)

Yield: 6 servings

Sauté barley in 2 tablespoons butter in skillet until golden brown. Remove barley to buttered baking dish. Add remaining 2 tablespoons butter, onion and mushrooms to skillet. Sauté until tender; add to baking dish. Pour 1 cup broth over barley mixture; mix gently. Bake at 350 degrees for 40 minutes. Add 1 cup broth; mix well. Bake for 40 minutes. Stir in remaining ½ cup broth. Bake for 30 minutes longer. Stir in almonds at serving time.

Grits and Vegetable Casserole

6	ounces Gruyère or Swiss cheese, chopped
1	quart skim milk
¼	cup butter or margarine
¼	teaspoon pepper
1	cup quick-cooking grits
1–1½	cups finely chopped onion
1	cup chopped fresh parsley
1–1½	cups chopped celery
1	cup chopped yellow and red bell pepper
3–5	cloves of garlic, minced
¼	cup butter or margarine
⅓	cup grated Parmesan or Romano cheese

Yield: 12 servings

Melt cheese in milk in saucepan over medium heat, stirring to blend well. Add ¼ cup butter, pepper and grits; mix well. Cook until thickened, stirring constantly. Sauté onion, parsley, celery, bell pepper and garlic in ¼ cup butter in skillet; drain in colander. Add to grits mixture; mix well. Spoon into greased 9x13-inch baking dish. Sprinkle with Parmesan cheese. Bake, covered, at 350 degrees for 30 minutes. Let stand for 20 to 30 minutes before serving. May substitute 2 tablespoons vegetable oil for ¼ cup butter or margarine for grits as well as for sautéing vegetables.

This dish freezes well and reheats easily in oven or microwave.

Nippies

1	cup flour
1/2	teaspoon salt
1	egg
1/4	cup (about) milk

Yield: 3 to 4 servings

Combine flour, salt, egg and milk in bowl; mix to form soft dough. Drop by teaspoonfuls into boiling water in saucepan. Cook for 10 to 12 minutes or until dumplings are cooked through; dumplings will not rise to surface. Garnish with butter or margarine to serve.

These are good served with sauerkraut and spareribs or beef stew.

Kugel Noodle Pudding

16	ounces uncooked medium noodles
6	eggs
2	cups buttermilk
1/2	cup melted butter
1/2	cup sugar
1/2	teaspoon salt

Yield: 15 servings

Cook noodles using package directions; rinse and drain. Beat eggs in mixer bowl until light. Add buttermilk, butter, sugar and salt; mix well. Add to noodles; mix gently. Spoon into greased 9x13-inch baking dish. Bake in preheated 350-degree oven for 1 hour.

This dish can be made in advance and chilled or frozen until needed. It is especially good with chicken or fish.

Orzo with Basil and Pine Nuts

2	ounces pine nuts
3	tablespoons olive oil
1	cup chopped fresh basil
	Salt and pepper to taste
16	ounces uncooked orzo
1	teaspoon salt
2	quarts boiling water

Yield: 6 to 8 servings

Sauté pine nuts in olive oil in small saucepan over high heat for 2 to 3 minutes or until golden brown. Stir in basil and salt and pepper to taste. Cook pasta with 1 teaspoon salt in boiling water in saucepan until tender; drain. Combine with pine nut mixture in large bowl; toss to mix well.

Orzo with Tomatoes

3/4	cup uncooked orzo
	Salt to taste
6	cups boiling water
1	teaspoon minced garlic
2	tablespoons olive oil
8	ounces plum tomatoes, cored, cut into 1/2-inch pieces
	Freshly ground pepper to taste
2	tablespoons loosely packed chopped fresh basil or Italian parsley
2	tablespoons freshly grated Parmesan cheese

Yield: 4 servings

Cook pasta in salted boiling water in saucepan for 10 minutes or just until tender; drain. Sauté garlic in olive oil in saucepan until tender; do not overcook. Add tomatoes, salt and pepper. Cook for 3 minutes, stirring constantly. Stir in pasta, basil and Parmesan cheese. Serve immediately.

Food Gathering ⁓

The group activity of food gathering is still practiced by Native Americans in the Southwest for piñons and acorns. Piñons (pine nuts) are picked in the fall or early winter. The nuts are high in protein and fat. Piñons can be shelled and eaten raw or roasted in the shell. They can also be boiled into a gruel, or ground and formed into cakes. Piñons are gathered for sale by the Hopi and Navajo. The nuts are highly prized for their flavor and are used in many cake, cookie and dressing recipes.

Acorns ripen in late July or August. They are gathered by Apache women who shell and grind them into meal, which is used to thicken stews or to flavor bread.

Green Rice

3	cups cooked rice
1	cup chopped fresh parsley or
	½ cup dried parsley
½	cup shredded Cheddar cheese
⅓	cup chopped onion
1	4-ounce can chopped green chiles
1	clove of garlic, minced
1	13-ounce can evaporated milk
2	eggs, beaten
½	cup vegetable oil
1	teaspoon salt
½	teaspoon pepper
1	tablespoon fresh lemon juice
	Paprika to taste

Yield: 6 to 8 servings

Combine rice, parsley, cheese, onion, chiles and garlic in greased 2-quart baking dish. Combine evaporated milk, eggs, oil, salt, pepper and lemon juice in bowl; mix well. Pour over rice mixture; sprinkle with paprika. Bake in preheated 350-degree oven for 45 minutes or until knife inserted at edge comes out clean.

Parsley and Rice Ring

3	cups cooked rice
1	cup chopped parsley
2	eggs, beaten
1	cup milk
1	tablespoon Worcestershire sauce
1½	teaspoons salt
2	teaspoons chopped green onions
¼	cup melted butter or margarine
½	cup shredded sharp Cheddar cheese

Yield: 6 servings

Toss rice with parsley in bowl. Add eggs, milk, Worcestershire sauce, salt, green onions and butter; mix well. Add cheese; mix lightly. Spoon into greased ring mold or baking dish. Place ring mold in large baking pan with 1 inch hot water. Bake at 325 degrees for 40 minutes. Unmold ring mold onto serving plate.

Wild Rice Casserole

1	7-ounce package long grain and wild rice mix
1	cup chopped celery
1/2	cup each chopped green and red bell pepper
1/4	cup butter or margarine
1	4-ounce can mushrooms, drained
1	8-ounce can sliced water chestnuts, drained
1/2	teaspoon salt
1	cup whipping cream, whipped

Yield: 6 to 8 servings

Cook rice using package directions, omitting seasoning packet. Sauté celery and bell peppers in butter in saucepan. Add to rice with mushrooms, water chestnuts and salt; mix well. Fold in whipped cream. Spoon into 2-quart baking dish. Bake at 325 degrees for 25 minutes.

Grandmother's Apple and Raisin Stuffing

6	medium tart apples, peeled, chopped
1	medium onion, chopped
3	stalks celery, chopped
1/2	cup butter, margarine or turkey or chicken fat
1	1 1/2-pound loaf of bread, cubed
1/2	cup raisins
2	teaspoons cinnamon
1/4	teaspoon nutmeg
3/4	teaspoon allspice
2	eggs, slightly beaten
4 1/2	cups chicken broth
1	tablespoon melted butter or margarine

Yield: 12 servings

Sauté apples, onion and celery in 1/2 cup butter in skillet until tender. Combine with bread cubes, raisins, cinnamon, nutmeg and allspice in bowl. Add mixture of eggs and chicken broth; mix lightly. Spoon into 9x13-inch baking dish. Brush top with 1 tablespoon melted butter. Bake at 350 degrees for 45 minutes or until puffed and brown.

May reduce recipe by 1/2 and bake in 8x8-inch baking dish if preferred.

Acoma Great Star

Desserts

Pineapple

The Spanish reported on another new food that they found amazing: "There are also some like the artichoke plant but four times as tall which give a fruit in the shape of a pine cone, twice as big, which fruit is excellent and it can be cut with a knife like a turnip and it seems very wholesome." They had discovered pineapple.

Pineapples became popular in Europe in 1514—before coffee was introduced and well before chocolate was brought from Mexico. At first, however, the pineapple was considered a curiosity and a challenge to the hothouse gardeners. In 1670, Charles II was made a gift of the first pineapple grown in England, and the fruit became a traditional gift to bring to a host or hostess in colonial America. Hence the use of the pineapple motif over doorways, on door knockers and in centerpieces for banquets and other social events. It was not until 1732, when Richard Bradley published his second cookbook, that a recipe for pineapple appeared in English.

Vanilla

Vanilla was also discovered by the native peoples of Mexico. Vanilla is the seed pod of only one of 35,000 orchids known to man. The first peoples to realize that the fermented seed pods have fragrance and taste were the Totonac peoples, who live in the Mexican state of Vera Cruz. More than 1,000 years ago the Totonacs discovered a method for curing the beans and brought the vine into intense cultivation. Vanilla beans became an integral part of Totonac culture and were used for perfume, flavoring, medicine and insect repellent.

When the Aztecs conquered the Totonacs, 500 years before the arrival of Cortés, they demanded vanilla beans as a part of their tribute. "Chocolatl," the dish of Aztec royalty, was made from cacao, maize, honey and vanilla.

By 1510, vanilla was introduced into Spain, where its popularity grew. By 1602, it was known in Great Britain and Queen Elizabeth I became a devotee of vanilla. In her later years, she is said to have eaten only food flavored with vanilla.

Date and Nut Torte

2	eggs
1	cup sugar
1	teaspoon vanilla extract
2	tablespoons flour
2	teaspoons baking powder
1¼	cups chopped dates
1	cup chopped walnuts
1	cup whipping cream, whipped

Yield: 6 to 8 servings

Beat eggs with sugar in mixer bowl until smooth. Stir in vanilla. Fold in mixture of flour and baking powder. Fold in dates and walnuts. Spoon into greased 8x8 or round 9-inch baking pan. Bake at 325 degrees for 30 minutes or until light brown. Serve with whipped cream.

This is also good with ice cream.

Old-Fashioned Apple and Spice Cake

4	cups chopped peeled apples
6	tablespoons brandy
2	eggs
2	cups sugar
½	cup vegetable oil
2	cups flour
2	teaspoons baking soda
2	teaspoons cinnamon
1	teaspoon nutmeg
½	teaspoon cloves
½	teaspoon salt
1	cup chopped walnuts
1	cup plumped raisins

Yield: 16 to 18 servings

Combine apples with brandy in bowl; mix well. Let stand to absorb flavor, stirring occasionally. Beat eggs with sugar and oil in large mixer bowl. Mix flour, baking soda, cinnamon, nutmeg, cloves and salt together. Add to egg mixture; mix well. Stir in apples, walnuts and raisins. Spoon into greased and floured 9x13-inch cake pan. Bake in preheated 325-degree oven for 1 hour or until wooden pick inserted in cake comes out clean. Serve warm or cooled.

This also may be baked in muffin cups.

Pineapple Cake

2	eggs
1	cup sugar
2	cups flour
2	teaspoons baking soda
1	20-ounce can crushed pineapple
1	cup chopped walnuts
1	teaspoon fresh lemon juice

Yield: 16 to 20 servings

Beat eggs and sugar in mixer bowl until smooth. Add flour, baking soda, undrained pineapple, walnuts and lemon juice; mix well. Spoon into bundt pan sprayed with nonstick cooking spray. Bake at 350 degrees for 40 minutes. Remove to wire rack to cool.

May bake in miniature muffin cups at 400 degrees for 12 to 15 minutes if preferred.

Gâteau Grand Marnier

1	cup butter, softened
1	cup sugar
3	egg yolks
1	teaspoon Grand Marnier
2	cups flour
1	teaspoon baking soda
1	teaspoon baking powder
1¼	cups sour cream
	Grated rind of 1 orange
1	cup chopped pecans
3	egg whites, stiffly beaten
½	cup sugar
1	cup orange juice
⅓	cup Grand Marnier

Yield: 10 to 12 servings

Cream butter and sugar in mixer bowl until fluffy. Beat in egg yolks 1 at a time. Add 1 teaspoon Grand Marnier. Sift flour, baking soda and baking powder together. Add to batter alternately with sour cream, mixing well after each addition. Stir in orange rind and pecans. Fold in egg whites. Spoon into greased 9-inch tube pan. Bake at 350 degrees for 50 to 55 minutes or until cake tests done. Combine ½ cup sugar, orange juice and ⅓ cup Grand Marnier in bowl; mix well. Pour over hot cake in pan. Cool in pan on wire rack. Invert onto serving plate.

This is a grand finale to any meal.

Party Cake Elegante

1   2-layer package yellow cake mix
1¹/₂ cups plain yogurt
1   6-ounce can frozen lemonade
      concentrate, thawed
1   14-ounce can sweetened condensed
      milk
4   kiwifruit, peeled, sliced
1   pint fresh strawberries or
      raspberries, sliced

Yield: 10 to 12 servings

Prepare and bake cake mix using package directions for two 9-inch cake pans. Remove layers to wire rack to cool. Split layers horizontally into halves. Combine yogurt, lemonade concentrate and condensed milk in bowl; mix well. Spread mixture over cake layers. Stack cake layers with fruit between, alternating kiwifruit and strawberries. Spread remaining lemonade mixture over top of cake; mixture will run down sides of cake. Decorate top of cake with concentric rings of remaining fruit. Chill until serving time.

Black Russian Cake

1   2-layer package yellow cake mix
1   3-ounce package chocolate instant
      pudding mix
1   cup vegetable oil
³/₄   cup water
4   eggs
¹/₄   cup vodka
¹/₄   cup Kahlua
      Confectioners' sugar
8   red and green candied cherries

Yield: 12 to 14 servings

Combine cake mix, pudding mix, oil, water, eggs, vodka and Kahlua in mixer bowl; beat at medium speed for 4 minutes. Spoon into greased and floured 10-inch bundt pan. Bake at 350 degrees for 55 minutes. Cool in pan on wire rack for 30 minutes. Invert onto cake plate. Sprinkle with confectioners' sugar. Cut red cherries into halves; arrange on top of cake. Cut green cherries into quarters; arrange on either side of red cherries.

Cherry and Almond Glazed Sponge Cake

1   cup butter or margarine, softened
1¹/₂ cups sugar
4   eggs
1   teaspoon almond extract
2   cups flour
1   21-ounce can cherry pie filling
¹/₄   cup sliced almonds
      Confectioners' sugar

Yield: 15 servings

Cream butter and sugar in mixer bowl until light and fluffy. Beat in eggs 1 at a time, beating well after each addition. Stir in almond extract. Add flour; mix well. Spread in greased 10x15-inch cake pan. Mark off 15 servings lightly with tip of knife. Spoon equal portions of pie filling into center of each square; sprinkle with almonds. Bake at 350 degrees for 30 to 35 minutes or until light brown. Cool in pan on wire rack. Sprinkle with confectioners' sugar. Cut into squares.

Pecan Roll

4   egg yolks
1   cup confectioners' sugar, sifted
4   egg whites, stiffly beaten
1   cup finely chopped pecans
1   cup whipping cream
2   tablespoons sugar
2   tablespoons baking cocoa
1   tablespoon confectioners' sugar

Yield: 12 to 14 servings

Beat egg yolks with 1 cup confectioners' sugar in mixer bowl until smooth. Fold in stiffly beaten egg whites and pecans. Spoon into greased 10x15-inch cake pan lined with greased waxed paper. Place in oven preheated to 400 degrees; reduce oven temperature to 375 degrees. Bake for 20 to 25 minutes or until light brown. Invert onto towel sprinkled with additional confectioners' sugar. Remove waxed paper. Roll up in towel; let stand until cool. Beat whipping cream, sugar and baking cocoa in mixer bowl until soft peaks form. Unroll cake; spread with cream mixture. Roll cake to enclose filling. Place on serving plate; sift 1 tablespoon confectioners' sugar over top.

Chocolate-Port Wine Torte

1	cup baking cocoa
2	cups boiling water
1	cup butter, softened
2¹/₂	cups sugar
4	eggs
1¹/₂	teaspoons vanilla extract
2³/₄	cups sifted cake flour
2	teaspoons baking soda
¹/₂	teaspoon salt
¹/₂	teaspoon baking powder
¹/₂	cup Port wine
1	cup red raspberry preserves
	Fudge Frosting

Yield: 1 (3-layer) cake

Combine baking cocoa and boiling water in bowl; beat with wire whisk until smooth. Let stand until cool. Combine butter, sugar, eggs and vanilla in large mixer bowl. Beat at high speed for 5 minutes. Sift dry ingredients together. Add dry ingredients ¹/₄ at a time to sugar mixture alternately with cocoa mixture, beginning and ending with dry ingredients and beating constantly at low speed. Do not overbeat. Pour batter into 3 greased and floured 9-inch round cake pans. Bake at 350 degrees for 25 to 30 minutes or until layers test done. Cool in pans for 10 minutes. Invert onto wire racks to cool. Sprinkle bottoms of layers with wine. Stack two of the layers top side down on cake plate, spreading each layer with ¹/₂ cup preserves. Place remaining layer top side up on cake. Spread Fudge Frosting over top and side of cake.

Fudge Frosting

1	cup semisweet chocolate chips
¹/₂	cup half and half
1	cup butter
2¹/₂	cups confectioners' sugar

Combine chocolate chips, half and half and butter in saucepan. Cook over medium heat until smooth, stirring constantly. Remove from heat. Add confectioners' sugar; mix well. Beat until of spreading consistency.

Cheesecake

2	pounds cream-style cottage cheese
1	8-ounce package cream cheese, softened
8	eggs
1½	cups sugar
2	tablespoons melted butter
2	cups sour cream
1	tablespoon flour
	Juice of 1 lemon
1	teaspoon vanilla extract
	Zwieback Cheesecake Crust

Yield: 10 to 12 servings

Combine cottage cheese and cream cheese in blender container; process until smooth. Add eggs, sugar, butter, sour cream, flour, lemon juice and vanilla gradually, processing constantly until smooth. Spoon into cooled Zwieback Cheesecake Crust. Bake at 350 degrees for 45 to 60 minutes or until puffed and evenly browned. Turn off oven; leave door ajar. Let cheesecake stand until oven is cool. Chill cheesecake overnight. Place on serving plate; remove side of pan.

Zwieback Cheesecake Crust

1	6-ounce package Zwieback
1	teaspoon cinnamon
1	cup sugar
½	cup melted butter

Process Zwieback, cinnamon and sugar in blender until Zwieback are finely crushed. Add butter; process until well mixed. Press into buttered 9-inch springform pan. Bake at 350 degrees for 10 minutes. Cool slightly.

Easy Low-Fat Cheesecake

1½	cups graham cracker crumbs
3	tablespoons melted margarine
1	cup low-fat cottage cheese
2	cups plain nonfat yogurt
½	cup sugar
1	tablespoon flour
1	egg
2	egg whites
2	teaspoons vanilla extract
2	cups raspberries, strawberries or blueberries

Yield: 10 servings

Mix graham cracker crumbs and margarine in bowl. Press firmly over bottom and part way up side of 8-inch springform pan. Bake at 350 degrees for 7 minutes; reduce oven temperature to 300 degrees. Cool crust on wire rack. Process cottage cheese and yogurt in blender for 1 minute or until smooth. Add sugar, flour, egg, egg whites and vanilla; process until smooth. Spoon into crust. Bake for 55 minutes or until center is nearly set when cheesecake is shaken. Cool on wire rack. Chill, tightly wrapped, for 8 hours to overnight. Top servings with berries.

Raspberry Essence Pots de Crème

1	cup chocolate chips
2	tablespoons sugar
	Salt to taste
1	tablespoon raspberry liqueur
1	egg
¾	cup milk, scalded, cooled

Yield: 6 servings

Combine chocolate chips, sugar, salt, liqueur, egg and milk in blender container; process for 1 minute or until smooth. Spoon into 6 ramekins. Chill for 4 hours or until firm. Garnish servings with whipped cream.

Lemon Soufflé with Raspberry Sauce

2	envelopes unflavored gelatin
1/2	cup cold water
2/3	cup fresh lemon juice
6	eggs
1 1/2	cups sugar
2	cups whipping cream, whipped
1	tablespoon grated lemon rind
	Raspberry Sauce

Yield: 12 servings

Tie collar of waxed paper around 1 1/2-quart soufflé dish. Set aside. Sprinkle gelatin over water in saucepan. Let stand for 10 minutes or until softened. Heat over low heat until gelatin dissolves, stirring constantly. Let stand until cool. Blend in lemon juice. Beat eggs with sugar in mixer bowl until thick and very pale yellow in color. Blend in gelatin mixture. Fold in whipped cream gently. Reserve a small amount of lemon rind for garnish. Fold remaining lemon rind into mixture. Pour into prepared soufflé dish. Chill overnight. Remove collar. Serve with warm or cold Raspberry Sauce. Garnish with reserved lemon rind.

Raspberry Sauce

1/2	cup raspberry jam
2	tablespoons sugar
1/2	cup water

Yield: 1 cup

Combine jam, sugar and water in saucepan. Bring to a boil, stirring constantly. Boil for 2 minutes, stirring constantly. May add Kirsch or almond or vanilla extract if desired.

Raspberry Soufflés

1	10-ounce package frozen raspberries, thawed
4	egg whites, at room temperature
1/2	cup sugar
1	cup whipping cream
2	tablespoons Grand Marnier

Yield: 6 servings

Butter 6 individual soufflé dishes; sprinkle with sugar. Process undrained raspberries in food processor until smooth. Beat egg whites in mixer bowl until soft peaks form. Add 1/2 cup sugar 1 tablespoon at a time, beating constantly until stiff peaks form. Fold in raspberry purée. Spoon into prepared dishes. Bake in preheated 375-degree oven for 12 to 15 minutes or until set. Whip cream with Grand Marnier in mixer bowl. Serve on soufflés.

Frozen Banana Split Delight

1 1/2	cups graham cracker crumbs
3	medium bananas, sliced
1/2	gallon Neapolitan ice cream, softened
1	cup finely chopped walnuts
1	cup chocolate chips
1/2	cup butter or margarine
1/2	cup evaporated milk
2	cups confectioners' sugar
1/2	teaspoon vanilla extract
1	12-ounce container whipped topping
1/2	cup graham cracker crumbs

Yield: 10 to 12 servings

Layer 1 1/2 cups graham cracker crumbs, bananas and ice cream in 9x13-inch pan; sprinkle with walnuts. Freeze until firm. Combine chocolate chips, butter, evaporated milk and confectioners' sugar in saucepan. Cook until thickened, stirring constantly. Cool to room temperature. Add vanilla. Spread over frozen dessert. Freeze until firm. Spread with whipped topping at serving time; sprinkle with 1/2 cup graham cracker crumbs.

Lemon-Orange Ice Cream

1/2	teaspoon each grated lemon and orange zest (optional)
2	cups sugar
1	quart milk
2/3	cup fresh lemon juice
1/2	cup fresh orange juice
2	cups whipping cream, whipped

Yield: 2 quarts

Process lemon and orange zest with sugar in food processor fitted with metal blade until very finely ground. Combine with milk, lemon juice and orange juice in bowl; mix well. Fold in whipped cream. Pour into covered freezer container. Freeze until firm, stirring once when partially frozen if desired. Serve alone or with fresh berries.

Arizona Sour Orange Pie

1 1/2	cups sugar
1 1/2	cups water
1/3	cup cornstarch
3	egg yolks, slightly beaten
3	tablespoons butter
1/2	cup sour orange juice
1	tablespoon grated sour orange rind
1	baked 9-inch pie shell
3	egg whites
	Pinch of salt
1/3	cup sugar

Yield: 8 servings

Blend 1 1/2 cups sugar, water and cornstarch in saucepan. Bring to a boil, stirring constantly. Cook for 1 minute. Stir a small amount of hot mixture into egg yolks; stir egg yolks into hot mixture. Cook for 1 minute longer; remove from heat. Stir in butter, orange juice and orange rind. Spoon into pie shell. Beat egg whites with salt in mixer bowl until soft peaks form. Add 1/3 cup sugar, beating constantly until stiff peaks form. Spread over pie, sealing to edge. Bake at 350 degrees for 12 minutes or until light brown. Cool on wire rack.

This is a tasty way to use the fruit of the decorative sour orange trees like those that grow in the courtyard and on the grounds of The Heard Museum. The fruit is also good for orange marmalade or used in the many ways that lemon juice is used.

Almond-Date Tarts

1	**egg**	
2	**tablespoons butter**	
1/2	**cup sugar**	
1/2	**teaspoon vanilla extract**	
1/2	**cup chopped dates**	
1/2	**cup raisins**	
1/2	**cup chopped almonds**	
	Tart Pastry	

Yield: 4 dozen

Combine egg, butter, sugar, vanilla, dates, raisins and almonds in food processor container. Process until well mixed. Shape Tart Pastry into 48 small balls; press each over bottom and side of miniature muffin cup. Spoon almond-date filling into prepared cups. Bake at 325 degrees for 25 minutes. Cool completely in pan. Store in airtight container in refrigerator for up to 2 weeks.

Tart Pastry

8	**ounces butter, softened**	
1/2	**cup confectioners' sugar**	
1/2	**teaspoon almond extract**	
1/2	**teaspoon vanilla extract**	
2	**cups flour**	
1/2	**cup finely chopped almonds**	

Cream butter and confectioners' sugar in mixer bowl until light and fluffy. Beat in flavorings. Add flour and almonds; mix well. Chill, covered, in refrigerator.

Amaranth ⌒

Amaranth grain is an ancient plant which has been rediscovered. Its high content of the essential amino acid lysine makes it a nutritious addition to other grains low in lysine. The seeds are usually roasted and ground into a sweet-flavored flour that is used for bread, cakes and mush. Amaranth grains can also be popped until light and crisp, then coated with honey for a snack.

Lemon Meringue Pie

1¹/₂	cups sugar
¹/₄	cup plus 2 teaspoons cornstarch
¹/₄	teaspoon salt
¹/₂	cup plus 1 tablespoon fresh lemon juice
¹/₂	cup cold water
5	egg yolks, beaten
2	tablespoons butter or margarine
1¹/₄	cups boiling water
1–3	teaspoons grated lemon rind
	Several drops of yellow food coloring
1	baked 9-inch pie shell
	Meringue

Yield: 8 servings

Combine sugar, cornstarch and salt in saucepan. Stir in lemon juice, cold water and egg yolks. Add butter. Stir in boiling water. Bring to a boil over medium heat, stirring constantly. Cook for 2 to 3 minutes. Stir in grated lemon rind and food coloring. Cool slightly. Spoon into pie shell; top with Meringue, sealing to edge. Bake at 350 degrees for 12 to 15 minutes or until golden brown.

Meringue

5	egg whites, at room temperature
¹/₂	teaspoon cream of tartar
¹/₂	cup plus 2 tablespoons sugar

Beat egg whites in mixer bowl until frothy. Add cream of tartar. Beat at high speed until soft peaks form. Add sugar gradually, beating constantly until stiff but not dry.

Yogurt Pie

2	8-ounce containers any flavor yogurt
1	8-ounce container whipped topping
1	baked 9-inch pie shell or graham cracker pie shell
	Peaches, strawberries, raspberries or kiwifruit

Yield: 8 servings

Combine yogurt and whipped topping in bowl; mix well. Spoon into pie shell. Top with fruit at serving time.

Pineapple Chiffon Pie

4	egg yolks
1	8-ounce can crushed pineapple
1/2	cup sugar
3	tablespoons lemon gelatin
4	egg whites
1/2	cup sugar
1	baked 9-inch pie shell or graham cracker pie shell
2	vanilla wafers, crushed

Yield: 8 servings

Combine egg yolks, undrained pineapple and 1/2 cup sugar in double boiler over hot water. Cook until thickened, stirring constantly. Add gelatin, stirring until dissolved. Cool to room temperature. Beat egg whites in mixer bowl until frothy. Add 1/2 cup sugar gradually, beating constantly until stiff peaks form. Fold into gelatin mixture. Spoon into pie shell; sprinkle with vanilla wafer crumbs. Chill until serving time.

Pumpkin Chiffon Pie

1	envelope unflavored gelatin
3/4	cup packed dark brown sugar
1/2	teaspoon salt
1/2	teaspoon nutmeg
1	teaspoon cinnamon
1	teaspoon ginger
1/2	teaspoon cloves
1/2	cup milk
1/4	cup water
3	egg yolks
1 1/2	cups canned pumpkin
3	egg whites
1/4	cup sugar
	Gingersnap Crust

Yield: 1 (9-inch) pie

Combine gelatin, brown sugar, salt and spices in double boiler. Add milk, water, egg yolks and pumpkin; mix well. Cook over boiling water for 10 minutes or until gelatin dissolves and mixture is heated through, stirring occasionally. Chill until mixture mounds when dropped from spoon. Beat egg whites until soft peaks form. Add sugar gradually, beating until stiff peaks form. Fold into gelatin mixture. Pour into Gingersnap Crust. Chill until firm. May substitute baked pie shell for Gingersnap Crust.

Gingersnap Crust

| 1 1/2 | cups gingersnap crumbs |
| 1/3 | cup butter, softened |

Combine gingersnap crumbs and butter in bowl; mix well. Press into 9-inch pie plate. Bake at 325 degrees for 10 minutes. Let stand until cool.

Chess Pie

1/2	cup butter or margarine, softened
2	cups sugar
1	tablespoon flour
1	tablespoon cornmeal
5	eggs, beaten
1	cup milk
1	teaspoon vanilla extract or grated lemon rind
1	tablespoon fresh lemon juice
1	unbaked 9-inch pie shell

Yield: 8 servings

Cream butter and sugar in mixer bowl until light and fluffy. Beat in flour and cornmeal. Add eggs, milk, vanilla and lemon juice; mix well. Spoon into pie shell. Bake at 350 degrees for 55 to 60 minutes or until pie tests done. Cool on wire rack.

Frozen Chocolate Pecan Pie

6	ounces bittersweet chocolate
1/4	cup sugar (optional)
1/2	teaspoon instant coffee granules
4	eggs, at room temperature
1	tablespoon dark rum
1	teaspoon vanilla extract
1 1/2	cups whipping cream, whipped Pecan Crust

Yield: 8 servings

Combine chocolate, sugar and coffee granules in double boiler. Cook over hot water until chocolate melts, stirring to mix well; remove from heat. Whisk in eggs, rum and vanilla gradually. Cool for 5 minutes. Fold in 2/3 of the whipped cream. Spoon into Pecan Crust. Freeze for 1 hour or until set. Top servings with remaining whipped cream.

Pecan Crust

2	cups finely chopped pecans, toasted
5	tablespoons packed brown sugar
5	tablespoons cold butter, chopped

Mix pecans, brown sugar and butter in medium bowl until mixture holds together. Press over bottom and side of 9-inch pie plate. Freeze for 1 hour or until firm.

Fudge-Pecan Pie

2	ounces unsweetened chocolate
2	tablespoons margarine
2	eggs
1	cup dark corn syrup
1	cup sugar
1	teaspoon vanilla extract
1/2	teaspoon salt
1	cup pecan halves
1	unbaked 9-inch pie shell

Yield: 8 servings

Melt chocolate with margarine in saucepan over low heat, stirring to mix well. Cool slightly. Beat eggs slightly in bowl. Add corn syrup, sugar, vanilla, salt and chocolate mixture; mix well. Stir in pecans. Spoon into pie shell. Bake at 350 degrees for 45 minutes or until knife inserted in center comes out clean. Cool on wire rack.

Easy Lime Pie

1	3-ounce package lime gelatin
1	cup boiling water
1	cup sugar
3	tablespoons fresh lemon juice
1	12-ounce can evaporated milk
2	8-inch graham cracker pie shells
1	8-ounce container whipped topping

Yield: 16 servings

Dissolve gelatin in boiling water in bowl. Add sugar and lemon juice, stirring to dissolve sugar. Chill until partially set. Freeze evaporated milk in freezer tray until crystals form around edge. Beat in mixer bowl until stiff peaks form. Fold into gelatin mixture. Spoon into pie shells. Spread with whipped topping. Freeze until firm. Garnish with fresh sliced lime or other citrus fruit.

Yucca ∼

The yucca was a valuable plant for early Native people in the Southwest. For thousands of years, the fiber was used to make sandals, headbands, brushes, rope and carrying nets. Yucca also provided food. The young flower stalk and blossoms are steamed to make a delicious pot of greens. The large fleshy fruit of the Banana Yucca (Yucca baccata) hangs like a bunch of small bananas from its long stalk. This fruit may be eaten raw or cooked. When it is cooked the pulp can be mashed and spread out to dry for later use. The cooked fruit may be made into a jam or used as a filling for pastries.

Oatmeal Carmelitas

1	cup flour
1	cup rolled oats
3/4	cup packed brown sugar
1/2	teaspoon baking soda
1/4	teaspoon salt
3/4	cup melted butter
1	cup semisweet chocolate chips
1	cup chopped pecans
3/4	cup caramel ice cream topping
3	tablespoons flour

Yield: 3 dozen

Combine 1 cup flour, oats, brown sugar, baking soda, salt and butter in mixer bowl; mix at low speed until crumbly. Press half the mixture into 7x11-inch baking pan. Bake at 350 degrees for 10 minutes. Sprinkle chocolate chips and pecans over baked layer. Blend ice cream topping and 3 tablespoons flour in bowl. Spoon evenly over pecans; top with remaining crumb mixture. Bake for 20 to 25 minutes longer or until golden brown. Cool on wire rack for 1 to 2 hours. Cut into bars.

Open Sesame Lemon Bars

1	cup flour
1/4	cup sugar
1/2	cup melted butter or margarine
3/4	cup sugar
2	tablespoons flour
1	teaspoon ground ginger
1/2	teaspoon baking powder
2	eggs
1/4	cup fresh lemon juice
1 1/2	teaspoons grated lemon rind
2	tablespoons sesame seeds

Yield: 2 dozen

Mix 1 cup flour and 1/4 cup sugar in bowl. Add butter; mix well. Press over bottom of 9x9-inch baking pan. Bake at 350 degrees for 18 to 20 minutes or until light brown. Mix 3/4 cup sugar, 2 tablespoons flour, ginger and baking powder in bowl. Add eggs and lemon juice; mix well. Stir in lemon rind. Spoon over baked layer. Bake for 20 minutes or until nearly set. Sprinkle evenly with sesame seeds; pat lightly. Bake until set. Cool on wire rack. Cut into bars.

Coconut Diamonds

1/2	cup butter or margarine, softened
1/2	cup packed brown sugar
1/2	teaspoon salt
1	cup sifted flour
2	eggs
1	teaspoon vanilla extract
1	cup packed brown sugar
1	tablespoon flour
1/2	teaspoon salt
1	3½-ounce can flaked coconut
1	cup chopped walnuts
	Lemon Glaze

Yield: 3 dozen

Cream butter, 1/2 cup brown sugar and 1/2 teaspoon salt in mixer bowl until light and fluffy. Add 1 cup flour; mix well. Press into ungreased 9x13-inch baking pan. Bake at 350 degrees for 12 to 15 minutes or until light brown. Beat eggs in mixer bowl. Add vanilla, 1 cup brown sugar, 1 tablespoon flour, 1/2 teaspoon salt, coconut and walnuts; mix well. Spread over baked layer. Bake at 350 degrees for 20 to 25 minutes or until set. Cool on wire rack. Spread Lemon Glaze over top. Cut into diamonds or squares.

Lemon Glaze

2½	cups confectioners' sugar
1/4	cup fresh lemon juice
	Grated rind of 1 lemon
2	tablespoons butter or margarine, softened

Combine confectioners' sugar, lemon juice, lemon rind and 2 tablespoons butter in mixer bowl; mix until smooth.

Chocolate Chip Bars

1	3-ounce package chocolate pudding mix
1	2-layer package chocolate cake mix
3/4	cup finely chopped nuts
1	cup chocolate chips

Yield: 3 dozen

Prepare regular or instant pudding mix using package directions. Stir in cake mix. Spoon into greased and floured 9x13-inch baking pan. Sprinkle with nuts and chocolate chips. Bake at 350 degrees for 30 to 35 minutes or until layer tests done. Cool on wire rack. Cut into bars.

Jack Horner Bars

1¹/₂	cups butter, softened
1¹/₄	cups sifted confectioners' sugar
3¹/₂	cups flour
1	cup finely chopped walnuts
2	cups plum preserves or jam
1	tablespoon flour

Yield: 4 dozen

Cream butter and confectioners' sugar in mixer bowl until light and fluffy. Stir in mixture of 3¹/₂ cups flour and walnuts. Press ²/₃ of the walnut mixture into greased 9x13-inch baking pan. Stir preserves until spreadable; spread over walnut mixture. Stir 1 tablespoon flour into remaining walnut mixture; sprinkle over preserves. Bake at 375 degrees for 25 to 30 minutes or until light brown. Cool. Cut into bars.

Other jams, such as apricot or mincemeat, may be used in this recipe.

Soft Granola Bars

1	cup packed brown sugar
1	cup vegetable oil
2	eggs
2	cups rolled oats
1¹/₂	cups flour
1	cup raisins or chopped dates
1	cup chopped nuts or flaked coconut
1¹/₂	teaspoons ground cinnamon
1¹/₂	teaspoons ground cloves
1	teaspoon baking soda
¹/₄	teaspoon salt
¹/₄	cup honey
2	tablespoons margarine

Yield: 4 dozen

Combine brown sugar, oil and eggs in large mixer bowl; beat until smooth. Stir in oats, flour, raisins, nuts, cinnamon, cloves, baking soda and salt. Spread in greased 10x15-inch baking pan; pat smooth with hands. Bake at 350 degrees for 17 to 22 minutes or until center is set but not firm. Cool on wire rack for 15 minutes. Combine honey and margarine in 1-quart saucepan. Cook over medium heat until margarine melts and mixture is heated through, stirring constantly. Drizzle over baked layer. Cool completely. Cut into bars.

Rocky Road Fudge Bars

6	ounces cream cheese, softened
1	egg
1/2	cup sugar
1/4	cup butter or margarine, softened
2	tablespoons flour
1/2	teaspoon vanilla extract
	Chocolate Crust
1	cup chocolate chips
2	cups miniature marshmallows
	Chocolate Frosting

Yield: 3 dozen

Combine cream cheese, egg, sugar, butter, flour and vanilla in bowl; mix well. Spread over Chocolate Crust. Sprinkle with chocolate chips. Bake at 350 degrees for 30 to 35 minutes or until set and light brown. Spread marshmallows over top. Bake for 1 minute or until marshmallows are puffed and soft; spread evenly with knife. Spread Chocolate Frosting over top; swirl into marshmallow layer with knife. Cool on wire rack. Cut into bars.

These bars freeze well.

Chocolate Crust

1/2	cup butter
2	squares unsweetened chocolate
1	cup flour
1	cup sugar
1	teaspoon baking powder
2	eggs
1	cup chopped pecans

Melt butter and chocolate in medium saucepan over low heat. Add flour, sugar, baking powder, eggs and pecans; mix well. Spread in buttered 9x13-inch baking pan.

Chocolate Frosting

1/4	cup butter or margarine
2	squares unsweetened chocolate
2	ounces cream cheese
1/4	cup milk
3	cups confectioners' sugar
1	teaspoon vanilla extract

Melt butter and chocolate in medium saucepan over low heat. Add cream cheese, milk, confectioners' sugar and vanilla; mix well.

Easy and Rich Brownies

1/2	cup unsalted butter
4	squares unsweetened chocolate
2	cups sugar
1	teaspoon salt
4	eggs, at room temperature
1	cup flour
1	teaspoon vanilla extract
1	cup chopped nuts

Yield: 3¹/₂ dozen

Melt butter and chocolate in 2-quart saucepan over low heat, stirring to blend well. Stir in sugar and salt; remove from heat. Beat in eggs 1 at a time. Add flour, vanilla and nuts; mix well. Spoon into greased 9x13-inch baking pan. Bake in preheated 350-degree oven for 20 to 25 minutes or until brownies test done. Cut with sharp knife while hot. Cool on wire rack. Store in airtight container.

These brownies freeze well.

Cheesecake Bars

1	cup butterscotch chips
5	tablespoons butter
1¹/₂	cups graham cracker crumbs
8	ounces cream cheese, softened
1/4	cup sugar
2	eggs
2	tablespoons flour
1	tablespoon fresh lemon juice

Yield: 16 bars

Heat butterscotch chips and butter in saucepan over low heat, stirring constantly. Remove from heat. Stir in graham cracker crumbs. Reserve ¹/₂ cup mixture. Press remaining mixture into 8-inch square baking pan. Bake at 350 degrees for 10 minutes. Beat cream cheese and sugar in bowl until light and fluffy. Add eggs, flour and lemon juice; mix well. Spread over baked layer. Sprinkle with reserved crumb mixture. Bake for 20 minutes longer. Let stand until cool. Cut into bars. Store in refrigerator.

Golden Raisin and Walnut Bars

1/2	cup butter or margarine, softened
1/2	cup packed brown sugar
1	cup flour
2	eggs
1	cup packed brown sugar
1	teaspoon vanilla extract
1	teaspoon grated lemon rind
2	tablespoons flour
1/2	teaspoon salt
1	teaspoon baking powder
1 1/3	cups golden raisins
1/2	cup chopped walnuts
1/2	cup coconut

Yield: 3 dozen

Cream butter and 1/2 cup brown sugar in mixer bowl until light and fluffy. Add 1 cup flour; mix well. Press into 9x13-inch baking pan. Bake at 375 degrees for 8 to 10 minutes or until light brown. Cool slightly. Beat eggs in mixer bowl. Add 1 cup brown sugar, vanilla, lemon rind, 2 tablespoons flour, salt and baking powder; mix well. Stir in raisins, walnuts and coconut. Spoon over crust. Bake at 350 degrees for 20 minutes. Mark into 36 bars while warm. Cool on wire rack. Cut into bars.

Toffee Walnut Bars

1	cup margarine, softened
1	cup packed brown sugar
1	teaspoon vanilla extract
2	cups flour
1	cup semisweet chocolate chips
1	cup chopped walnuts

Yield: 3 1/2 dozen

Cream margarine, brown sugar and vanilla in mixer bowl until light and fluffy. Add flour; mix well. Stir in chocolate chips and walnuts. Press into 9x13-inch baking pan. Bake at 350 degrees for 25 minutes or just until layer tests done; do not overbake. Cut into bars while warm. Cool completely on wire rack.

Chocolate-Coconut Mound Bars

2	cups graham cracker crumbs
1/2	cup melted butter
2	tablespoons sugar
1	14-ounce can sweetened condensed milk
1 1/2	cups fine coconut
1/2	teaspoon vanilla extract
1/4	teaspoon almond extract
1 1/3	cups semisweet or milk chocolate chips

Yield: 4 dozen

Combine graham cracker crumbs, melted butter and sugar in bowl; mix well. Press firmly into lightly greased 9x13-inch baking pan. Bake at 350 degrees for 10 minutes. Combine condensed milk, coconut and flavorings in bowl; mix well. Spread over baked layer. Bake for 10 minutes longer. Sprinkle with chocolate chips. Let stand for 2 minutes; spread chocolate evenly. Cool on wire rack. Cut into bars.

Oatmeal-Raisin Bars

2	cups raisins
1	14-ounce can sweetened condensed milk
1	tablespoon grated lemon rind
1	tablespoon fresh lemon juice
3/4	cup butter or margarine, softened
1	cup packed brown sugar
1 1/2	teaspoons vanilla extract
2 1/2	cups rolled oats
1	cup flour
1 1/2	cups chopped walnuts
1/2	teaspoon baking soda
1/4	teaspoon salt

Yield: 3 1/2 dozen

Combine raisins, condensed milk, lemon rind and lemon juice in saucepan. Cook over medium heat until thickened, stirring constantly; remove from heat. Cream butter and brown sugar in mixer bowl until light and fluffy. Add vanilla, oats, flour, walnuts, baking soda and salt; mix well. Reserve 2 cups oat mixture; press remaining oat mixture into greased 9x13-inch baking pan. Spread raisin filling over top. Pat reserved oat mixture lightly over top. Bake at 375 degrees for 25 to 30 minutes or until light brown. Cool on wire rack. Cut into bars.

Split Levels

1/2	cup butter or margarine, softened
1	egg
1 1/2	cups flour
1/2	teaspoon baking powder
1/4	teaspoon salt
3/4	cup sugar
1/4	teaspoon almond extract
	Chocolate Filling

Yield: 3 dozen

Combine butter, egg, flour, baking powder, salt, sugar and 1/4 teaspoon almond extract in large bowl; beat at low speed until crumbly. Press half the mixture into greased 9x9-inch baking pan. Spread Chocolate Filling over top; sprinkle with remaining crumb mixture. Bake at 375 degrees for 20 to 25 minutes or until light brown. Cool on wire rack. Cut into squares.

Chocolate Filling

1	cup semisweet chocolate chips or butterscotch chips
1	3-ounce package cream cheese
1/3	cup evaporated milk or light cream
1/2	cup chopped nuts
2	tablespoons sesame seeds
1/4	teaspoon almond extract

Melt chocolate chips and cream cheese with evaporated milk in double boiler over hot water, stirring constantly to blend well. Stir in nuts, sesame seeds and 1/4 teaspoon almond extract.

Praline Kisses

1	egg white
1/2	teaspoon salt
1	cup packed brown sugar
1	cup chopped pecans

Yield: 1 1/2 dozen

Beat egg white in mixer bowl until frothy. Add salt. Add brown sugar gradually, beating constantly until stiff peaks form. Fold in pecans. Drop by small spoonfuls 1/2 inch apart onto greased baking sheet. Bake at 250 degrees for 45 minutes. Let stand on baking sheet for several minutes. Remove to wire rack to cool completely

Crunchy Oatmeal Cookies

3/4	cup shortening or softened margarine
1	cup packed brown sugar
1/2	cup sugar
1	egg
1	teaspoon vanilla extract
1/4	cup water
1	cup sifted flour
1/2	teaspoon baking soda
1	teaspoon salt
3	cups quick-cooking oats
1/2	cup chopped nuts (optional)
3/4	cup raisins (optional)

Yield: 4 dozen

Combine shortening, brown sugar, sugar, egg, vanilla and water in mixer bowl; beat until smooth. Sift in flour, baking soda and salt; mix well. Stir in oats, nuts and raisins. Drop by teaspoonfuls onto greased cookie sheet. Bake at 350 degrees for 12 to 14 minutes or until light brown. Remove to wire rack to cool.

Chocolate-Nut Cookies

1 1/2	cups plus 1 tablespoon sifted flour
1 1/2	teaspoons baking powder
1/2	teaspoon salt
3	squares unsweetened baking chocolate
1/4	cup butter or shortening
3/4	cup sugar
1	egg
3/4	cup milk
1/2	teaspoon vanilla extract
1	cup chopped walnuts

Yield: 3 dozen

Sift flour, baking powder and salt together 3 times. Melt chocolate and butter in double boiler over hot water; cool to lukewarm. Add sugar; mix well. Beat in egg. Add flour mixture alternately with milk, mixing just until moistened. Stir in vanilla and walnuts. Drop by teaspoonfuls onto ungreased cookie sheet. Bake at 375 degrees for 9 minutes or until cookies test done. Cool for several minutes on cookie sheet; remove to wire rack to cool completely.

Vermont Maple Cookies

1/2	cup shortening
1	cup packed brown sugar
1/2	cup sugar
2	eggs
1	cup sour cream or evaporated milk
1	tablespoon maple extract
2 3/4	cups flour
1/2	teaspoon baking soda
1	teaspoon salt
1	cup chopped pecans
	Maple Glaze

Yield: 7 dozen

Combine shortening, brown sugar, sugar and eggs in mixer bowl; beat until smooth. Stir in sour cream and maple extract. Add flour, baking soda and salt; mix well. Stir in pecans. Drop by teaspoonfuls onto greased cookie sheet. Bake at 375 degrees for 10 to 15 minutes or until light brown. Remove to wire rack to cool. Glaze with Maple Glaze. Let stand until dry. Store in airtight container.

Maple Glaze

1/2	cup butter
2	teaspoons maple extract
2	cups confectioners' sugar
2–4	tablespoons hot water

Heat butter in saucepan until golden brown; remove from heat. Add maple extract and confectioners' sugar; mix well. Add enough hot water to make of spreading consistency.

Benita's Meringue Cookies

2	egg whites
1/2	teaspoon cream of tartar
1/8	teaspoon salt
1	teaspoon vanilla extract
3/4	cup sugar
1	cup semisweet chocolate chips
1/4	cup chopped pecans or walnuts

Yield: 2 dozen

Beat egg whites with cream of tartar, salt and vanilla in mixer bowl until soft peaks form. Add sugar gradually, beating constantly until stiff peaks form. Fold in chocolate chips and pecans. Drop by rounded teaspoonfuls onto brown paper-covered cookie sheet. Bake at 300 degrees for 25 minutes.

Brownie-Nut Morsels

1/3	cup baking cocoa
1/2	cup plus 2 tablespoons melted butter or margarine
1	cup sugar
2	eggs, beaten
1 1/2	teaspoons vanilla extract
1 1/4	cups flour
1/2	teaspoon baking powder
3/4	teaspoon salt
3	cups chopped nuts

Yield: 5 dozen

Sift baking cocoa into melted butter in bowl; mix well. Add sugar, eggs and vanilla; mix well. Stir in flour, baking powder and salt. Mix in nuts. Drop by small teaspoonfuls onto lightly greased cookie sheet. Bake at 350 degrees for 6 to 9 minutes or just until set. Cool on cookie sheet for 2 minutes; remove to wire rack to cool completely.

For variety, omit chopped nuts, drop into lightly greased miniature muffin cups and top each with 1 pecan half; bake for 9 to 10 minutes.

Fork Cookies

1	cup shortening
1	cup sugar
1	cup packed dark brown sugar
2	eggs
2	cups quick-cooking oats
2	cups coconut
1	teaspoon vanilla or almond extract
2	cups flour
4	teaspoons baking powder
1	teaspoon baking soda
1/2	teaspoon salt
72	candied cherry halves or chocolate chips

Yield: 6 dozen

Cream shortening, sugar and brown sugar in mixer bowl until light and fluffy. Add eggs, oats, coconut and vanilla; mix well. Sift in flour, baking powder, baking soda and salt; mix well. Shape into 1-inch balls; place on cookie sheet. Press with fork to flatten. Top each with candied cherry half. Bake at 350 degrees until light brown. Remove to wire rack to cool.

Oatmeal Coconut Cookies

1	cup margarine, softened
1	cup packed brown sugar
1	cup sugar
2	eggs, beaten
1	teaspoon vanilla extract
2¹/₂	cups flour
1	teaspoon baking soda
³/₄	teaspoon salt
2	cups rolled oats
1¹/₂	cups Angel Flake coconut
¹/₂	cup chopped walnuts
2	cups crushed corn flakes

Yield: 6 dozen

Cream margarine, brown sugar and sugar in mixer bowl until light and fluffy. Beat in eggs and vanilla. Add flour, baking soda and salt; mix well. Stir in oats, coconut, walnuts and corn flakes. Drop by spoonfuls onto cookie sheet. Bake at 375 degrees for 12 minutes. Remove to wire rack to cool.

Old-Fashioned Lemon and Almond Cookies

³/₄	cup unsalted butter, softened
1	cup sugar
1	egg
1¹/₂	tablespoons grated lemon rind
¹/₃	cup finely ground almonds
1¹/₂	cups flour
2	tablespoons sugar

Yield: 3 dozen

Cream butter and 1 cup sugar in mixer bowl until light and fluffy. Add egg, lemon rind and almonds; mix well. Add flour gradually, mixing well. Chill, covered, for 2 hours to overnight. Shape into 1-inch balls; place 2 inches apart on lightly greased cookie sheet. Press to 2-inch diameter with bottom of glass which has been moistened and dipped in 2 tablespoons sugar. Bake at 350 degrees for 10 to 12 minutes or until light golden brown around edges. Remove to wire rack to cool.

Greek Butter Cookies

1	pound unsalted butter
1	egg yolk
3	tablespoons whiskey
2	tablespoons orange juice
1/4	teaspoon vanilla extract
1/4	teaspoon baking soda
3	tablespoons confectioners' sugar
5	cups (about) flour
1	1-pound package confectioners' sugar

Yield: 4 to 5 dozen

Melt butter in saucepan over low heat. Cool to room temperature. Pour off clarified butter, discarding milk solids which settle to bottom. Beat butter in mixer bowl until thick. Add egg yolk, whiskey, orange juice, vanilla, baking soda, 3 tablespoons confectioners' sugar and 1 cup flour; mix well. Add remaining flour gradually, mixing well to form firm dough. Shape into crescents; place on ungreased cookie sheet. Bake at 375 degrees for 15 to 20 minutes or until light brown. Remove carefully to wire rack to cool. Sift enough remaining confectioners' sugar over cookies to coat well. Store in airtight containers.

Country Raisin Gingersnaps

3/4	cup shortening
1	cup sugar
1	egg
1/4	cup molasses
2 1/4	cups flour
2	teaspoons baking soda
1/2	teaspoon salt
1	teaspoon ginger
1/2	teaspoon cinnamon
1/4	teaspoon ground cloves
1 1/2	cups seedless raisins
3	tablespoons sugar

Yield: 3 1/2 dozen

Cream shortening and 1 cup sugar in mixer bowl until light and fluffy. Beat in egg and molasses. Sift in flour, baking soda, salt, ginger, cinnamon and cloves; mix well. Stir in raisins. Chill, covered, for 2 hours to overnight. Shape into 1 1/2-inch balls; roll in 3 tablespoons sugar. Place on lightly greased cookie sheet. Bake at 375 degrees for 10 to 12 minutes or until surface is cracked and light brown. Cool on cookie sheet for 2 minutes; remove to wire rack to cool completely.

Red Lips

1	cup butter, softened
1/2	cup sugar
2	cups sifted flour
	Red jam

Yield: 5 dozen

Cream butter and sugar in mixer bowl until light and fluffy. Add flour; mix well. Shape into 1/2-inch balls; place 2 inches apart on lightly greased or nonstick cookie sheet. Press indentation in center of each ball; fill with jam. Bake at 375 degrees for 12 to 15 minutes or until light brown around edges. Cool on cookie sheet for several minutes; remove to wire rack to cool completely.

Melting Moments

1/2	cup butter, softened
1/3	cup confectioners' sugar
1	teaspoon vanilla or almond extract
1/4	teaspoon salt
1	cup sifted flour
1	teaspoon baking powder

Yield: 3 dozen

Cream butter, confectioners' sugar, vanilla and salt in mixer bowl until light and fluffy. Add mixture of flour and baking powder; mix well. Chill, covered, for 2 hours. Shape by teaspoonfuls into balls; place on ungreased cookie sheet. Flatten with fork dipped in flour. Bake at 350 degrees for 8 to 10 minutes or until edges are light brown. Cool on cookie sheet.

May decorate cookies with candies or colored sugar before baking. Do not substitute margarine for butter in this recipe.

Italian Festival Cookies

5	cups flour
2/3	cup sugar
1 1/2	tablespoons baking powder
1	cup margarine or butter
3	eggs
1/2	cup milk
1	tablespoon vanilla extract
	Festival Filling
2	cups confectioners' sugar
3	tablespoons milk
1/2	teaspoon vanilla extract

Yield: 8 dozen

Mix flour, sugar and baking powder in bowl. Cut in margarine until mixture forms coarse crumbs. Combine eggs, 1/2 cup milk and 1 tablespoon vanilla in small bowl; mix well. Add to crumb mixture; mix to form dough. Knead lightly until dough is no longer sticky, adding additional flour if needed. Roll into thin 3x6-inch to 3x8-inch strips. Spoon Festival Filling down center of strips. Bring up long edges to enclose filling; press to seal, rolling into filled cylinders. Cut diagonally into 2-inch pieces. Place seam side down on greased cookie sheet. Bake at 350 degrees for 20 to 25 minutes or until light brown. Combine confectioners' sugar, 3 tablespoons milk and 1/2 teaspoon vanilla in bowl; mix until smooth. Spread on cookies.

These cookies freeze well.

Festival Filling

12	ounces dried figs
4	ounces pitted dates
8	ounces raisins
1/2	cup sugar
1	tablespoon light corn syrup
2/3	cup crushed pineapple
1 1/2	teaspoons whiskey (optional)
1/2	cup chopped walnuts
1	teaspoon nutmeg
1	teaspoon cinnamon
	Grated zest of 1 orange

Pour boiling water over figs to rinse; drain well, discarding tips. Grind figs, dates and raisins together or process in food processor until finely chopped. Combine with sugar, corn syrup, undrained pineapple, whiskey, walnuts, nutmeg, cinnamon and orange zest in bowl. Let stand, tightly covered, overnight to blend flavors.

Snickerdoodles

1	cup butter or margarine, softened
1½	cups sugar
2	eggs
2¾	cups flour
2	teaspoons cream of tartar
1	teaspoon baking soda
½	teaspoon salt
¼	cup sugar
1	tablespoon cinnamon

Yield: 6 dozen

Combine butter, 1½ cups sugar and eggs in mixer bowl; beat until smooth. Sift in flour, cream of tartar, baking soda and salt; mix well. Chill for 30 minutes. Shape into 1-inch balls; roll in mixture of ¼ cup sugar and cinnamon, coating well. Place 2 inches apart on ungreased cookie sheet. Bake at 375 degrees for 8 minutes or until light brown. Cool on cookie sheet for several minutes; remove to wire rack to cool completely.

Oatmeal Lace Cookies

1	1-pound package light brown sugar
2¼	cups quick-cooking oats
1	cup unsalted butter, melted, slightly cooled
1	egg, slightly beaten
3	tablespoons flour
1	teaspoon vanilla extract
1	teaspoon salt

Yield: 6 dozen

Combine brown sugar, oats, butter, egg, flour, vanilla and salt in mixer bowl; mix well to form thin batter. Chill for 30 minutes. Drop by teaspoonfuls 2 inches apart onto ungreased cookie sheet. Bake in preheated 375-degree oven for 7 minutes or until brown around edges. Cool on cookie sheet for 3 to 5 minutes or until cookies can be easily removed; remove to wire rack to cool completely. Store in airtight container. May freeze until needed.

No-Roll Sugar Cookies

1	cup margarine, softened
1	cup sugar
1	cup confectioners' sugar
2	eggs
1	cup vegetable oil
1	teaspoon vanilla extract or grated lemon rind
4 1/2	cups flour
1/2	teaspoon baking soda
1	teaspoon baking powder
1	teaspoon salt
	Sugar

Yield: 6 dozen

Combine margarine, 1 cup sugar, confectioners' sugar and eggs in mixer bowl; beat until smooth. Add oil and vanilla; mix well. Sift flour, baking soda, baking powder and salt together. Add to batter 1/3 at a time, mixing well after each addition. Shape into 1-inch balls; place on ungreased cookie sheet. Flatten with glass dipped in additional sugar. Bake at 350 degrees for 10 minutes. Cool on cookie sheet for several minutes; remove to wire rack to cool completely. May freeze until needed.

Orange and Pecan Refrigerator Cookies

1	cup butter, softened
1/2	cup sugar
1/2	cup packed brown sugar
1	egg
1	tablespoon orange juice
1	tablespoon grated orange rind
2 3/4	cups flour
1	teaspoon baking soda
1/2	cup chopped pecans

Yield: 3 to 3 1/2 dozen

Cream butter in mixer bowl until light. Add sugar, brown sugar, egg, orange juice and orange rind; beat until smooth. Stir in flour and baking soda. Add pecans; mix well. Shape into rolls 2 inches in diameter. Chill, wrapped in waxed paper, overnight. Cut into thin slices; place on cookie sheet. Bake at 350 degrees for 10 to 12 minutes or until light brown. Cool on cookie sheet for several minutes; remove to wire rack to cool completely.

Apache Butterfly

Miscellaneous

Manioc

Manioc is a tuber that is the staple food crop of most of the native peoples of the Caribbean and lowland South America. Manioc is also known as cassava or yuca, not to be confused with the yucca of the Sonoran Southwest. Given enough moisture, manioc grows well in most soils and especially well in poor soils. The Spanish first observed manioc in what is today Cuba, where the Taino peoples warned them that the tuber was poisonous when raw. The Taino peeled and grated the root and then squeezed out the juice. When boiled, the juice becomes a harmless sauce which the world knows today as tapioca. Manioc pulp is then formed into flat cakes which are cooked on a griddle. The resulting bread, cassava bread, was a staple food of the people. It was quickly adopted by the Spanish and later the French, not only because it is delicious, but also because it can be stored for up to three years without loss of flavor or nutrition.

In the 16th century, manioc was introduced by the Portuguese into Africa, where it became an important crop. Mature manioc tubers remain in the ground for up to two years without harm, thus negating the need for specialized storage. Locusts, the scourge of African harvests, do not attack the plant.

Manioc is still the primary food crop of the indigenous peoples of lowland South America. It also is eaten as a bread with many traditional dishes in the Caribbean, and frequently prepared like French fries in many areas of Central America.

Amaretto Sauce

8	ounces ricotta cheese
8	ounces cream cheese, softened
1/2	cup sugar
2	tablespoons whipping cream
1/4	cup Amaretto

Yield: 2¹/₂ cups

Process ricotta cheese and cream cheese in blender or food processor until smooth. Add sugar, cream and liqueur; process until smooth. Chill until serving time. Serve with fresh fruit and pound cake.

Quick Sour Orange Marmalade

1	large or 2 medium sour oranges
	Sugar

Yield: 1 to 1¹/₂ cups

Rinse orange and cut into large pieces, discarding seeds. Process in food processor until evenly chopped. Measure fruit and juice, adding water to juice if needed to just cover fruit. Combine with equal amount of sugar in 2 to 3-quart glass dish. Microwave, uncovered, on High for 6 minutes or until mixture coats spoon. Cool. Mixture will continue to thicken; reheat with water if mixture becomes too thick. Spoon into clean jar. Store in refrigerator.

Remarkable Fudge

4¹/₂	cups sugar
1	12-ounce can evaporated milk
1/4	cup butter
2	cups semisweet chocolate chips
1	4-ounce bar German's sweet chocolate
1	8-ounce bar chocolate candy
1	7-ounce jar marshmallow creme
1	tablespoon vanilla extract
1	cup coarsely chopped walnuts

Yield: 6 pounds

Bring first 3 ingredients to a boil in saucepan. Boil for 8 minutes or to 234 degrees on candy thermometer, soft-ball stage; remove from heat. Add chocolate chips, sweet chocolate, candy bar, marshmallow creme and vanilla; mix until smooth. Stir in walnuts. Spread in greased 11x17-inch pan. Let stand until firm; cut into squares. Store in airtight container for up to 6 months.

Mexican Chocolate Fudge

2	cups sugar
3	tablespoons butter
1	teaspoon cinnamon
1/2	teaspoon salt
1	cup evaporated milk
1/2	cup miniature marshmallows
1 1/2	cups chocolate chips
2/3	cup chopped pecans
1	teaspoon vanilla extract

Yield: 64 servings

Combine sugar, butter, cinnamon, salt and evaporated milk in large electric skillet set at 280 degrees. Bring to a boil. Cook for 5 minutes, stirring constantly; turn off heat. Add marshmallows, chocolate chips, pecans and vanilla; mix until marshmallows and chocolate chips are melted. Spoon into buttered 8x8-inch dish. Let stand until cool. Cut into squares.

Peanut Butter Fudge Sauce

1/2	cup whipping cream
2/3	cup semisweet chocolate chips
2	tablespoons creamy peanut butter

Yield: 1 cup

Combine whipping cream and chocolate chips in 4-cup glass measure. Microwave on High for 1 to 1 1/2 minutes or until mixture boils vigorously, stirring 2 or 3 times. Add peanut butter, stirring until smooth. Microwave for 30 seconds longer. Serve over ice cream, frozen yogurt or strawberries.

Turtles

108	pecan halves
1	14-ounce package caramels
2	tablespoons evaporated milk
1	tablespoon butter
1	cup semisweet chocolate chips
2	tablespoons grated paraffin

Yield: 36 servings

Arrange pecan halves in 36 groups of 3 on buttered waxed paper. Melt caramels with evaporated milk and butter in medium saucepan, stirring to mix well. Spoon onto center of each group of pecans. Cool for 30 minutes. Melt chocolate chips with paraffin in double boiler over hot water over low heat. Spoon over caramel mixture. Let stand until cool. Store in airtight container.

Lemon Marmalade

6   **medium lemons**
6   **cups water**
6½   **cups sugar**
      Sugar
1   **1¾-ounce package powdered pectin**

Yield: 6 cups

Cut lemons into 30 thin slices, discarding ends and seeds. Mix with water and 6½ cups sugar in bowl. Let stand, covered, in cool place overnight. Bring to a boil in saucepan. Boil for 10 minutes; remove from heat. Let stand, covered, overnight. Measure lemon mixture and add equal amount of sugar. Add pectin. Stir in and bring to a rolling boil. Boil for 3 minutes. Cool to room temperature. Skim surface. Spoon into hot sterilized jars; seal with paraffin.

Prickly Pear Jelly

2½   **cups prickly pear juice**
1   **1¾-ounce package powdered pectin**
3   **tablespoons fresh lemon or lime juice**
3½   **tablespoons sugar**

Yield: 4 cups

Bring prickly pear juice and pectin to a boil in saucepan, stirring constantly. Add lemon juice and sugar. Bring to a rolling boil. Boil for 3 minutes; remove from heat and skim surface. Spoon into sterilized jelly jars; seal immediately with paraffin.

Prickly Pear Juice ⌒

Wear heavy gloves and use metal tongs to collect red prickly pears. Brush with vegetable brush or rub with heavy cloth or sponge to remove spines. Rinse the fruit; cook in water to cover in large saucepan for 1 hour or until tender. Press with potato masher to break skins. Strain through several thicknesses of cheesecloth into bowl. Juice may be frozen until needed.

Apricot Balls

1	cup chopped pecans
16	ounces dried apricots, chopped
1	cup vanilla wafer crumbs
8	ounces coarse coconut
1	14-ounce can sweetened condensed milk
	Confectioners' sugar

Yield: 2 dozen

Combine pecans, apricots, wafer crumbs, coconut and condensed milk in bowl; mix well. Shape into 1-inch balls; coat with confectioners' sugar. Store in airtight container for several days or freeze.

Spiced Figs

3	cups sugar
3/4	cup vinegar
1 1/4	cups water
2	cinnamon sticks
1	tablespoon whole cloves
3–4	pounds figs

Yield: 4 to 6 cups

Combine sugar, vinegar, water, cinnamon sticks and cloves in large saucepan. Bring to a boil. Add figs. Boil for 20 minutes; remove from heat. Let stand in syrup overnight. Repeat boiling and cooling steps on second and third days. Spoon into hot sterilized jars; seal with 2-piece lids.

Serve as accompaniment to meats and poultry.

Spiced California Grapes

4	cups Ribier or Emperor grapes
3	cups white vinegar
3	cups sugar
2	cinnamon sticks
1	teaspoon whole cloves
1/2	teaspoon allspice
1/2	teaspoon ground coriander
1/4	teaspoon mace
3	strips orange peel
3	strips lemon peel

Yield: 1 quart

Place grapes in sterilized 1-quart jar. Bring vinegar and sugar to a boil in saucepan, stirring to dissolve sugar. Add cinnamon, cloves, allspice, coriander, mace, orange peel and lemon peel. Simmer for 5 minutes; remove from heat. Cool slightly. Pour over grapes; seal with 2-piece lid.

Hollandaise Sauce

4   egg yolks
2   tablespoons lemon juice
1/4 teaspoon salt
1/4 teaspoon hot pepper sauce
1   cup butter

Yield: 1¹/₄ cups

Combine egg yolks, lemon juice, salt and
pepper sauce in blender container; process at
low speed until smooth. Heat butter in small
saucepan until very hot but not brown. Add
gradually to egg yolk mixture, blending
constantly. Serve immediately or keep warm
by placing in pan with 2 inches hot water. If
sauce becomes too thick, process briefly with
1 tablespoon hot water at serving time.

Fresh Cucumber Pickles

6   unpeeled cucumbers, sliced
1   cup white vinegar
2   cups sugar
1   cup sliced onion
1   teaspoon salt

Yield: 1 quart

Combine cucumbers, vinegar, sugar, onion and
salt in bowl; mix well. Spoon into 1-quart jar;
seal. Store in refrigerator.

Corn Relish

1/4 cup chopped onion
1   teaspoon celery seeds
1/4 teaspoon ground turmeric
1/2 teaspoon dry mustard
1/2 teaspoon salt
1/2 cup vinegar
1/3 cup sugar
1   12-ounce can whole kernel corn,
       drained
1/4 cup chopped green bell pepper
1/4 cup chopped red bell pepper

Yield: 2 cups

Combine onion, celery seeds, turmeric, dry
mustard, salt, vinegar and sugar in saucepan.
Bring to a boil. Add corn and bell peppers.
Cool to room temperature. Chill for 24 hours.

***May substitute Mexicorn for corn and omit
bell peppers.***

Sauerkraut Relish

1	green bell pepper, finely chopped
1	small onion, finely chopped
3	stalks celery, finely chopped
1	16-ounce can sauerkraut
1	cup chili sauce
1/3	cup packed brown sugar
1	teaspoon paprika
3	tablespoons fresh lemon juice
	Pepper to taste

Yield: 4 to 5 cups

Combine green pepper, onion, celery, sauerkraut, chili sauce, brown sugar, paprika, lemon juice and pepper in bowl; mix well. Chill until serving time. Serve cold.

Red Pepper Relish

6	red bell peppers
6	green bell peppers
6	onions
1	small head cabbage
1	bunch celery
1	cup sugar
2	tablespoons salt
1	quart cider vinegar

Yield: 6 to 8 pints

Grind peppers, onions, cabbage and celery. Combine in bowl; mix well. Spoon into 6 to 8 sterile 1-pint jars. Bring sugar, salt and vinegar to a boil in saucepan. Pour into jars; seal with 2-pint lids. Let stand for 2 weeks to improve flavor.

May heat vegetables in boiling mixture and pack into jars if preferred.

Cucumber and Yogurt Sauce

3	long thin cucumbers
1	teaspoon salt
2	teaspoons white wine vinegar
2	cups plain yogurt
2	tablespoons finely chopped fresh dill
1/4	teaspoon cayenne pepper

Yield: 2 1/2 to 3 cups

Peel cucumbers and cut into halves lengthwise; remove and discard seeds. Chop cucumbers coarsely. Combine with salt and vinegar in small bowl. Let stand for 1 hour or longer; drain and pat dry. Combine with yogurt, dill and cayenne pepper in serving bowl; mix well. Serve chilled with fish.

Cranberries in Wine Sauce

1	cup dry red wine
1	cup packed brown sugar
1/2	orange, peeled, sectioned
8	fresh or frozen unsweetened whole strawberries, sliced
1	12-ounce package cranberries

Yield: 2 1/2 cups

Combine wine and brown sugar in saucepan. Bring to a boil. Boil for 2 minutes, stirring occasionally. Add orange sections and strawberries. Bring to a boil. Add cranberries. Cook until cranberries pop, stirring occasionally. Chill.

Fresh Cranberry Relish

1	12-ounce package cranberries
2	medium tart apples, cored
2	medium oranges, peeled, seeded
1	cup sugar
2	tablespoons brandy

Yield: 3 1/2 cups

Put cranberries, apples and oranges through medium blade of food grinder; place pan beneath grinder to catch juices. Combine ground fruit with juices, sugar and brandy in bowl; mix well. Chill in refrigerator overnight.

This relish will keep for several days in the refrigerator or will freeze well.

Cocktail Sauce

3	tablespoons prepared horseradish
2	teaspoons fresh lemon juice
1	teaspoon Worcestershire sauce
3	drops of hot pepper sauce
3/4	cup chili sauce
1	cup catsup

Yield: 2 cups

Combine all ingredients in bowl; mix well. Store in covered container in refrigerator.

Pickled Gingerroot

8	ounces fresh young gingerroot
2	tablespoons salt
1	cup white vinegar
3/4	cup sugar

Yield: 1 pint

Peel gingerroot and cut into thin slices. Sprinkle with salt in bowl. Chill, covered, overnight. Rinse and drain well. Heat vinegar and sugar in 2-quart saucepan until sugar dissolves. Add gingerroot. Bring to a boil. Cook for 2 minutes. Spoon into clean 1-pint jar; seal with 2-piece lid. Cool to room temperature. Store in refrigerator for up to 1 year.

Make this relish in the summer when fresh young gingerroot is available in the market.

Kumquat Chutney

1–2	pounds kumquats, chopped
1	cup raisins
1–2	tart apples, peeled, chopped
1	teaspoon ground ginger or candied ginger
2	tablespoons brown sugar
1	cup sugar
1/2	teaspoon salt
2	cups water

Yield: 4 to 5 cups

Combine kumquats, raisins, apples, ginger, brown sugar, sugar, salt and water in saucepan. Cook until thickened, stirring occasionally. Cool to room temperature. Chill until serving time.

May store in refrigerator for months.

Bibliography

For those who may be interested in additional information on the native plants and foods of the Southwest, a list of references follows:

Elkort, Martin. **The Secret Life of Food**. Jeremy P. Tarcher, Los Angeles, 1991.

Foster, Nelson, and Linda S. Cordell. **Chilies to Chocolate**. The University of Arizona Press, Tucson, 1992.

Fussell, Betty. **The Story of Corn**. Alfred A. Knopp, New York, 1992.

Josephy, Jr., Alvin M. **The Indian Heritage of America**. Bantam, New York, 1968.

Kavasch, Barrie. **Native Harvests**. Random House, New York, 1979.

Kavena, Juanita Tiger. **Hopi Cookery**. University of Arizona Press, Tucson, 1980.

Nabhan, Gary Paul. **Gathering the Dessert**. University of Arizona Press, Tucson, 1987.

Neithammer, Carolyn. **American Indian Food and Lore**. Collier Books, Macmillan Publishing Company, New York, 1974.

Peeler, Tom. "Great Moments in Snack History." **American Way**. December 1983.

Sekaquaptewa, Helen. **Me and Mine**. University of Arizona Press, Tucson, 1969.

Sokolov, Raymond. "Columbus' Biggest Discovery." **Natural History**, August 1987. "America's First Food Writer." **Natural History**, October 1992.

Tannahill, Reay. **Food in History**. Stein and Day, New York, 1973.

Viola, Herman J. and Carolyn Margolis. **Seeds of Change**. Smithsonian Press, Washington, D.C., 1991.

Weatherford, Jack. **Indian Givers**. Crown Publishers, Inc., New York, 1988.

HEARD MUSEUM GUILD

Contributors

The Cookbook Committee expresses its appreciation to the Heard Museum Guild members and friends for contributing and testing recipes for this cookbook.

Ginger Allingham
Nancy Andre
Kit Applegate
Liná K. Austin
Kay Benedict
Lee Berry
Rose Berry
Gretchen E. Bock
Betty Bool
Marie Borgmann
Ann Bradeen
Pat Branom
Virginia Breitmeyer
Ruth Brill
Vonna Brown
Lillian Burke
Marie Byrne
Helen Cacheris
Sandy and Ted Charveze
Virginia Childs
Stephanie Clayton
Mary Coe
Bev Cooper
Lois Cox
Martha Cozzi
Flora Cullison
Marie Daniel
Pinney Deupree
Sylvia Diamond
Virginia Douglas
Ruth Dumbauld
Dorathy Engle
Peggy Fairchild
Barbara Fenzl
Eleanor Fiftal

Doris Gaffney
Janis Gallison
Gloria Gardner
Diana Sobo Gast
Anne M. Girand
Pat Greenberg
Bobbie Greenslade
Jean Grossman
Bobbie Haas
Polly Hartzler
Barbara Heard
Marcella Henderson
Joan Hill
Jean Humlicek
Donna L. Johnson
Skip Jones
Grace H. Kaiser
Cecelia Kline
Irene Kline
Barbara Knosp
Diane Kopp
Chuck Krevitsky
Thelma Krevitsky
Margaret Lavidge
Martha K. Lee
Joan Lincoln
Evelyn Lundquist
Barbara Maiwurm
Frederic Marquardt
Ann Marshall
Sharon Mayer
Carolyn McClure
Sue McGavock
Louis Menk
Martha Milner

Faye Mitchell
Nancy Moore
Carolyn Morgan
Gloria Murison
Betty F. Neal
Patricia Pasbach
Pat Pfister
Lynn Portis
Dorothy Powers
Vivian Price
Mary Rainey
Alma Rand
Pat Redinger
Carolyn Reid
Harriette Repenning
Louise M. Riedel
Lois Rogers
Jean Rupley
Ardith Sachtjen
Wilma Sain
Jeanette Salerno
Sheila Schecter
Patty Sipe
Louise Slotta
Sharon Spease
Nan Steiner
Anne Suguitan
Daune Turner
Elizabeth Van Zandt
Mary Vincent
Leanne Walgren
Jody Willoughby
Margaret Wood
Gladys Wright
Virginia Yates

Index

Heard In The Kitchen Cookbook Order Form

Heard Museum Guild Cookbook
The Heard Museum Shop
22 East Monte Vista Road
Phoenix, Arizona 85004-1480   **Phone: 1-800-252-8344**

Please send me _____ copies of ***Heard In The Kitchen*** @ $18.95 each $_____

Add postage and handling @ $2.95 each $_____

Total enclosed $_____

☐ Check   ☐ Money Order

Please make check or money order payable to The Heard Museum Shop.

Mail to:

Name _____   Phone (_____)

Address _____   Apt. _____

City _____   State _____   Zip _____

- -

Heard In The Kitchen Cookbook Order Form

Heard Museum Guild Cookbook
The Heard Museum Shop
22 East Monte Vista Road
Phoenix, Arizona 85004-1480   **Phone: 1-800-252-8344**

Please send me _____ copies of ***Heard In The Kitchen*** @ $18.95 each $_____

Add postage and handling @ $2.95 each $_____

Total enclosed $_____

☐ Check   ☐ Money Order

Please make check or money order payable to The Heard Museum Shop.

Mail to:

Name _____   Phone (_____)

Address _____   Apt. _____

City _____   State _____   Zip _____